11/00

32.50

D0961858

Robert Lawrence Stine

What's So Scary About R.L. Stine?

Patrick Jones

Scarecrow Studies in Young Adult Literature

The Scarecrow Press, Inc.
Lanham, Maryland & London
1998

SCARECROW PRESS, INC.

Published in the United States of America
by Scarecrow Press, Inc.
4720 Boston Way
Lanham, Maryland 20706

4 Pleydell Gardens, Folkestone
Kent CT20 2DN, England

British Library Cataloguing in Publication Information Available

Library of Congress Cataloging-in-Publication Data

Jones, Patrick, 1961-
    What's so scary about R.L. Stine? / Patrick Jones.
        p.   cm. -- (Scarecrow studies in young adult literature)
    Includes bibliographical references (p.   ) and index.
    ISBN 0-8108-3468-5 (alk. paper)
    1. Stine, R.L.--Criticism and interpretation. 2. Young adult fiction,
American--History and criticism.   I. Title. II. Series.
PS3569.T4837Z74   1998
813'.54--dc21
                                        98-8374
                                        CIP

To Erica

CONTENTS

EDITOR'S FOREWORD

Welcome to the first volume in the Scarecrow Studies in Young Adult Literature series. Controversy is inherent in anything to do with teenagers, and so it is appropriate that the first volume in the series focuses on one of the most hotly debated issues in recent years—the value of popular reading, particularly as it is exemplified by the best-selling juvenile writer of all time, R.L. Stine. Future volumes are planned on leading YA authors such as Robin McKinley, Ann Rinaldi, and Margaret Mahy; on multicultural issues such as Asian and Asian-American fiction for young adults; and on controversial topics such as gay and lesbian literature for teens and the portrayal of empowered girls in YA fiction. Suggestions for subjects and authors are welcomed by the editor.

PREFACE

I was just beginning to work as a young adult (YA) librarian when Stine's first YA thriller *Blind Date* was published in 1986. Since then, I have read his books for fun, used them for booktalks, reviewed them for library professional magazines, read them for my work on the Recommended Books for the Reluctant Young Adult Reader committee, spoken about them at conferences, and listened to and then reviewed recorded book versions of his work. I have written about Stine before, both in my book *Connecting Young Adults and Libraries, 2nd ed.* (Neal-Schuman, 1998) and in the reference book *Twentieth Century Young Adult Writers* (Gale, 1995). I have also written about the thriller genre in magazines and in the book *Children's Books and Their Creators* (Houghton Mifflin, 1996).

I was at first very enthusiastic about Stine and the thriller genre, primarily because they were books that boys were actually excited about. Like many librarians, however, I became concerned about the level of violence and pulled back, adopting the "Well, at least they're reading something" party line. In re-reading both Stine's own work and articles about him in preparation for this book, I realized I was wrong in my disclaimer. To say "Well, at least they're reading something" devalues not just Stine and recreational reading in general, but devalues the reader as a person. This attitude debases the reading experience by creating a caste system of books; it is elitist and counterproductive. Rather than discounting and dismissing Stine, we should be praising him for finding a formula that produces positive reading experiences for young people as kids learn that reading is exciting and interesting and they want to do more of it. Maybe more means Stephen King; maybe it means Henry James; maybe it means *We All Fall Down* by Robert Cormier, or maybe it means the next *Fear Street* title. Regardless, more reading is the result.

In planning this text, I realized my approach would need to differ from other books of literary criticism about young adult authors. Most of the other books in the field examine respected authors and seek to explain the importance of their works. That the subject is important and worth analyzing is a given. This book is radically different because Stine is not respected, at least in YA literature circles, nor is his work seen as important. In fact, some see Stine and his writings as dangerous, debasing, and detrimental. Moreover, debate about Stine has become a prism through which we view questions about youth and reading. Should children read horror? Is horror harmful? Should they read series fiction? Should genre fiction be in libraries? To explain the importance of Stine is to consider these larger questions also before us. I have an advocacy agenda as well. I don't want to just serve Stine by this argument but also thrillers and recreational paperback original fiction. Despite what you may have heard, this is not such a scary territory.

ACKNOWLEDGMENTS

This book would have been a much scarier experience for me without the help of others. The staff of Houston Public Library's Heights branch was courteous and helpful in dealing with my ILL blitz. Dr. Mary K. Chelton provided inspiration, but more than that, blazed the trail for the acceptance of genre fiction. Thanks to Mark and Sandy Morris, Charles Novo, and Patricia Taylor for their contributions to this manuscript. I am grateful to Patty Campbell for choosing me for this project knowing that we have opposing viewpoints about Stine. I would like to thank Erica Klein for supporting me, putting up with my writing habits, and being pretty damn funny to boot. Also, thanks to my mother Betty Jones who nurtured my love of reading and has always supported my writing pursuits. I would like to thank the hundreds of kids who have spoken with me about Stine and thrillers. It was their enthusiasm for the genre that convinced me there was something more to these books than just a collection of cheap thrills—not to discount the genius of creating cheap thrills. In particular, I'd like to acknowledge my friend Brent Chartier's son Adam who talked with me about *Goosebumps*, *Fear Street*, and his reading habits and interests. Adam provided me with the suggestion of which *Fear Street* to analyze in detail (*Secret Admirer*), but something more important: a reminder of the readership for whom Stine is writing. What is lost in the debate among librarians, critics, and teachers about Stine are the voices of his readers, like Adam, who wonder why adults just don't "get it." I hope this book helps adults "get it."

CHRONOLOGY

1943   Robert Lawrence Stine is born in Columbus, Ohio on October 8.

1952   Begins writing at age nine.

1962-1965   Edits humor magazine, *The Sundial*, at Ohio State University.

1965   Graduates from Ohio State University, B.A. in English.

1965-1966   Teaches junior high social studies classes in Columbus.

1966   Moves to New York City, starts writing career.

1968-1971   Hired by Scholastic, becomes associate editor at *Junior Scholastic*.

1969   Marries Jane Waldhorn on June 22.

1972-1975   Editor, *Search* magazine.

1975-1983   Editor, *Bananas* magazine.

1978   Publishes (as Jovial Bob Stine) his first book, *How to Be Funny.*

1980   Son, Matthew Daniel, born on June 7.

1982-1989   Publishes several multiple storyline books. Takes many other writing assignments, including head writer for children's TV show, *Eureka's Castle.*

1984-1985   Editor, *Maniac* magazine.

1985   Leaves Scholastic.

1986   Publishes first thriller, *Blind Date.*

1987   Publishes second thriller, *Twisted.*

1989   Publishes first *Fear Street* title, *The New Girl*, and *The Baby Sitter*, first of four *Baby Sitter* books.

1990   Publishes two humorous novels, *Phone Calls* and *How I Broke Up With Ernie.*

1991   Publishes first *Fear Street Super Chiller*, *Party Summer.*

1992   Publishes first *Goosebumps* title, *Monster Blood,* and first *Fear Street* trilogy, *Cheerleaders*

1993   Publishes historical horror trilogy, *Fear Street Saga.*

1994   *Goosebumps*mania begins as Stine dominates
                USA Today's best-seller list.

1995   Named one of *People* magazine's most intrigu-
                ing people. Publishes first adult novel, *Super-
                stitious*. *Goosebumps* TV show premiers. Attack
                article   by Diana West published in new con-
                servative magazine, *The Weekly Standard*.

1996   The merchandising of *Goosebumps* explodes,
                producing *Goosebumps* T-shirts, hats, etc. Spin-
                off book series, such as the *Fear Street Sagas*
                and *Goosebumps Presents*, begin. *Goosebumps*
                CD-ROM released.

1997   Publishes, with friend Joe Arthur, juvenile
                autobiography, *It Came From Ohio: My Life as
                a Writer*. Scholastic's stock drops 40% on
                announcement that sales of *Goosebumps* are off
                and series probably has peaked. *Goosebumps*
                identified by the American Library Associa
                tion's Office for Intellectual Freedom as the
                most challenged books during 1996. *Fear Street*
                series moves from Archway to Golden Books as
                Stine signs a contract rumored to be for $13
                million. Movie deal signed between Stine and
                Fox Family Films for first *Goosebumps* movie.

1998   *Goosebumps 2000* series debuts as *Goosebumps*
                takes on a scarier edge. *Goosebumps* made the
                subject of a Disney World attraction.

INTRODUCTION:
WHY R.L. STINE?

Since the publication of *The Outsiders* by S.E. Hinton and *The Pigman* by Paul Zindel in the 1960s, the literary genre known as young adult (YA) literature has continued to mature and produce outstanding books by talented writers. Authors like S.E. Hinton, Paul Zindel, M.E. Kerr, Robert Cormier, and a host of others represent the best that YA literature offers, proving that books for teenagers are not "dumbed-down" adult books, but rather a literature with unique voices and virtues. This literature stands up under the critic's beam, over the test of time, and in the eyes of young readers. Because of this, their works have been deemed worthy of numerous journal articles as well as books of literary criticism. Added now to that roster of esteemed young adult writers worthy of study is . . . R.L. Stine? The author of countless joke collections, multiple storyline books, and even bubble gum cards, Stine has earned a notoriety that stems primarily from his *Fear Street* series and other YA thrillers. Stine expanded his publishing empire in 1992 with the *Goosebumps* series for pre-teens, which catapulted him to the status, since 1994, of the best-selling author in the U.S. No one writing for youth is in the same league as R.L. Stine when it comes to book sales.

Stine, however, is obviously not of the same literary quality as titans of YA literature like Robert Cormier, Rosa Guy, and their ilk. Let's get that out of the way first. One constant in reviewing or critiquing literature is to compare and contrast one author with others in the same field. A problem arises here because Stine is not really in the same category as Cormier or Guy, not only because of the quality of his writing, but also because of his themes, motives, and even philosophy. Stine has more in common with Rosie O'Donnell than he does with Rosa Guy; he's a writer as entertainer, not an author as artist. Comparing Stine to these authors serves no one—not Stine, nor Cormier, nor Guy, nor the YA reader. Instead, given Stine's tremendous popularity, the real question is not "Are these books quality?" but rather "What is it about these books that makes them so popular?" To dismiss his work as "junk" reading not only insults his readers, but also fails to teach us anything. We know readers respond to his books, yet other than saying the books are "fun to read," we don't analyze what is causing that response in readers. Looking closely at Stine's work allows us to learn a great deal about an area rarely discussed in detail in the field of YA literature: popular young adult paperback fiction. Since this type of book is a huge part, if not the biggest part, of the YA publishing industry, ignoring it also serves no one. Instead, by studying Stine's fiction we can learn a great deal about YA readers, YA books, and the connections between the two. In addition, we can learn how a poor kid from Columbus, Ohio, who wrote silly humor magazines, became the publishing powerhouse known as R.L. Stine.

THE KING OF ALL MEDIA

On 21 February 1997, Scholastic Inc., publishers of Stine's *Goosebumps* series, saw its stock drop 40% after an announcement that its earnings would not meet expectations. Blame for this dramatic drop fell on the decline in sales figures of the *Goosebumps* franchise, in particular their older titles. Five years into the life of the series, it has "simply peaked."[1] The wide coverage given this news—which ended up on the front page of most newspaper business sections—demonstrates the impact and importance of R.L. Stine. One writer, it seems, influences the fate of an entire company. Few in the history of publishing have had that distinction. No one in the history of young adult books has even come close.

Nor has anyone else in the history of young adult literature sold (or for that matter written) as many books as R.L. Stine. Admittedly, a great many of the titles bear the *Goosebumps* brand name and are aimed at children, but it was Stine's YA thriller series, *Fear Street*, that made *Goosebumps* possible. Even without *Goosebumps*, Stine's *Fear Street* titles for Archway/Pocket Books and nonseries thrillers for Scholastic place him in sales far above that of the most respected names in YA literature. Stine is also, without a doubt, the most famous of all young adult writers. Perhaps only Judy Blume in her heyday rivals Stine in this regard. *People* magazine profiled Stine, even selecting him as one of its "most intriguing people" for 1995.[2] He has appeared on countless television shows, helped create two successful television series (*Goosebumps* and *Eureka's Castle*) and has been written about in just about every major news source. His first adult novel earned a big advance and a movie deal. The *Goosebumps* brand name appears on fast-food drink cups, snack foods, calendars, clothing, and everywhere else in the retail world. His books sprout audiotape versions and CD-ROM games, generate movie deals (a *Goosebumps* movie, to be produced by Tim Burton, was inked in December 1997), are transformed into television shows then released as best-selling videos. Kids' unofficial *Fear Street* and *Goosebumps* tribute pages fill the World Wide Web, and Stine has been a popular guest on America Online. He is not just a writer; he is, with apologies to Howard Stern, bucking to become the King of All Media.

Yet, while Stine's young fans devour his work, adults (parents, teachers, librarians, and critics) have devoured Stine. His books are attacked, assailed, insulted, and banned. As paperback originals, his books are infrequently reviewed and the notices are far from glowing. Even those who don't attack Stine dismiss his work with the backhanded compliment of "Well, at least they're reading something." The final totals will perhaps show that this "something" has been read and enjoyed more than books by any other author for kids. Given that much quantity, there is obviously a quality to his writing. Maybe the quality is only the ability to write best sellers, but that alone demonstrates a unique talent that can't be ignored or dismissed.

What kids are reading (and reading and reading) are the works of a great entertainer. Like Stephen King, to whom he is often compared, Stine knows how to tell a story. He knows how to keep readers interested and involved and, most important, how to satisfy them. Stine isn't breaking any new literary ground. Trying to analyze his books along those lines doesn't work. Stine is not creating well-rounded characters; he is not using imagery, symbolism, metaphor or any of the other tricks of *that* trade in his writing. Instead, he practices the tricks of his own trade: that of entertaining people with "cheap thrills." He uses humor, rollercoaster plots, suspenseful chapter endings, "gross outs," credible teen dialogue, and a bare-bones style to get to the point, which is to thrill, scare, and thus entertain his readers. He is not interested in educating, enlightening, or informing; he is only interested in entertaining. Further, Stine believes that "kids as well as adults are entitled to books of no socially redeeming value."[3] But his books do have value—the value of reading. Never has a writer for kids been so flagrant about his motives; never has a writer for kids been so successful in achieving these goals.

STINE AND LITERARY CRITICISM: AN OXYMORON?

YA authors like Robert Cormier and Richard Peck earn stacks of positive reviews, literary awards, and mentions on annual Best Books lists. Some have won the Margaret Edwards Award for lifetime achievement in the field of young adult literature; classes in secondary schools and students in young adult literature courses study their works. Almost all of these authors command the respect and admiration of teachers, educators, and librarians. The artistry of their writings shows that the terms "young adult literature" and "literary criticism" belong in the same sentence. The same could not be said about R.L. Stine. The most common response I received after telling colleagues about this book was that Stine and "literary criticism" was an oxymoron. He will never win a lifetime achievement award; neither are his books studied, nor is Stine respected or admired by adults. Instead, he is, as was once a popular YA expression, "dissed" by them.

Stine does deserve, and indeed requires, both respect and a closer look. Anyone who writes books that are so popular must do something right. The task here is to try to explain what that something is. Perhaps this is literary criticism, but it is also cultural criticism because the Grand Canyon of opinions about Stine has a great deal to do with the perceived purpose of literature for kids. If you believe that books for youth should be lasting, treasured, and enlightening, you won't like R.L. Stine. If you believe that horror, violence, or anything else scary does not belong in books for youth, then Stine is not for you. Finally, if you believe that all books must be meaty literature and that light snack-food reading has no value, then you'll want to pass on the R.L. Stine plate.

The people who don't like Stine share many of those beliefs. Yet, I would also advance that many share a lack of respect and understanding of youth and their reading. The failure to accept and respect Stine is not so much a prejudice against popular culture—although that is a huge part of the problem—but a lack of understanding of kids and reading. Critics of Stine seem only focused on their own reactions to his work, not those of kids. This is fine with Stine since he seems to be writing without any concern for what adults think of his work: he seems to care only about his audience. Since adults fail to understand why his books are popular, they'll never understand what makes R.L.

Stine an important figure in contemporary books for youth.

This condescending attitude comes out in reviews, which almost always contain a phrase like "It's no Agatha Christie" or other disparaging comparisons with respected authors. The question about Stine's work shouldn't be whether it is as good as something else, but whether it is good on the level that it inhabits. Is it scary? Is it suspenseful? Is it satisfying? More important, is it these things to his readers? The reactions of adults, teens, and children are very different. That is something Stine knows; it is also something his critics seem to forget.

There is also the matter of taste. One of Stine's fortes is the "gross out" scene in which one of his teen characters will find a dead maggot-ridden rat on the doorstep or blood in a lunchbag. Such scenes are not to everyone's taste. Stine's books contain acts of violence, and often there is blood. Stine's horror show is, by the very nature of the subject matter and the rules of the genre, going to turn lots of readers, especially adult readers, away. Stine's detractors substitute subjective tastes for an objective judgment of the quality of the work itself. You may be grossed out by blood, yet it is difficult not to appreciate the creative genius of Hitchcock's shower scene in *Psycho* or the finely crafted shock sequences in Stine's *Fear Street Saga* trilogy. Instead of being put off by the "blood" in Stine's writing, it is time to explore the "guts" that make his work so successful.

WHY STUDY R.L. STINE?

For all the reasons listed above, studying R.L. Stine seems appropriate. To not study the most popular author writing for young adults fails to show the range of books available for teens. Further reasons for study include:

1. Impact on readers. The goal of anyone writing for kids is to connect with readers. Stine has achieved this to the nth degree. Readers respond to his work, but is it only because the books are suspenseful, or could it be because he strikes other chords within readers? Just because a book is escapist or rec-

reational reading does not mean that is the *only* level it works
on, especially with the young teens. He's writing formula
fiction and the formula works. Is it just the plotting, or are
there are other elements that make Stine so popular? There
are plenty of other thrillers, but Stine stands above them all.
If his books are as bad as his critics claim, then how come
readers think they are so good? Further, his critics claim his
books have a negative impact. Rolling out arguments reminiscent of the anti-comic book debates from the 1950s, they
claim Stine isn't just a bad writer, but that his books are
harmful. Are they? Is Stine helpful, harmful, or harmless?
Which is it?

2. Importance to the literature. While Stine didn't create the YA
   thriller, he was one of the founders, and he did create the first
   and most successful thriller series with *Fear Street*. Since the
   late 1980s, thrillers have dominated the YA book world.
   They have filled bookstores, libraries, and school book fairs.
   Other YA authors saw their older works republished in new
   thriller covers, while many YA authors who had never written series or paperback originals started penning thrillers.
   Where did this genre come from? Why did this whole genre
   succeed? Why do people want to be scared?

3. Impasse between kids and adults. Stine represents a very serious split between readers of YA fiction and reviewers of
   YA fiction. The field has seen this before, most noticeably in
   the romance series explosion that occurred in the years before thrillers took over the marketplace. Librarians have been
   battling over the role of series fiction in libraries for almost a
   hundred years. How is it that while kids are devouring these
   books, librarians are questioning whether they belong in a library? Why is it that at the same time critics are moaning
   that young people don't read, they are denouncing Stine's
   books that are read by millions?

4. Insight into Stine. How is it that a joke book writer, magazine
   editor, and multiple storyline book author became the biggest
   name in youth publishing? In particular, how did those for-

mer writing jobs influence Stine and help him develop his YA thrillers? In other words, how did the person Robert Lawrence Stine become the phenomenon known as R.L. Stine? How is he so productive? Was it because at an early age, as Stine says, "I was really hooked on writing"?[4] All of Stine's fans know the bare bones of his life and career, but I'll try to look at themes and patterns. Are these books autobiographical? How does he get his ideas? How does he write so many books? What are his influences?

5. Investigating Stine's style. Stine is not the only writer penning horror for young adults and pre-teens, but he is without a doubt the most successful. What gimmicks does he use? What are the elements of his success? What are those "cheap tricks" he employs? By looking at a few individual titles, as well as groups of books, we find that the elements of Stine's often imitated but never duplicated style become clear. Yes, it is formula fiction and it works. So, what are the ingredients? What makes Stine, Stine?

APPROACHING THE SUBJECT

In this book, I'll hope to answer these and other questions about Stine, his work, and his influence. The other volumes of YA literary criticism recap every book by the subject author, but that approach doesn't seem prudent here, nor possible. With close to 250 published books to examine, the "annotated" Stine would be a book in itself. I will look at some individual titles in depth, but the focus will be more on discovering the themes and techniques that run throughout his work, and the connections from his work in one genre to another. Rather than comparing Stine to other YA authors, most of the comparisons and allusions here are from the world Stine lives in: popular culture. To understand and appreciate Stine, a critic must have an understanding and appreciation of popular culture. If you can value only fine dining, then you'll never understand how others enjoy a drive-through meal at McDonald's. Yet the fact that millions of people do enjoy fast food and fast culture—series paperbacks, professional wrestling, and TV sitcoms—cannot be denied. If we want kids to appreciate good literature in the future, we must not be judgmental toward the literature that they like now. To endorse and validate popular reading isn't pulling kids away from a quest for fine literature, but rather encouraging a step toward it by making a connection.

To prepare for this book, I reread almost everything Stine had written for YAs, including as many of the early humor books as I could find through interlibrary loan and used-bookstore shopping. In addition, I read everything written about Stine, including reviews, but in particular articles featuring interviews. A personal interview with Stine for this book could not be arranged, so I will be quoting from Stine's remarks in previously published sources and his autobiography. While certainly a dialogue with Stine and his associates would have been very beneficial to this book, Stine has been very forthright in his published interviews about his work and what it means. By following his story from joke teller to plot twister to horror master, I hope to do more than explain his books and his influence by providing an insight into Stine's writing life and style. Throughout all of these incarnations, one constant has remained. R.L. Stine writes books that entertain people, from his self-produced humor magazines written at age nine up to the latest *Fear Street* and *Goosebumps* installments. That fact—that his books entertain— is one that escapes many adults, but is never forgotten by R.L./Robert Lawrence/Jovial Bob Stine.

NOTES

1. "Between the Lines, " *Entertainment Weekly* (14 March 1997): 72.

2. "R. L. Stine," *People Weekly* (25 December 1995): 102-3.

3. *Contemporary Authors,* New Revision Series. Ed. Deborah Straub. (Detroit: Gale Research, 1988): 450.

4. R.L. Stine, as told to Joe Arthur, *It Came From Ohio: My Life as a Writer* (New York: Scholastic, 1997): 26 ; hereafter cited in text as *Ohio.*

CHAPTER ONE

DON'T GO IN THE ATTIC

It was a terrifying scene, a madhouse where "boys were crying and girls were screaming."[1]

The Ritz Carlton hotel in suburban Washington, D.C. in 1995 was packed with over 2,000 kids. That number represented less than half of those who wanted in—the police estimated the crowd at 5,000. Finally, the police asked him to come out and speak, using a megaphone, to all those trying to get into the building. He told them it was just impossible for him to see them all. The lucky ones who got inside stood silent, their eyes focused and in rapt attention because *he* was here.

R.L. STINE HAS LEFT THE BUILDING

He was R.L. Stine. On this day, however, he seemed more like Elvis. Police had to escort him in and out of the building. At the Reading is Fundamental Fair at the Ritz Carlton, Stine was the star attraction—and not only among children. At a related cocktail reception, high-ranking government officials, reporters and other members of D.C. society came up to Stine to get their son's or daughter's book autographed. Stine signed, smiled, and answered questions. He had heard the questions before, like "What does R.L. stand for?" (Robert Lawrence). In addition to answering questions during appearances on TV programs like the *Today Show*, he gets a truckload of mail every week. Some

1

reports say it is 400 letters, while others peg it as high as 2,000.[2] The letters, like the personal appearances, have taken on a mob scene quality not normally associated with a writer of books for kids. Maybe it happened, maybe it didn't, but when R.L. Stine finally made his way through the crowd to exit the Ritz Carlton that day, one could easily imagine hearing the announcement, "R.L. Stine has left the building."

It was not the first time Stine had drawn an overflow crowd. Soon after the D.C. chaos, Stine reduced his personal appearances, not only because they take time out of his busy schedule, but also because they were becoming too dangerous, and for the many who couldn't get in, too disappointing. A bookstore appearance in Texas in May 1996 brought similar results. Hundreds of children waited for hours, some getting in line as early as 6:30 a.m. for Stine's noon appearance. Once again, there was not enough time or space for all the kids to meet Stine. Stine "had to be ushered out the back door into a waiting van much like a movie or rock star. His departure was marked by enthusiastic shouts of 'There he is! There he is!'"[3]

This phenomenon was first documented when Stine appeared in his hometown of Columbus, Ohio, in 1994. One of the big events was a bookstore signing at a mall. Stine almost missed it. On his way there, the car he was in became stuck in a traffic jam. He thought there must have been an accident; instead, it was the crush of cars of people trying to get to the mall to bring their sons and daughters to see him. Once inside, Stine "spent five hours autographing books for about a thousand children."[4]

At the time of the Ritz Carlton appearance in 1995, Stine was at the absolute height of his fame. *USA Today* had proclaimed him the best-selling author in America since 1994.[5] Meanwhile, a TV show based on his *Goosebumps* series was just beginning, kicking off with a show that drew huge ratings.[6] Merchandise bearing the *Goosebumps* brand name was starting to appear in stores on all sorts of products. He was crowned the "king of creepy."[7] If Stine's books deal with nightmares, then this return to Columbus had to be like a dream. He was rich, successful, and famous, which were not exactly the circumstances in which he left Columbus back in the 1960s. Then, he was a young man who had a goal of moving to New York, becoming a successful writer, and editing his own humor magazine. Returning years later, those dreams had been fulfilled perhaps beyond his wildest imaginings. Yet in many ways success had not changed him at all. He was the same—his sense of humor, his desire to entertain, but most of all his love, his absolute love of writing, never left him.

Those three elements made him, like Elvis, the king of his chosen field. Like Elvis, Stine is loved by fans, both boys and girls, and hated by many of their parents. His ability to please his audience, to give them exactly and repeatedly what they want, defies those who seek to pick apart his work. He cranks out hits on a regular basis like someone punching a golden goose clock while his critics decry the quality of his books. Stine's success goes beyond his own work. His shadow falls not just on one genre, but on a whole industry. Finally, Stine's life, like Elvis's, is an American Dream success story. It is a story about a kid who grew up without much and was considered—by his own admission—a bit of an outsider, but who had a dream he pursued with determination, hard work, and unbending drive. When the time came, he was the right person with the right skills in the right place at the right time. As a joke writer, he must have known the last factor was perhaps the most important. Timing was everything.

CHILDREN PLAY WITH SCARY THINGS

There was a time when Robert Lawrence Stine was not in the right place at the right time: his birthday. It seems fitting that the man who made his fame and fortune delivering scary tricks and treats would have been born on Halloween. Instead, he was born a few weeks earlier, October 9, 1943, to Lewis and Anne Stine. Three years later his brother William was born. William figures prominently in most of Stine's childhood stories—mostly anec-

dotes about Bob and Bill trying to scare each other. The younger
brother is also a stock Stine character, showing up in books as a
wise guy, playing practical jokes and sneaking up behind people
and causing a dreadful fright. Looking back over Stine's childhood and young adult years, it is easy to see the influences and
experiences that led him to be such a success. As a child, he
liked telling stories that gave the listener, his brother,
"goosebumps"; as an adult, he would write stories giving them
to his readers.

Stine admits to a childhood fascination with scary things. He
was, by his own admission, "a fearful kid" (*Ohio*, 10) who didn't
take risks and found the world terrifying. In his autobiography
Stine tells about an experience at summer camp. He was supposed to dive into a pool and take a swimming test to earn a Red
Cross merit badge. Terrified, he could not dive and instead
walked away. It was a moment of supreme embarrassment and
panic. And later inspiration. As Stine says, he tries to use the
"same feeling of fear" in his books (*Ohio*, 12). The combination
of horror and humiliation would be part of the new ground that
Stine and fellow YA thriller author Christopher Pike would
stake out. Not only did bad things happen to teen characters,
they happened to them in public. Often the worst teen terror is
not fear of a villain, but fear of embarrassment among a peer
group. This situation at camp was also the perfect "fight or
flight" dilemma. In his thrillers, he would have his characters
face similar moments of decision. Each of them, however, would
not flee; instead they would always jump ahead to see what was
on the other side of the door or in the darkened room. Moreover,
youthful readers who have had similar moments of fear or failure can show their toughness by making it through one of Stine's
scary creations. Stine must realize that many kids feel as he
did—scared, shy, and unsure of themselves—and so reading
about scary things is almost as therapeutic as it is entertaining.

Despite his fears, or perhaps because of them, Stine enjoyed
scary entertainment as a child. He was a fan of radio programs
such as *The Shadow*. Stine recalled "being real scared . . . listen-

ing to these scary things on the radio. I loved that."[8] One program—*Suspense* – Stine said "terrified me" (*Ohio*, 7). He enjoyed radio programs other than thrillers, including those of Jean Shepherd. Shepherd was a storyteller broadcasting out of New York City telling humorous homespun tales about his childhood and family. Shepherd was a huge influence, according to Stine, because listening to the storyteller started him "someday going to New York" (*Ohio*, 7-8) and writing for a living.

Stine loved the B horror movies of the 1950s. He was coming of age when the "creature feature" genre was in full swing. He and his brother would go into a theater packed with other kids and they would "scream and kick the seats" (*Ohio*, 33) at the monsters on the screen. Another big influence came from television's *Twilight Zone* with its unique mix of irony, humor, and horror. But mostly Stine liked the trick endings the show was famous for. He said the show "hooked me from the start" (*Ohio*, 47). Although viewers knew there would be a surprise ending, they tuned in each week to be tricked again. Much the same, Stine's readers "tune in" with each new monthly installment of *Fear Street* or *Goosebumps* knowing full well a trick ending is coming after a story full of shocks and jolts.

Stine also enjoyed the horror comics and magazines of the 1950s like *Tales from the Crypt*. While he was a fan, according to Stine, his mother was not. Stine said, "My mother wouldn't let me bring them into the house. She said they were trash. So I had to read them at the barbershop. I used to get a haircut every week" (Gilson, 1995). Stine also became a fan of the new magazine *Mad*. The magazine, Stine recalled, "absolutely blew me away. I couldn't believe anything could be so funny."[9] He later said, "*Mad* magazine changed my life."[10] Stine was like a lot of kids growing up in the 1950s—fascinated by horror but also enjoying the slightly subversive *Mad* humor that was just coming into vogue. But Stine's biggest childhood influence wasn't the work of anyone else; his biggest influence was in his own house.

THE THING IN THE ATTIC

Stine grew up in Bexley, a suburb of Columbus, Ohio. The house had a big yard, lots of trees, and three stories. The third story, however, was merely an attic. An attic that his mother refused to let him enter. The existence of the attic and his mother's cryptic explanations as to why he was not allowed there got young Robert Lawrence Stine's imagination flowing as he would wonder, *"What terrible thing is up there in the attic?"* (*Ohio*, 2-3). He imagined monsters because his mother provided him with no other explanation. It was almost as if his mother had given him the title "Don't go in the attic," and Stine was writing the story. Stine started sharing these spooky thoughts and other scary stories with his brother Bill. Stine recalled:

> When my brother and I were kids, we gave each other goosebumps every night. We would lie in our beds in the room we shared and take turns telling each other scary stories. We tried to frighten one another—and it was easy . . . Our stories were about ghosts and haunted houses, werewolves and mummies staggering to life. Some were about walking in the woods in back of our house . . . In our stories there were creatures buried under the rocks, hideous monsters who pushed away the stones and came stalking after us . . . After a while, I developed a storytelling technique that drove my brother crazy. I would tell my story slowly, quietly, building to the horror. Then, when the three-headed bat was about to swoop to attack, when the mummy had his putrid decaying hands wrapped around a throat, when I reached the very peak of suspense—I'd say "To be continued tomorrow. Good night." And I'd leave my brother begging me to continue while I fell asleep with a cruel smile on my face.[11]

The cliffhanger "trick," as Stine himself calls it, came early.

It was similar to the trick that his mother had played on him regarding the attic. By not telling Stine *what* was there or *why* he could not see the attic, she generated more suspense and fueled his imagination. His fascination with the attic came to a head when his parents decided to sell the house and move when he was "about seven"(*Ohio*, 12). Sensing he might not have many more chances, Stine decided to go up into the attic. Once there, he was profoundly disappointed—there were no monsters, no old trunks, no mooseheads hanging on the walls; it was nothing like he imagined. There was hardly anything interesting at all, with one exception: "I found an old typewriter in the attic. I brought it downstairs and started typing up stories and little joke magazines. I've been writing ever since." [12] With that discovery, everything changed in the life of young Bob Stine. The typewriter led him to writing, which would become the central element of his life, so much so that Stine later said, "I didn't really have a childhood. I was nine years old and typing, typing."[13]

TYPING, TYPING

Stine began typing his own magazines. The first was called the *All New Bob Stine Giggle Book*. It overflowed with jokes, but by his own admission, had a badly drawn cover. Stine loved comic books and wanted to draw them but did so "in the worst way!" (*Ohio*, 8). *The Giggle Book* was tiny: three by four inches, only ten pages long—five of which were blank. After the *Giggle Book* came *HAH For Maniacs Only* (*Maniac* would be the name of a humor magazine Stine created as an adult) and a host of others in rapid succession. He spent hours in his room typing and illustrating the only copy. He let his brother see it and then brought it to school for his friends to pass around, read, and crack up over.

Stine's writing as a youth showed a particular talent that would greatly influence his later works. He was already finding he could work fast and funny. He saw this as an avenue to popularity, but also he found these magazines fun to do. He got to see the effect the magazines had on his schoolmates. He got to watch them laugh at something he wrote. Stine was writing for his peers—the style, the vocabulary, the type of wit and humor, all of it aimed at boys eight to twelve years old. When he wrote his humor magazines as an adult, he perhaps remembered that style and those magazines. One of Stine's greatest attributes as a writer for youth is that he never seems to be writing or talking

down. Instead, his voice is very much that of a peer. His joke
books, for example, do not seem to be by someone trying to
write jokes an adult might think a ten-year-old would find funny.
Instead, they seem much more like the jokes a ten-year-old
would tell. Or later, the type of horror story a teenager might
tell.

Writing, according to Stine, was his passion: "Mainly I
loved writing and typing" (*Something 1994*, 222). The typing
soon got easier when his parents bought him a new typewriter
for his bar mitzvah. The magazines were becoming more popular
as well, in part because of their irreverence in the style of *Mad*.
This often attracted the attention of a disapproving principal or
teacher who failed to see humor in Stine or his magazines and
would ask, "You think you're pretty funny, don't you?" (*Ohio*,
28). His subject matter was usually parodies, often related to
school, such as an article called "How to Read This in Class."
His titles, including one called *BARF*, aimed for the junior high
funny bone.

Despite the success of these magazines, Stine didn't find
himself embraced in school by the popular crowd, in part because he was, by his own admission, "pretty nerdy" (*Ohio*, 33).
He played clarinet in the band unsuccessfully and sang in the
chorus but didn't play on any sports teams. Although he lived in
the wealthy suburb of Bexley, his parents were not rich. Stine
said, "We lived in this tiny house three doors from the railroad
tracks, surrounded by big houses owned by wealthy people . . . I
felt like an outsider."[14] At school Stine was surrounded by kids
with nicer clothes and newer cars. He recalled that "I was shy to
begin with. All my friends got Thunderbirds when they turned
16. I think that's one of the reasons I became a writer" (Gilson
1995). Stine's friendships in school were based on a shared
sense of humor. He and his pal Jeff recorded comedy tapes, and
his buddy Norm was a wisecrack artist. Stine and his friends
were products of the fifties' youth culture: they cruised the
streets, went to drive-ins, or just rode around with the radio

turned up and the windows rolled down, honking the horn constantly at everyone they knew.

Stine's typewriter was also in constant use. In addition to continuing to write magazines, he tried his hand at a novel, *The Lovable Bear*, and wrote lots of stories. He was also writing articles for the school newspaper and essays for contests. He entered and won such contests mainly, he said, because "I loved seeing my picture in the papers" (*Ohio*, 38). He also wrote, in his own words, the "world's all time funniest" senior class skit (*Ohio*, 48). If writing was his obsession in junior high and high school, it was about to become his golden opportunity.

BOB STINE, BUCKEYE

To his surprise, Ohio State University accepted him as a student—a surprise because he had spent his time in high school "writing little magazines instead of studying" (*Ohio*, 50). Stine says he was "the kind of student who didn't have to work hard to get B's. I think every report card would say 'Bob could do much better, he isn't really working up to the best of his ability' . . . I remember being bored a lot in school, being more interested in things like radio shows, TV and writing" (*Something 1994*, 222). Since Ohio State was located in his hometown of Columbus, Stine could live at home and use his nonclass time writing. Ohio State, like most large university campuses, had several opportunities for budding writers, one of which was the humor magazine *The Sundial*. Stine said he had always "dreamed about writing for the magazine" (*Ohio*, 53) which once had James Thurber on staff. As a freshman Stine applied for, and got—again to his surprise—the job of editor of the magazine. Primarily, Stine said, this was because the board making the decision wanted someone who would not be a "troublemaker" (*Ohio*, 53).

Stine's *Sundial* exploded with cartoons, parodies, fake interviews, made-up ads, and other comedy staples. *The Sundial* also engaged in practical jokes such as Stine running for student body president with the slogan "Elect a clown for President"

(*Ohio,* 60). During his *Sundial* years, Robert Lawrence Stine became "Jovial Bob" in an effort to "create a personality to sell the magazine."[15] Stine got his first taste of criticism when the student newspaper, *The Lantern,* ran reviews of *The Sundial* that were, in Stine's words, "downright nasty" (*Ohio,* 62). He also made lifelong friendships. Several old *Sundial* cronies would show up later in his life, including Joe Arthur, who helped pen Stine's autobiography. Arthur remembered that when he met Stine in *The Sundial* office, Stine was "writing the whole magazine" (*Ohio,* x). Stine described *The Sundial* as "mainly what I did at Ohio State. I'd hang out at this magazine office in the Student Union and put out this magazine every month" (*Something 1994,* 222). It was the first step to fulfilling his dream.

To do that, however, meant moving to New York City where he imagined that all writers lived. After finishing college, Stine began readying himself for the move. To raise cash he took a job as a teacher, first as a substitute, then as a junior high history teacher. Stine did not care much for history nor did he find his students interested in it either, so he emphasized reading. Awarding students for good behavior during the week, Stine made Friday a free reading day where he encouraged all types of reading, in particular comic books. Perhaps Stine learned valuable lessons at this time—the importance of leisure reading and not to be condescending toward the reading choices made by young people. He also gained from his year of teaching some up close and personal interaction with kids from an adult viewpoint that would help him craft dialogue for his later books. But it was only a year. Stine was not happy teaching and while the principal never criticized him, he did not, in Stine's words, "nominate me for Teacher of the Year" (*Ohio,* 66). Teaching was not his dream; being a writer in New York City was.

THE RIGHT PLACE

Stine arrived in New York in 1966, found an apartment in

Greenwich Village and looked for work as a magazine writer. His first job was with a trade magazine called *Institutional Investor*, where he talked his way into a job professing knowledge of the inner workings of magazine production from his *Sundial* days. He was fired almost immediately when it became apparent to everyone, including himself, that he had no such knowledge. What he did know how to do, however, was write. He eventually landed a job at a teen fan magazine. With the woefully uncreative title of *15*, this fanzine was edited by a middle-aged woman out of her apartment. In this job, he wrote "interviews" with various celebrities, but he never actually talked with any of them. Instead, he would build the article out of newspaper clippings and photos. Stine went on lots of such "interviews," including one with The Beatles, before the magazine went bust. Before that happened, however, he managed to publish his first horror story, "Bony Fingers from the Grave," under the name Robert Lawrence for the magazine *Adventures in Horror*, which had the same publisher as *15*. Although this job did not last long, it gave Stine valuable experience in writing for teenagers. Stine said, "It was great training. In a way it was very creative work because we had to make up everything" (*Something 1994*, 222). If *15* was at all like other teen fanzines, the writing style had to be crisp and lively. It had to be readable yet not talk down or seem juvenile. The ability to write that way, reinforced through all Stine's pre-*Fear Street* days, would be one of the keys to his success. Rather than only coming up with his own inspiration for articles, Stine was also fed ideas and subjects by his editor. That too would prove to be a pattern in his writing life.

Stine's next job was quite different, as he became a writer for a trade magazine called *Soft Drink Industry*. It was a basic "nine-to-five grind" job, which Stine found "boring" (*Ohio*, 77). Later Stine admitted that the job "helped train me . . . as far as writing very fast. I would have to do twenty articles a day from stacks of news clippings on my desk. It taught me to not stop and think about it, just sit down and write" (*Something 1994*, 222).

While Stine was momentarily derailed professionally, his personal life was undergoing great change. He met Jane Wald-horn, also a magazine writer, at a party, and the two soon became engaged. They married on June 22, 1969. Back in Columbus, his younger brother Bill was working on *The Sundial* and met his wife-to-be, Megan, and the couple soon moved to New York. Stine's father retired and relocated to northern California. With all of that change in the air, Stine decided to join in by leaving *Soft Drink Industry* to work as a staff writer for Scholastic, which turned out to be exactly the right place for R.L. Stine.

BANANAS AND MANIACS

Scholastic was one of the top publishing houses in New York, with a very specific, albeit huge, market. Their target audience was students. They distributed their books through book fairs and their magazines through classroom subscriptions. The Scholastic brand name was everywhere in schools, as the company had publications for just about every niche of the educational market. Stine and his wife Jane both started working for Scholastic as staff writers; he for *Junior Scholastic*, she for the magazine *Scope*. Stine soon moved over to edit *Search*, Scholastic's social studies magazine. *Search*'s audience was junior high students, but the writing was on a fourth-grade level. Although Stine had little interest in social studies, he had great interest in seeing the magazine succeed. Just as he had made history more interesting in the classroom, he tried to make learning entertaining in this magazine. He recalled:

> It was a real challenge for me to be the editor of a social studies magazine. And it was perfect for the reader because . . . they didn't like school and couldn't read well. It was a very creative magazine. We did all kinds of things in disguise, interviews, simulations, that sort of thing. We had tremendous mail responses from teachers saying the kids loved it. (*Roginski*, 208)

Stine did not say so, but he probably knew that "couldn't read well" was a code phrase for boys. Stine's solution was humor. Other than *Sports Illustrated*, easily the most popular boys' magazine at that time was *Mad*. From his first magazine at age nine up to *The Sundial*, Stine knew intuitively that humor would reach readers that other writing could not.

Scholastic knew all about humor magazines. Its laugh riot, *Dynamite*, was one of the most successful children's magazines in the country, selling over a million copies each month. When the editor of *Dynamite* left, Jane moved into that chair, while Scholastic let her husband create a humor magazine for teenagers. Named *Bananas*—and soon to be loaded with gross jokes about food and lots of TV parodies—it was a combination of the juvenile humor of *Dynamite* with the mocking humor of *Mad*. For a while Stine edited both *Search* and *Bananas*. When the time came to choose, it was no choice. Stine said, "I had to choose one. I took *Bananas*. It was what I really wanted to do from the time I was nine years old. I was thirty-two and I'd achieved my life's ambition" (*Roginski*, 209).

Magazine writing meant Stine had to write fast, write well, and then move on to the next piece. It was the perfect training ground for someone who later in life would be writing at least two books a month. Magazine writing meant constant deadlines, the need to come up with new material, and also retain material that readers liked. Humor magazines like *Mad* depend not only on recognition humor such as TV parodies, but also repetition humor. Readers want to see certain bits in every issue, like *Mad*'s famous back cover or the "Spy vs. Spy" feature. Stine perhaps learned another valuable lesson: if something is funny enough (later he would translate this to "scary enough"), it is not only okay to use it over and over, but expected. What would an issue of *Bananas* be, for example, without more banana jokes each issue? Much the same, what would a *Fear Street* be without a prank telephone call, a mistaken identity, and a dead rat? In humor and horror, familiarity does not breed contempt; it breeds expectations and popularity.

Another important skill Stine honed during these years was writing for kids. Maybe since Stine started writing humor (and telling scary stories) as a child, he always allowed that sensibility to dominate his writing. His books do not talk down to kids; they greet them on their own level. The vocabulary, the sentence structure, the nuts and bolts are aimed at kids. From his work at *Search*, Stine also gained experience writing for reluctant readers. The way to do that was to appeal to the short attention span of many teenagers, in particular boys. And it was primarily boys who bought, loved, and passed around *Bananas*.

WE HAVE NO BANANAS

Although popular, *Bananas* never reached the sales of *Mad*. The humor was basic: lots of fake lists, TV and movie parodies, goofy cartoons, jokes, and riddles. Nonetheless, Scholastic began having some financial difficulties, and sliced *Bananas* while downsizing. Stine took an assignment to start a new magazine called *Maniac*, which lasted about a year. Soon after, Stine found himself without a job.

Not only did Stine edit *Bananas* and *Maniac,* he was also their creator. During his Scholastic years, Stine was involved in two other very important creations. The first was the birth of his son, Matthew, on June 7, 1980. Stine rarely writes about Matt in his books, although he is the model for the cover of *Fear Street's The Perfect Date* and Matthew is the name of the main character/vampire in *Goodnight Kiss*. Matt is also the name of the character in *The Protectors* series Stine wrote in the late 1980s under the pen name of Zachary Blue. Matt professes profound disinterest in his father's work . Stine commented, "My son has NEVER read one of my books! He won't read them—because he knows it drives me CRAZY!"[16] Matt does, however, provide inspiration. In interview after interview, Stine says about Matt and his friends, "I spy on them, listen to their music and see how they dress" (*Scholastic*). For most of Matt's childhood Stine said he "stayed home, the happy homemaker" (*Ohio*, 97).

A few years after Matt's birth, the Stines were involved in the creation of Parachute Press, a company formed by Jane Stine and their friend Joan Waricha. It soon became Stine's distribution channel for much of his free-lance writing. Rather than being sold directly to publishers, Stine's work would be owned and edited by Parachute Press. For many of Stine's 1980s books this did not make a difference, but it had tremendous impact when *Goosebumps* hit. It became the equivalent of having a license to print money.

But that was all to come later. Although he had written several humor books before leaving Scholastic in the mid-1980s, Stine was on his own as a free-lance writer. Understanding Stine's magazine days, as well as his free-lance work writing humor and multiple storyline books, is the key to understanding how *Fear Street*, then *Goosebumps*, achieved their great success. But before he ever learned to be frightening, R.L. Stine (also known as Jovial Bob Stine) was funny.

NOTES

1. Laura Blumenfeld, "Frightfully Glad to Meet You," *Washington Post* (8 December 1995): F1.

2. Kit Alderdice, "R.L. Stine: 90 Million Spooky Adventures," *Publishers Weekly* (17 July 1995): 209; hereafter cited in text as Alderdice.

3. Monica Stavish, "Children's Writer Worth Wait for Fans," *Fort Worth Star-Telegram* (10 March 1996) http://neterrant.net:80/news/doc/1047/1:NE11/1:NE11031096.html. (14 February 1997).

4. Nancy Gilson, "Of Shivers & Goosebumps," *Columbus Dispatch* (30 September 1995): H1; hereafter cited in text as Gilson, 1995.

5. Jacqueline Blais, "Spooky Stine Tackles TV Next," *USA Today* (6 April 1995): D4.

6. Alan Bash, "Goosebumps Spreading Fast," *USA Today* (1 December 1995): D1.

7. Eve Becker, "The King of Creepy," *Chicago Tribune* (12 July 1994): Sec. 7:1.

8. *Something About the Author: Facts and Pictures about Authors and Illustrators of Books for Young People*, vol. 76, ed. Diane Telgen (Detroit: Gale Research, 1994): 222; hereafter cited in text as *Something 1994*.

9. James W. Roginski, *Behind the Covers: Interviews with Authors and Illustrators of Books for Children and Young Adults* (Littleton CO: Libraries Unlimited, 1985): 208; hereafter cited in text as Roginski.

10. "Authors Online, Meet the Author: R.L. Stine," *Scholastic Network* http://network.scholastic.com/network/authors/gallery/stine/ (14 February 1996); hereafter cited in text as *Scholastic*.

11. R.L. Stine, "Why Kids Love to Get *Goosebumps*," *TV Guide* (28 October 1995): 24; hereafter cited at *TV Guide*.

12. *Speaking for Ourselves, Too : More Autobiographical Sketches by Notable Authors of Books for Young Adults*. ed. Donald R. Gallo (Urbana IL: National Council of Teachers of English, 1993): 203; hereafter cited in text as *Speaking*.

13. R.L. Stine, "Ghost Writer," *Life* (December 1994): 112.

14. Dan Santow and Toby Kahn, "The Scarier the Better." *People Weekly* (14 November 1994): 115.

15. Nancy Gilson, "Safely Scary," *Columbus Dispatch* (10 March 1994): G8; hereafter cited in text as Gilson, 1994.

16. "Authors Online, R.L. Stine." *Scholastic Network* http://network.scholastic.com/network/authors/gallery/stine/transcript.htm (14 February 1996).

CHAPTER TWO
JOKE TELLER

Like a character in one of his thrillers, Stine's life changed because of an unexpected phone call.

> "My name is Ellen Rudin," the voice on the other end of the line said. "I'm a children's book editor at E.P. Dutton."
> "A children's book editor? Why would a children's book editor be calling me?"
> "I think your magazine is very funny," she continued. "I'll bet you could write funny children's books." (*Ohio*, 89)

Rudin suggested that Stine try such a book and let her read it. Stine responded with *How to Be Funny*. While seemingly a how-to-do-it book, it was really a vehicle for Stine's *Bananas*-style humor, like the fake "how to" story. Stine's first book was merely an extension of his day job. When editing *Bananas*, Stine found that he could use the same gags, gimmicks, and tricks over and over again because they worked. His audience didn't seem to care if the jokes were old as long as they were funny.

HOW TO BE FUNNY

While there are many jokes in *How to Be Funny*, the first and foremost joke is Stine playing with his new book format. As Jon Szieszka would do years later in his fractured fairy tale *The Stinky Cheese Man*, Stine made the book format into a gristmill for gags. The table of contents tells very little about the contents, but a great deal about Stine's humor:

> Chapter Three. Chapter Three has been lost. We're substituting Chapter Seven in its place. Only we're calling it Chapter Three. Please don't tell anybody.
> Chapter Four. Why must every book have a Chapter Four?   Wouldn't it be much faster to go on to Chapter Five?
> Chapter Five. How To Be Funny with Chapter Four. Whoops—your book doesn't seem to have a Chapter Four. Better skip this chapter, too. Why not go back and reread the Introduction while everyone else reads Chapter Five?[1]

The last item in the table of contents, not surprisingly, is the introduction. In the first couple of pages, Stine has introduced readers to exactly what they are going to be getting: zany humor that will not make room for real content. What was important for Stine was not to convey information about telling jokes, but to tell jokes.

After a long list of supplies needed for the lessons in this book (items listed include a rhinestone weasel whip, a warm doorknob, and a wet llama), Stine's introduction further cracks the form. Like a good how-to book, Stine's is written in second person, but that, of course, is the joke: "Has this ever happened to you?   You pick up a new book. You just start to read the introduction. And suddenly the books asks, 'Has this ever happened to you?" (*Funny*, 1). Not content to tell the joke once, Stine uses comedy's golden spike, repetition: "If this has happened to you—don't stop reading. It may happen to you again! Has this ever happened to you?" (*Funny*, 1).

The introduction also serves up Stine's other trick of the comic trade, that hallmark of juvenile humor, the pun: "You haven't done your metric system homework....your math teacher is embarrassing you....by saying, 'What should I do with you?' You turn to him and say 'Take me to your liter'" (*Funny*, 3). The humor isn't sophomoric; it just aspires to that level. But it is also developmentally correct. By ages eight and nine, kids have a big enough vocabulary and sense of humor to appreciate puns, as entertainer Rosie O'Donnell discovered with her 1997 book *Kids Say the Punniest Things*. While Stine had no way of knowing back in 1977 the future controversy over his books, he suggests a motive for escapist entertainment: "When you're in a jam, when things get tense, when you have problems—big problems—that's the time to crack a joke, walk into a wall, fall on the floor. Does it help? It can't hurt!" (*Funny*, 2). It is a nice metaphor: recreational reading doesn't harm kids; instead it provides a pleasurable experience.

The first chapter would be familiar to *Bananas'* readers: the fake quiz. As he would do later in his multiple storyline books, Stine invites his readers' involvement by providing them with interactive sections. (Maybe this is where the librarian antagonism toward Stine began, as the library copy of *How to Be Funny* I had was marked up in pen by a reader who took the quizzes.) This chapter also contains a fill-in-the-blanks section (putting a joke together), a series of nonsense words, and an exercise which consists of matching straight lines with punch lines. In the last gag, the straight lines and punch lines don't match, but as the subtitle of the book suggests, this is going to be "an extremely silly guidebook."

The rest of the book continues to provide instruction on how to be funny in various settings: in school, at the dinner table, at parties, and with soup. Along the way, Stine introduces several characters, all the age of his readers. One such character is Dexter Brewster, who spends six months practicing walking backward only to have it end in comic disaster. Brewster is the kid for whom nothing goes right. All of his gags seem to backfire. When he pulls out an eight-foot-long, fifty-pound pencil to demonstrate pencil-sharpening shenanigans, he gets splinters in his hands. He is fairly helpless; he is also hysterical. Brewster is just one of the many silly names Stine uses here; others include Gene Wilikers, Foster Badhabits, and Hector Whipple.

Another gimmick Stine uses to great effect is the list. Lists include: "Rules for being funny with soup, such as placing your feet in your soup" (*Funny*, 37) and "What isn't funny, such as being the new kid in school" (*Funny*, 64). That last line is also telling because many of Stine's *Fear Street* titles would be about new kids in school, including the first volume, *The New Girl*.

The review questions at the end of chapters are another spoof of how-to books. The questions have no answers and have little to do with the preceding chapter: "What are the two funniest places to stick your fork when you are told not to play with your silverware?" (*Funny*, 29). In an eerie foreshadowing, the chapter on how to be funny at parties ends with this review question: "True or false—a party needn't end in blood to be truly funny" (*Funny*, 46).

The book ends, not with the introduction as promised, but with a final gag: a fake bibliography. Here Stine mocks a book convention, uses a list, uses funny names (including Jovial Rob Shine), and piles on the silly sentences:

> Mark Thyme, How *to Be Funny with Apricots*. Duck Press, 1975. A good idea that doesn't work—mainly because apricots are not at all funny and never will be. Author has a few good suggestions for funny things with an apricot pit, but once you've got them up your nose, what do you for an encore? (*Funny*, 71)

"NO SOCIALLY REDEEMING VALUE"

For Stine, an encore was called for again and again as *How to Be Funn*y launched his career in the children's book industry, although Stine claims the book didn't sell. He said, "Everyone says they want it—bookstores, librarians. . . . But it doesn't sell." (*Roginski*, 210). Nor did the book get particularly good reviews. *Publishers Weekly* noted that Stine's readers will "love laughing with him" [2] and *Kirkus* simply stated, "It's funny." [3] Others were quite negative. Many reviewers, Stine's said, were "confused" (*Roginski*, 210). The review in *School Library Journal* foreshadowed later critiques of Stine: praising his work yet dismissing it at the same time: "While Jovial Bob isn't exactly on a par with Woody Allen (or Woody for juveniles) there may be a bon mot here to gladden nine to 12 year olds."[4]

Woody Allen? This seems indicative of what was to come later with assessment of Stine's YA thrillers: an incorrect critical comparison. He's being compared to Woody Allen, a writer with whom Stine has little in common save the same broad category of humor. Allen is a writer for adults and older teenagers, which is not Stine's market. Actually, a better comparison would have been to a rising young comic, Steve Martin. The audience Stine was trying to reach was not Woody Allen's sophisticated cultish crowd, but Steve Martin's mass audience. Martin's success stemmed from his desire to go for the punch line at all costs, either by telling stupid jokes ("Let's get small") or just looking stupid (the fake arrow through the head gag).

Stine promoted his book with such a gag. He recalled:

> It was a Saturday afternoon and I was in the children's department. To promote being funny I sat there with bunny ears on my head. So there I was sitting there with these ears on my head. A grown man! No one would come near me! We didn't sell one book. . . . I think I terrified a lot of kids. (*Roginski*, 209)

That memory of terrifying children must have stuck. Another strange foreshadowing of his scary books was the reaction of adults, in particular librarians, to *How to Be Funny*. Stine recounted reviews of the book which again bear an all-too-weird similarity to later shots at his scary fiction. Stine said, "It was called, in one instance, 'a dangerous book.' Another said, 'If this book gets in the hands of kids, the kids will try some of the things in it. This will be a world of tears, not a world of laughter. Not recommended'" (*Roginski*, 210).

What is interesting is the pattern of overreaction Stine started with book one. Adults worried about the social impact of writings that Stine would claim have no "socially redeeming value. It's just fun"(*Roginski*, 210). While dismissing the quality of

Stine's books, the same critics worry that children will act out what they read on the page. The reaction to his first book, like the reaction to his later books, showed that the critics missed the point that these books are just entertaining and not meant to be taken seriously.

How to Be Funny served as a model for Stine's future humorous monographs. Borrowing from the *Bananas* style guide, Stine set down the rules: don't be afraid to be too juvenile, use language that kids like, such as puns and funny names; don't aim too high or anywhere other than the funny bone, make the humor relate to their lives, stay with what works, and finally pile the jokes on top of the jokes. Like the movie *Airplane*, part of the joke in Stine's books is that everything is a joke. Either he knew instantly what the right formula was or the reaction to the book told him to trust his instincts.

Along with the first book, Stine began to develop a philosophy of writing for kids:

> The whole problem with doing humor for children comes from adults. A lot of people seem to think that if a book or magazine is just funny, it's trash. Adults have the right to read or watch trash. Adults have the right to pick out a book that's just entertainment, nothing else. But many adults seem to feel that every children's book has to teach something, has to be uplifting in some way. My theory is a children's book doesn't have to teach them anything. It can be just fun. I'll sit down and watch some TV program, some garbage, just for entertainment. I have that right. Kids somehow don't have that right. It seems to me they should. There's nothing wrong with something that's just fun. (*Roginski*, 209-210)

Stine's vision of juvenile book publishing stuck with him when he was writing thrillers. Although talking specifically about humor here, he was really talking about all popular books. This would be his standard line of defense against the attacks on his thrillers.

It is easy to see why Stine chose this philosophy. First, because he had never in his writing career, save pit stops at trade magazines, tried to write anything but entertainment. Second, the humor and horror genres do not get any respect from book critics, educators, nor those who bestow film awards. Horror and comedy films don't, with rare exceptions, win Academy Awards; they are considered too lowbrow. Yet, horror and comedy films consistently make a great deal of money. The tastes of the public differ greatly from the critical establishment. Stine perhaps realized that since he could not please the select few, he would elect to please the many.

PIG, MONSTER, AND SOUP JOKES

Writing books that were just fun became Stine's part-time job for the next decade. In addition to his magazine duties, Stine cranked out over twenty joke and humor books. Almost all were collaborative efforts involving an illustrator, and several were co-written with his wife Jane. Stine's humor books during this period were of three main types. First, like *How To Be Funny*, there were parodies of "serious books," such as *Bored with Being Bored! How to Beat the Boredom Blues*. Second, there were those published under the title of one of his magazines, such as *Bananas Looks at TV*. Third, there were joke books, nothing but page after page of jokes with accompanying illustrations, like *Jovial Bob's Computer Joke Book*.

Stine did joke books about pigs (*The Pigs' Book of World Records*), videogames (*Blips*), and—to no surprise—monsters (*One Hundred and One Silly Monster Jokes*). This mix of humor with horror would be Stine's trump card in *Goosebumps*. Even more interesting is *101 and One Wacky Kid Jokes*—interesting not so much because of the jokes, like "'Why are you wolfing down those cookies?' 'I want to eat as many as I can before I lose my appetite,'"[5] but because of the cover that features a young boy wearing a green mask and scaring his sister. The cover looks strangely like that of one of Stine's most popular *Goosebumps* books, *The Haunted Mask*.

A book like *The Beast Handbook* is a pastiche combining the

best of all three models. The character of the Beast was first introduced in *Bananas.* The "handbook" approach used lists and
the usual fake bibliography, plus page after page of jokes. Most
of the parodies would use humor not only on subjects of interest
to kids, but also situations that might cause them some stress. As
Stine wrote in *How to Be Funny,* when confronted with a big
problem, be funny. It may not help, but it can't hurt.

One of the better examples of this type of book is *The Sick of
Being Sick Book,* co-written with his wife Jane. He explained
their working relationship:

> It is very hard to work together, to collaborate. . . . We work very dif-
> ferently. I have to work from the beginning from the very first word on
> the first page and right through. I don't like to revise at all. I'm too self
> satisfied. I always think if it's typed, it's a masterpiece, it's perfect. So I
> don't change a word. Jane loves to revise! She writes the back and
> thinks about it. Then she writes the middle. Then the introduction. She
> goes back and forth all the time. It drives me crazy. Consequently, the
> books get better. (*Roginski,* 211)

The writing partnership dissolved, according to one account,
when "Jane ended a shouting match by locking her husband in a
closet for 15 minutes."[6] This professional collaboration would
flourish, however, when they adopted the writer/editor professional relationship.

Sick of Being Sick resembles *How to Be Funny* in many
ways. There is the same use of lists:

- Ten things that won't make you feel better, such as "a doctor....
  asking if you are a boy or a girl." [7]
- Ten most popular medicines of the Middle Ages, most related to
  tree bark. (*Sick,* 23)
- Twenty things you can do with tissues, such as "wear white socks.
  Stuff them with 400 tissues. Ask people to sign your cast." (*Sick,*
  26)

There is also the fake bibliography, featuring authors such as
Ann Gree Hacker, Hank R. Cheef, and Chu Litely. There is how-

to advice (how to survive daytime TV); a test (what's your PQ? patient quotient), a sick kids' hall of fame (more funny names and gags), and the continued fascination with the humorous properties of soup (souper bowl team-up recipe). This fascination climaxed in Stine's send-up of etiquette books with *Don't Stand in the Soup*. While the subject matter was all new, the formula was kept the same because it worked.

FORCED HUMOR AND FATIGUED JOKES

The reviews for *Sick of Being Sick* were much less friendly, with the reviewer in *School Library Journal* writing "that such silliness could continue at book length is too much for even hard-core *Mad* readers. A stack of comics would be funnier and cheaper." [8] At least this reviewer got the point, even if she missed most of the jokes: these books are supposed to be silly, not educational. This fact seems lost on many of the reviewers of Stine's humor titles, who are critical of the lack of real advice and the preponderance of dumb jokes. A reviewer of *Cool Kids' Guide to Summer Camp* wrote that the book was nothing more than "forced humor and fatigued jokes about food and crafts, interspersed with genuine nuggets of advice." [9] The *Kirkus* review of the same title noted "minimally funny advice. . . . The jokes perhaps qualify as camp humor, a concept comparable to that of military music. . . . it's forced and flat."[10] *School Library Journal's* review of *Don't Stand in The Soup* carped that the book contains "useless advice for young readers." [11] More telling is the failure of the reviewers to see these books through the eyes of the intended readers. Perhaps to an adult "camp humor" is an oxymoron, but to many kids it is not. Witness the success among teens of the movie *Meatballs,* released about the same time as *Cool Kids' Guide to Summer Camp.* Like later reviewers who don't appreciate the thoughtless scares of Stine's thrillers and instead would want them to be "better," these reviews wanted real advice and sophisticated humor. Real advice and

sophisticated humor might be fine things, but they were not what
Stine was offering. This is the equivalent of expecting real news
from *Saturday Night Live*'s Weekend Update segment.

One of Stine's most negative reviews was in *School Library
Journal*'s notice on *Bored with Being Bored*: "Thoughtful children and their parents will find some of the targets questionable,
especially when they see the author's fondness for comic clichés. Old jokes can sound new to young ears; the humor's vin-
tage is not the problem. Offensiveness is."[12] This sounds like
not so much a matter of critical judgment but of taste. *Bored
with Being Bored* is not a Newbery candidate, but it is very successful in the context of humor books. That's the correct standard. Although Stine said *How to Be Funny* was "a really offensive book for parents" (*Something 1994*: 223), most of his
humor books are fairly tame given the genre. Humor makes fun
of things and making fun can be offensive to those being lampooned. Kids' big targets of humor are those in power over their
lives, in particular teachers and parents (and perhaps librarians),
because humor is one of the few weapons that kids have at their
disposal. Yet, Stine's humor, for the most part, is not offensive;
his jokes are silly, not sharp or sarcastic. "Thoughtful children"—whatever that term means—are not Stine's audience. His
audience is readers who just want to have thoughtless fun. The
SLJ reviewer might be shocked to learn this group could include
"thoughtful children" who want thoughtless recreational reading.

Philosophical discussion aside, it is hard to say, on a text
level, what the reviewer was so negative about. *Bored with Being Bored* is one of Stine's funnier humor books, with lots and
lots (and lots) of lists.   One of the best bits is another biblio-
graphic parody called "Books that no one has ever checked out"
containing fake book titles like *Learn to Sing the Metric System*, *The Big Book of Lettuce*, and *Nature's Playmate: The
Grubworm*. Stine has tapped into something quite real
here—kids' natural inclination to find things boring (Isn't "This
is *boring!"* the natural lament of every nine-year-old?) and to

make fun of them. Although the silly things that kids do are targets, more often adults get lampooned.

Some of Stine's reviews for his humor books were positive, usually noting, like the review of *First Dates*, that "kids will love it." [13] The ambivalence of the reviews, as would be the case with his thrillers, has very little to do with the books themselves, but rather the purpose. Stine's critics seem to want his book to *do* something, while Stine is content (and successful) in just being entertaining. They note the negative reactions they fear young readers will have while failing to note the most obvious positive reaction: laughter.

WHAT WORKS

Much of the humor, especially in the joke books, is just plain silly. The jokes are often nothing more than puns, using the familiar question and answer approach, such as:

What's the vampire's favorite holiday? Fangsgiving.
What's a monster's favorite skyscraper? The Vampire State Building. [14]

The humor books rely on a similar dose of silliness, but there is an undercurrent of making fun of things adults do and say. For example, *Bored with Being Bored* lampoons, but the jokes don't pierce by being offensive. As he would with the thrillers, Stine is pulling punches. Certainly in a book about boredom he could have jabbed harder at teachers, but he doesn't. It is also reflective of Stine's rapport with his audience and his own past. He thought school was boring and lots of kids do as well, so let's have some fun with that.

Stine continued to write this type of humor book as late as 1990. He would then adapt his work habits and formulas for his new career as a thriller writer. What he learned in writing humor is obvious: find something that works and stick to it. Kids won't mind the repetition if they like what is being repeated. In Stine's humor books, he uses the same gags or gimmicks over and over, just as he would use the same gags or gimmicks repeatedly in his thrillers. The books were about taking normal or stressful situations (being sick, going to camp) and making them funny. Stine claims that the best kind of humor is "recognition humor. Things they recognize from their own lives. . . . They love this kind of material" (*Roginski*, 209). Much the same, the thrillers would be about recognizable emotions, settings, and situations. The difference is that rather than the punch line being a knee-slapper, it would be a skin-crawler.

The differences between humor and horror, however, are not great: lots of humor is offensive, especially that of young adolescents who are exploring the boundaries. Similarly, there's a tad of rebellion in humor, again a very distinctive characteristic of pre-teens and teens. Other elements of humor, such as timing, sentence construction, use of stereotypes, and occasional gross outs are the very same elements which make up Stine's horror books. Although he couldn't have known it at the time, these years writing joke books turned out to be the perfect training ground for writing horror.

Perhaps Stine also learned during these years to accept that his paperbacks have a temporary shelf life, to accept negative reviews by adults of his work, and to accept that kids loved his work. This fact surprised Stine as he said, "I still can't believe people actually pay me money to write the things I write. I feel as if I'm getting away with something, as if I should be paying them!" (*Roginski*, 212) Stine learned about impact. If you write a joke, you want someone to laugh. If you write a scary scene, you want someone to be scared. Unlike other writers for young adults who came out of different traditions, Stine emerged from a background where speed, sales, and audience response, not critical praise and awards, were the desired result. When writing jokes Stine practiced the economy of entertaining: set up the joke, hit the punch line, then move on. When it came time to write a monthly installment for the next *Fear Street,* that pace was nothing new to Stine—it was one he was used to. Moving on from Jovial Bob Stine to "scary" R.L. Stine wasn't such a big leap at all. But first he had to play a game of "find your fate."

NOTES

1. Jovial Bob Stine, *How to Be Funny: An Extremely Silly Guidebook,* (New York: E.P. Dutton, 1978): i; hereafter cited in text as *Funny.*

2. *Publishers Weekly* (10 July 1978): 136.

3. *Kirkus Reviews* (15 July 1978): 753.

4. *School Library Journal* (November 1979): 82.

5. Jovial Bob Stine, *101 Wacky Kid Jokes,* (New York: Scholastic, 1988): 20.

6. Denise Gellene, "Scary up Scads of Young Readers," *Los Angeles Times* (7 August 1996) A:1; hereafter cited in text as Gellene.

7. Jovial Bob Stine and Jane Stine, *The Sick of Being Sick Book* (New York: Scholastic, 1980): 20; hereafter cited in text as *Sick.*

8. *School Library Journal* (August 1980): 840.

9. *School Library Journal* (November 1981): 98.

10. *Kirkus Reviews* (1 April 1981): 436.

11. *School Library Journal* (August 1982): 122-23.

12. *West Coast Review of Books* (November/December 1983): 68.

13. Jovial Bob Stine, *101 Silly Monster Jokes* (New York: Scholastic, 1986): 22.

CHAPTER THREE
PLOT TWISTER

In 1979 Bantam Books launched the *Choose Your Own Adventure* paperback series. The premise was simple: a book written directly to readers that involved them through decision-making and interaction with the text. Written in second person, the books led the reader/main character to a decision at the end of each chapter. If they made one choice, they turned to a certain page. Another choice took them to a different page. Each subsequent page-turning led to another chapter ending; another choice, and another turn of the page. The genre became known as "multiple storyline books" and imitators followed. The books were successful (the series is closing in on its 200th volume), in part because they reached a market that YA publishers longed for: middle school boys. Although certainly girls read these books, the settings, situations, and covers seemed to reflect and to be designed to attract the male market.

But having a marketing idea is not the same as having a successful series. Many publishers had been trying and failing to launch a boys' series throughout the 1980s. So why did these multiple storyline books succeed? Writing in the *English Journal*, Jeffrey S. Copeland proposed that the reasons for their popularity could be "grouped into four categories: readers as protagonists, plot format, levels of excitement generated, and availability." [1]

Copeland looked at each element's contribution to the success of the genre. He noted, "The reader is told nothing of the reader/protagonist's sex, outlook, age, physical characteristics, or the like. . . . The reasons for this are clear: for these books to succeed, the 'you' must be allowed to be developed by and take on the characteristics of the reader" (*Copeland,* 53). All good YA books attempt to write characters to whom teen readers can relate. The multiple storyline books went one better by providing the one character to whom each teen could most easily relate: themselves. As Copeland observed, the "you" actually "becomes either the reader or, in many cases, the character the reader would like to be" (*Copeland,* 53).

These were simple wish-fulfillment books taken to a new level by simplifying the process of a reader interacting with the text. Copeland noted these books are nothing more than an interconnected series of plots, some of which end badly for the reader. If that occurs, the reader can start over again and trace a new plot. Better, Copeland notes, "readers can actually become the writer of the story, deciding what should happen as it happens" (*Copeland,* 53).

Because of this technique these books are about action, about characters stuck in scary, dangerous, or tricky situations that require them to do something. But these titles also allow readers to control the level of excitement: they can play it safe or they can take risks. Although they are books, the texts become more than that. They are almost like games. This last notion is well known to readers, as Copeland noted that they "can take great pride in escaping an early end. In essence, for many readers, it is not enough just to read the story; it becomes a challenge to see how far they can get in the book before being eaten by a wild creature, becoming lost in a cave forever, or falling into a raging river" (*Copeland,* 53). Finally, Copeland pointed out the large quantity of titles. Almost every YA publisher had released at least one series. Thus, the books were easily available, exciting, easy to read, and allowed reader participation—the same elements of success Stine would use in his thrillers. What more,

Copeland asked, "could a young adult want in a book?" (*Copeland,* 54)

THE TIME RAIDER

Scholastic published Stine's first multiple storyline book, *The Time Raider,* in 1982. Although Stine was an established author, this was a new genre for him. He needed to learn the basics of fiction writing: character, setting, and conflict, and he needed to construct page-turning plots with lots of action. For his first book, he chose a genre he had enjoyed as a youth: science fiction. Stine has said that he read speculative fiction as a child because "I loved traveling to the future and to other worlds"(*Ohio,* 44). *The Time Raider* allows the reader to do just this by allowing them to pretend they've stepped into a time machine. Right away, a decision is called for as the first chapter ends with an option of going forward or backward in time. The choice the reader makes leads to another chapter, which features more decision points. Thus every one of the fifty or more scenes in the book leads up to a cliffhanger. For example, one segment ends with "The tall woman wearing the silver star is still holding you up to the crowd. You cannot escape."[2]

Stine was perfecting his staccato style here. There are many chapters of nothing but one-sentence paragraphs, some of which are merely sentence fragments, which is a very effective tool in writing suspense. YA mystery author Jay Bennett was a master of this wide-margin style in the pre-*Fear Street* days. There is also, this being an R.L. Stine book, plenty of humor. For example, since Stine is playing around with a time machine, there are lots of possibilities for funny twists, such as a segment that ends: "You fall into a deep snowdrift and didn't get there in time. Edgar and Frank are both lost. That means you were never born. You'd better put this book down. It is meant only to be read by people who were born!" (*Time,* 47) Another example is a scene that ends on page 91 telling readers are trapped in a time warp, so turn to page 93. Page 93 informs them to turn to page 91.

The book is very short, only 94 pages, and several of those consist of full or half-page illustrations. While these books were rarely reviewed, there was critical consensus about them. Many librarians and teachers, like Copeland, were very positive toward the books, although always with the disclaimer of the need to move readers on to something better. What is missing, however, in the few reviews and articles about these books, is any recognition of the talent it takes to put such a book together, not only telling one story, but multiple stories, and making each segment interesting enough on its own so the reader chooses to follow that plot strand. Moreover, the ability to make the plots different—allowing for one risky choice and one safe choice—takes creativity. Finally, even with all the tricks and gimmicks, books like The *Time Raider* need to be entertaining. The plots or premises not only have to hold readers' interest, but also must be clever and yet recognizable, and the writing has to actively engage the reader for an amusing and entertaining wild ride. The reader "wrote" the book, but Stine supplied all the raw materials.

BOOKS AS GAMES; GAMES AS BOOKS

The plethora of plot twists and endings in *The Time Raider* were nothing compared to another publishing venture for Scholastic. Taking the interactive element one step further, several of the multiple storyline series imitated the success of role-playing games. In these game books, the players are on a quest and along the way have to make decisions not only about what to do, but whom to trust, what to carry, etc. More than a multiple storyline book, Stine's *Badlands of Hark* is a book as a game and a game as a book. It is a maze fleshed out.

The premise of the game book is that there is priceless treasure that the reader will find if he or she follows the right path. The book starts with a list of the rules:

1. There is only one correct path through badlands. . . . One wrong choice—and the game is over. You must go back to the beginning and start your journey again.

2. The game is divided into 250 sections. Each section is numbered at the top. Begin your journey through the Badlands with section 1. Then make your choice of where to go next. Each section advances the action.

3. If you move well through the Badlands, you will be awarded points.

4. Throughout the journey you will come upon signs and scrolls and other items.[3]

Those rules sum up the book nicely. Every page contains a short section, sometimes half a page long, sometimes only a few sentences. Some pages contain up to five of these game segments. Each section describes the action and presents a decision, except those that end with the words GAME OVER. This is not a book in any traditional sense—the action is fragmented. None of the sections can build any suspense because there is little detail. You come upon something, you pick it up or don't pick it up, something happens, and eventually you die. Yet these game books are entertaining and challenging, not challenging in the same way as a good novel, but challenging as any puzzle or maze. Challenging, one would imagine, as well for the writer to execute. Stine also wrote several of these game books for Avon's *Wizard Warrior and You* series.

MACHO MEN FIND THEIR FATE

Stine continued to pen multiple storyline books for Scholastic in the *Twist-A-Plot* series, which included Stine's first published dive into horror with 1984's *Horrors of the Haunted Museum*. Stine also wrote multiple storyline books for Ballantine. The most successful combined the crispness of the multiple storyline books *and* the popularity of a successful movie character in the *Indiana Jones* books that Stine penned in the *Find Your Fate* series. These were not as densely plotted as the *Hark* game books (which were plotting at its absolute apex), but managed to meet the requirements of the genre.

The main innovation made up for the greatest weakness of

the multiple storyline books: character. While the reader was the protagonist in books of this type, there were rarely other characters of any interest—stock villains, but no other heroes. For some readers, being the hero of the book might be fun. Ballantine and Stine must have figured that readers would enjoy even more being the hero along with another colorful hero: Indiana Jones.

The *Indiana Jones* books are, if nothing else, exciting. Stine's style continued to grow by shrinking. The descriptions were getting tighter, and lots of pages were full of one-sentence paragraphs and probing questions. The books were a bit longer, around 120 pages containing upwards of seventy chapters and thirty endings. There is heavy use of cliffhangers, a mix of ones that are scary and ones that are just decisions, like which of two doors to enter. The books had exciting and exotic settings, lots of action, and more than a little humor. They also read like rough drafts for the thrillers to come:

> You run to the office door and struggle to pull it open. Indy is right behind you.
> "Let me try it kid," he says. He turns the knob and pulls with all his might. "It's been secured from the outside," he says, giving up. "We're locked in here!"
> "What's that hissing sound?" Marla Evans asks, walking up behind you.
> You look down. "Gas!" you yell. Green gas is seeping into the room from under the door.
> "We're trapped! Trapped!" Marla cries in terror. [4]

Ballantine reprinted these titles, with flashy new covers and Stine's name very prominently displayed, in 1996.

Stine continued in this vein, adapting books with two other popular male characters: James Bond and G.I. Joe. The Bond book is a movie tie-in, based on a film at that time (*A View To Kill*) with the same setting and villains. Rather than following the dual-hero formula in *Win Lose or Draw*, the reader becomes James Bond. The Bond book, however, does not really work.

Somehow without the sex or special effects, the story does not really click, nor are the villains or cliffhangers very interesting. The *G.I. Joe* books are better, with many more engaging, reliable action sequences.

After writing a couple of *G.I. Joe* books in the *Find Your Fate* series, Stine penned a few *G.I. Joe: a Real American Hero* series titles, including the first *Siege of the Serpentor*. These were not multiple storyline books but straight series action fiction. One such title, *Jungle Raid*, Stine published even after finishing his first two thrillers. Seeds and saplings of the thriller style are certainly present:

> "That guy sure didn't look like any brother of Hawk's," Mainframe said.
> "A lot of brothers don't look much alike," Falcon said. "My brother's five feet two and weighs two-eighty. I used to use him for a bowling ball."
> Mainframe laughed. "I still don't get it about Hawk," he said. "I didn't know Hawk even had a brother. And how in the blazes did his brother find him in the middle of the jungles of San Juego?"
> Falcon started to reply. Suddenly, a powerful blast shook the base. It was followed by another. The lights dimmed. The roar of heavy weapons seemed to surround them.
> "I don't believe this!" Falcon cried, grabbing up his pistol. "Mainframe—give the alert! We're being ATTACKED!!" [5]

The elements are the same: confusion about identity, characters asking the same questions readers are asking, the abundance of exclamation marks, the short action-packed paragraphs, the use of humor, and finally the cliffhanger ending. This is basic macho action writing with lots of gunfights and buddyship. None of these plot-heavy books requires great characterization, but at least in thrillers Stine can get his audience to relate to the emotions of the protagonists, something that he can't do in army books.   In addition, Stine later admitted he was perhaps not qualified to be writing army books, confessing, "I didn't know a rifle from a golf club" (*Ohio*, 99).

Stine did a number of these, some under pen names. Several

of the *G.I. Joe* books came out under the pseudonym Eric Affabee, and Stine wrote two books under the pen name Zachary
Blue for Scholastic's *The Protectors* series. These series were
very much products of their times, the Reagan eighties. With the
popularity of hit movies like *Rambo*, the military was back in
style as the good guys. Stine also penned a series of novels for
Scholastic called *Space Camp*, mixing science fiction, adventure,
and, of course, wacky humor (the last title in the series was *Bozos in Space*). None of these series lasted long, and Stine's use
of a pen name is a curious decision and unexplained in his
autobiographies or interviews. Nor are these books that Stine
looks back on fondly. He said, "Every once in a while someone
realizes that I wrote *G.I. Joe* books. Now, I'm very embarrassed."[6] At the time, though, Stine must not have been too embarrassed because he got his brother William and his sister-in-
law Megan involved in writing these titles. These projects stayed
in the family, as titles included the note "Editorial services by
Parachute Press."

These series books, however, were not Stine's only source of
income. In addition to the humor books, he was also doing
movie tie-ins, picture books, and a host of other projects, such
as:

> Mighty Mouse coloring books. It was good money, one sentence a page
> at about $500 a book. I wrote bubble gum cards. The lowest of the
> lowest thing I ever wrote was a series of books based on some rubber
> balls called Mad Balls. . . . They were rubber balls with ugly faces on
> them, you can't get lower than that. (*Webchat*)

But one choice for a writing assignment would transport him,
like some character in a multiple storyline book, to an exciting
new place: television.

EUREKA!

The Nickelodeon cable TV network was just getting off the
ground in the mid-1980s when Stine joined the program

Eureka's Castle as head writer. Despite never having written for television or preschool children, Stine headed up a staff of ten writers. The show was similar in some ways to Sesame Street, but as Stine recalls, *Eureka's Castle* "didn't teach kids anything!" (*Ohio*, 100) Stine and his writers created all the bits for the show, which featured a group of puppets. The show was a hit both with kids and, for once, with critics, as it won an Ace award for best children's show. Stine helped write 100 hours of regular scripts, as well as several specials. Although he does not discuss it much in his autobiography or in interviews, it seems clear that Stine is quite proud of his work on the show. While it was different, it was also more of the same, demonstrating Stine's ability to entertain young people.

THE PROVING GROUNDS

Though Stine himself dismisses a lot of his work from this period, its importance to his development can't be overlooked. In writing multiple storyline books, Stine learned a great deal about plotting. He learned to write short, punchy, action-packed scenes, and learned to put his characters in harm's way at the end of one chapter and take them out in the next. He also learned to involve readers in a story not so much by writing rounded characters, but by allowing the reader to be, or mirror, the main character. While that was easy to do in second-person multiple storyline books, Stine would adapt this technique in the thrillers by making his characters reflective of the target audience. Although lots of his books for boys never hit big, Stine probably knew there was something he could write that would appeal to males but that he had just not found it yet. His style was also developing, consisting of lots of chapters filled with more action than description and short bursts of dialogue-loaded paragraphs, lots of one-sentence paragraphs, heavy use of a staccato fragmented sentence style to build suspense, cliffhanger chapter endings, and a sincere fondness for question marks and exclamation points. Grafting these new skills for fiction writing onto those learned in the funny business, Stine's voice was growing stronger.

But perhaps most of all during this period Stine reinforced his belief that kids deserve books that are just entertaining without any other value attached to them. From writing movie tie-ins to bubble gum cards, Stine demonstrated that words were entertaining. In a youth culture drowning in sound, video, and image, Stine spent the mid-1980s trying to show readers, in particular male readers, that reading was fun. That's a basic value that Stine teaches in every book among all his twisting plots.

NOTES

1. Jeffrey S. Copeland, "Multiple Storyline Books for Young Adults," *English Journal* (December 1987): 52; hereafter cited in text as Copeland.

2. R.L. Stine, *The Time Raider* (New York: Scholastic, 1982): 15; hereafter cited in text as *Time*.

3. R.L. Stine, *The Badlands of Hark* (New York: Scholastic, 1985): i.

4. R.L. Stine, *Indiana Jones and the Cult of the Mummy's Crypt (Find Your Fate #7)*. (New York: Ballantine Books, 1985): 95.

5. R.L. Stine, *Jungle Raid (G.I. Joe, a Real American Hero #5)* (New York: Ballantine Books, 1988): 12.

6. "Webchat Broadcasting System Interview with R.L. Stine," *Internet Roundtable* (11 November 1985) http://www.irsociety.com/recent /transtin/html (5 May 1997); hereafter cited in text as *Webchat*.

CHAPTER FOUR
A BLIND DATE

It was an offer he couldn't refuse.

Stine was lunching with his friend Jean Feiwel, a former associate from Scholastic whose main claim to fame was coming up with the concept of the hugely successful *Baby Sitters Club* series. When she set up the lunch with Stine, she perhaps had two things in mind. First, that the success of Christopher Pike's *Slumber Party* indicated that there was a market among teenagers for thriller/horror books. Second, she knew that Stine could work fast, that he could write for kids, and that he could be entertaining. Stine recounted the conversation:

> "Did you ever consider writing a YA horror novel?"
> "Well, I've always liked horror," I told her. "But I never thought of writing it."
> "Well, why don't you give it a try," she suggested. "Go home and write a book called *Blind Date*." (*Ohio*, 107)

This conversation is interesting on several levels. Not only does it mirror an interchange he had almost a decade earlier with Ellen Rudin at Dutton, but it was an offer pitched to many YA writers in the 1980s and 1990s as YA paperback editors were desperate to get more horror books to the shelves. It is hard to imagine any of the authors like Richard Peck or Robert Cormier jumping at this offer. Again, that is yet another thing that sets Stine apart: he seems utterly without pretensions. His entire

41

writing career had been built around wanting to entertain readers, not with providing them with life-moving emotional experiences, nor with constructing a literary masterpiece, nor even
with writing something that would be considered quality literature. Instead, from the beginning of his writing career, Stine
dealt more with quantity: write it quickly, meet the deadline, get
a laugh or a scream, move on to the next project, repeat process.
Therefore, when Jean Feiwel made the offer, she perhaps knew
Stine wouldn't turn her down with a speech about sacrificing his
artistic integrity. Instead, he realized it for what it was: a golden
opportunity to entertain a lot of people.

The title *Blind Date* was a metaphor. Like a person on a
blind date, Stine had an opportunity that might turn into something big. He began his venture, however, with high hopes and
very little information. Sitting down to write his first novel,
Stine didn't know what he was about to get himself into. He
couldn't have known he was taking the first steps to creating a
genre, as well as a great deal of controversy. Nor could he have
know that this "blind date" would lead to a long term relationship with scary stories.

THE TITLE COMES FIRST

Despite never having written a horror novel before, Stine was
confident he could take Feiwel's title and make something of it.
Stine recalled, "When you're starting out as a freelancer, you
don't know how to say no" (*Alderdice, 200*). Armed with just a
title, Stine spent three months writing *Blind Date*. This "title
comes first" approach for Stine became his standard procedure.

> If I can get a title first, then I start getting ideas for it. Like *The Baby
> Sitter*. You start to think what's scary about being a baby-sitter? Or
> *The Stepsister*. What would be scary about getting a new stepsister?
> The title will lead me to an idea about what the book should be.[1]

Although Stine had not written horror before, save two multiple
storyline books, he was well versed, having grown up reading

Tales from the Crypt and similar horror comics. In addition,
while horror was not Stine's genre, suspense and action were, as
demonstrated by his prodigious output of *Indiana Jones* and *G.I.
Joe* books. Stine bought some YA thrillers and mysteries by Lois
Duncan, Joan Nixon, and Christopher Pike. Later he wrote, "I
liked the books. . . . But I had some different ideas" (*Ohio*, 108).

More than having his own ideas, Stine had a background that
was perfectly suited. He had learned from his magazine writing
to be concise, and from his work writing multiple storyline and
series books he certainly learned the importance of plot, action,
and using cliffhangers. Finally, from his humor writing he had
learned two important things: how to set up a gag and how to
write to get a physical reaction from his audience. This time
around instead of making them laugh Stine would make them
scream.

THE SOUND OF BONE BREAKING

Blind Date opens with the sound of violence: "At first, when
Kerry heard the sound of the bone breaking, he thought it was
his."[2] The broken bone, however, turns out to be that of Sal
Murdoch, the high school team's star quarterback. Kerry Hart is
the back-up quarterback. It looks to the other team members as if
Kerry broke Sal's leg on purpose so he could be the starter, despite his insistence it was an accident. The accident sets in motion a chain of events. Kerry gets kicked off the team by the
coach and is threatened by other teammates and by Sal's girlfriend:

> A voice . . . called out. "There could be another accident. Know what I
> mean?" Suddenly the back window was rolled down. Sharon Splinter
> stuck her head out. "You ruined his life! I'm going to pay you back!"
> (*Blind*, 11)

Kerry's salvation throughout all this turmoil is his best friend
Josh. Josh is a prototypical wiseass, with smart aleck come-
backs for everything, who likes to ridicule the "jocks" to their

faces. His dialogue is filled with puns and jokes, like a Stine humor book. A Josh-like character would show up in almost every *Fear Street* to provide comic relief.

When Kerry returns home he talks with his younger brother Sean, wonders how his father will take the news, thinks about his mom (his parents have recently divorced), and, as he did in the coach's office, thinks about his older brother, Donald, who has recently disappeared. Donald was a star football player whose shadow Kerry has been living under for years. Exhausted, Kerry goes to his room and just wants to feel sorry for himself.

> The phone rang.
> He waited for Sean to pick it up.
> A second ring.
> Come on Sean, get off the couch and pick it up.
> A third ring.
> Kerry . . . fumbled around in the dark for the phone.
> "Hello." It was a girl's voice. "Is this Kerry?"
> He cleared his throat. "Yes, it is."
> "Hi Kerry," it was the sexiest voice he had ever heard. "I'm your Blind Date." (*Blind*, 14)

Bang. Like a joke, Stine sets up the situation, then delivers with a punch line, which just happens to be the title of the book. The shared vernacular between humor and horror is known well to Stine, who said, about *Fear Streets* and *Goosebumps*, "Every chapter ends in some kind of punch line" (*Webchat*).

In many ways, this first chapter is a blueprint for Stine's later thrillers. There's action from the first moment, threats, a faked death, and a mysterious phone call. There are Stine character types like the vindictive cheerleader, the funny best friend, and a missing mysterious family member. Kerry is very much a Stine type: a normal kid who just wants to be popular and get along in his life, only to have a series of threats, pranks, and violent acts throw his life into chaos. The notion of revenge would drive many *Fear Street* titles in the future. What is radically different from later *Fear Street*s, however, is not what is written, but how it is written.

The first chapter of *Blind Date* is fourteen pages—oversized by Stine's later standards. It contains five scenes: the accident, the aftermath with the players and Sharon, the talk with the coach, the walk home with Josh, and the scene at home with a phone call. The "he's dead" fake out comes on page five. In later books, such a statement would end the chapter. The next would open with the revelation that, of course, the person is not dead, they are just . . . something. Here, Sal has merely passed out from shock. In this chapter Stine gives more than usual attention to his character's home situation, in particular Kerry's feeling toward his parents. In later books, Stine might have parents make a cameo appearance, but rarely did they rate emotional involvement by a character. The exception to this would be in *Missing*, one of Stine's earliest and spookiest *Fear Streets*, where the parents failure to appear is the plot.

The chapter ends and the thriller begins with the phone call. It's a great set-up. Phones dominate Stine's teen environment. Almost every book requires a phone, and in several thrillers, such as *Wrong Number* and *Call Waiting*, it drives the plot. The apex of Stine's phone fascination comes in his humorous novel *Phone Calls*, which consists of nothing but telephone conversations. For a teenager, at least before the arrival of computer networks, the telephone was a lifeline. It was not just a place to talk, gossip, and plan, but it represented a step into adulthood. This step into adulthood, in every Stine book, leads to horrific consequences.

In *Blind Date*, the telephone also seems like an invitation into another adult practice: sex. Later in the book, as he goes to meet the blind date, Kerry wonders about her body and if she will "go all the way" (*Blind*, 31). Stine's just hinting, yet already there is more sexual overtone than would show up in most of his YA books:

Her voice was kittenish, a soft purr. . . .
Her laugh was driving him crazy. It was such a *dirty* laugh.
"I guess you like to tease a lot," Kerry said, growing bolder.
"Well," she adopted a little girl's voice. "I don't always tease. Maybe
you will find that out." (*Blind*, 15-16)

Through the conversation, Kerry attempts to guess the identity
of the caller with the "sexy laugh" (*Blind*, 19). It turns out she
has just moved into town. She ends the call quickly, giving
Kerry her name (Amanda) and address and instructing him to
pick her up on Saturday night. The "new girl" or "new boy"
character would soon become a Stine staple. It allows him to
bring in a character with secrets, someone who won't talk a great
deal about his or her past, although sometimes, as in *The Best
Friend*, a character will claim to have a past that no one remembers.

Another scene early in the book which is very unlike Stine is
a long intense confrontation between Kerry and his police offi-
cer father. Kerry confesses to his dad that he is off the football
team. Rather than responding to his son, the father talks about
Donald and his contribution to the school's football program,
forcing Kerry to shout, "Dad—we're not talking about Donald! .
. . You're supposed to react to ME!" (*Blind*, 21). Kerry then
proceeds into a half-page monologue recalling that his brother is
gone because "something happened" that involved a car, but
Kerry can't remember the details. He explodes in anger and an-
guish as his father tells him "Don't try to remember what happened, Kerry, just accept it" (*Blind*, 22). As his father drives
away, the headlights of the squad car prompt another memory in
Kerry: what happened with Donald involved headlights. Thus,
Stine has set up a second mystery: what happened to Donald?

Then comes another phone call. It is another female voice,
but one that sounds faked—like someone talking while pinching
her nose—telling Kerry that "sticks and stones can break *your*
bones" (*Blind*, 25). She then mockingly sings, "The toe bone is
connected to the foot bone" before hanging up. A Stine thriller

will almost always contain such threats, most of them containing some sort of gimmick like a song or fake name. Now, Stine has three mysteries going and it is only page twenty-six. Like Stine's multiple storyline books, *Blind Date* gives the reader lots of puzzles to solve.

Behind all of these new threats lies Kerry's real fear that because of the accident the kids at school are going to hate him. He realizes he will never be as popular as Donald and thinks, "It was scary to be disliked" (*Blind*, 26). While Kerry may not be, in literary terms, a well-rounded character, he is very real and his fears are those of Stine's readers, fears not of being stalked or getting strange calls, but of being unpopular. As Kerry is driving to Amanda's house, he is thinking these thoughts. In this scene, Stine gives us a nice description of the town, in particular of fancy Sycamore Street with its huge old mansions that look a lot like those on Fear Street. Amanda's residence is nothing of the sort. It is a run-down mess that looks abandoned, like a haunted house.

THE VANISHING HITCHHIKER

When no one answers the door, Kerry thinks someone has played a trick on him, and he utters a phrase that would appear in many a Stine novel: "It's all a joke" (*Blind*, 36). Just as he is about to leave, two figures appear at the door:

> They stared back at him. Their expressions revealed fear and surprise.
> Finally, Kerry regained his senses. "Hi, is Amanda home?"
> The man's eyes bulged behind the square eyeglasses. "What?"
> "Is Amanda home, I'm her date."
> The woman screamed and dropped her teacup to the floor just inside the door. "*No ! No No!*" she screamed, her eyes rolling up to the ceiling.
> The man didn't scream, but he seemed about to faint. He closed his eyes. His voice came out in a hoarse whisper, "Amanda is *dead.*"
> (*Blind*, 37)

Bam, the chapter ends.

Stine has talked about recognition humor; here he is using recognition horror. This story—a man goes to meet a woman only to learn she is dead—is a variation on the "vanishing hitchhiker" urban legend. Although there are many versions, the core of this urban legend is the story of a young man who meets a young woman, usually hitchhiking, who leaves an object in his car. When he returns to the woman's house to return the object, her parents inform him—as in the scene on Amanda's porch—that the girl is dead and has been dead for some time.[3] Most teen urban legends revolve around many of the same issues presented by Stine in his first foray into horror—the step into adulthood and independence being a very scary step to take.

Sitting in the car, Stine lets Kerry become the reader asking questions:

> "Who was Amanda? Why was she dead? . . . Did he even know her? .
> . . And the girl on the phone? . . . Had she called him as part of a cruel
> joke? Was she Amanda too?" (*Blind*, 40)

This is another Stine staple: a scene where the protagonist begins to question everything. This type of scene serves two purposes. First, it lets red herrings swim. The character begins to suspect everyone, thus adding to the suspense by raising the possibility that every character could be "the one." Second, it explains for the reader the questions needing answers in the upcoming scenes. Stine has his characters push forward the plot by showing what questions require explanation and what action needs to take place. As a writer of joke books and interactive fiction, Stine knew many in his audience were not "good readers." These scenes allow readers to sort out what is going on up to a certain point in the story. It foreshadows what is to come, but also recaps what they already know. As Kerry runs through all the possibilities, he thinks a girl named Margo might have set him up on the date. He calls her from a pay phone to no avail, but mysteriously, after hanging up the phone, it rings. The voice is not Amanda, but the "other" voice repeating the phrase "the foot bone is connected to the leg bone" (*Blind*, 44). This is a prototypical Stine chapter. It answers the question posed by the cliffhanger from the previous chapter, then asks the unanswered questions of the protagonist/ reader. It ends with, if not a cliffhanger, a shocker of another terrifying phone call.

By contrast, chapter five is a mess. It is long and contains several scenes, including another phone call from the blind date. Kerry learns her name is Mandy, not Amanda, and that she lives on Sizemore, not Sycamore. He makes arrangements to meet her as she again hangs up in a hurry. Immediately the phone rings with the "other" caller who escalates: "Sticks and stones will break your bones. Are you ready to die?" (*Blind*, 49) It is odd pacing. This rather significant plot development of a murder threat is treated almost like a throwaway—three lines in the middle of this long chapter.

This is followed by another long conversation between Kerry and his father where they discuss the newspaper headline about Sal's injury. Kerry imagines the headline reads: "Superstar quarterback ruined for life by bumbling idiot who should be murdered" (*Blind*, 52). Kerry tells his dad about the threatening calls, only to have his father, the policeman, dismiss it as "just a 'teenage prank'" (*Blind*, 55). This type of adult dismissal is common in Stine's books. The parents are often uninterested, absent, or too busy working. What all this does, of course, is force his teen characters to assume adult roles and assert independence. Given the number of single-parent households, this is perhaps a responsibility that many of his readers have had to assume. It is, paradoxically, when teens assume adult roles in a Stine book that the trouble often begins. The chapter ends with Kerry and Josh threatened by a group of football players from their school.

DAYDREAM BELIEVER

In chapter six, Stine introduces one of his favorite devices:

the "Is it real or is it a dream?" scene. As the football players are ready to attack Josh and Kerry, Kerry lunges at them, and like some cartoon super-hero, tosses them around. The fight ends when Sharon appears on the scene to tell everyone that Sal is all right and they all apologize to Kerry. This action, while seemingly real, turns out to be only a daydream.

In reality, the football players pound on Kerry and bloody his face (the first of many appearances of blood in Stine's books). The scene is disturbing, the violence is graphic, and readers can feel Kerry and Josh's pain as they are pummeled by the football thugs. It is also out of character; all of Stine's books contain violence, but there is an unrealistic quality to it. While many of Stine's critics would attack him for the randomness of the violence in his books, it seems clear that those sudden shocks might actually be preferable to this more realistic approach.

Stine pulls out two more items from his growing bag of tricks back to back in the next two chapters. Chapter seven features a long conversation between Kerry and Amanda that ends at Kerry's vandalized locker. Lockers appear often in Stine books and with good reasons. Obviously they are a part of everyday YA life, but more than that they do represent a zone of privacy, thus safety, for teenagers. To have someone attack a locker merely underscores the vulnerability of the protagonist and increases the sense of danger: "His textbooks—all smeared, all covered with blood" (*Blind*, 76). But chapter eight begins with the realization that the red substance is not blood, only red paint. This is another Stine staple: the "It is not blood, it is—" trick. But real blood shows up throughout Stine's books as well. While Stephen King used blood for gross-out effect, he also used it symbolically in *Carrie* (a novel of menstruation horror). Stine uses blood almost like he used "soup" in his joke books. It is also a word guaranteed to get a reaction. Further, today's teen readers, like it or not, given a childhood of television and movie viewing, expect to see blood and guts. Stine doesn't drown them in it, but uses a minimum amount to maximum effect to keep the suspense heated.

Stine is building sympathy for his hero and adding heat to the story by the constant pounding that Kerry is taking. He has been beaten-up, terrorized by phone calls, kicked off the football team, and will get in trouble at school with both a principal and a teacher. Worse, though, is the fact that everyone at school hates him for injuring Sal. More than simply having readers "relate" to his protagonist, Stine is trying to get them to feel sympathy for the character as well as pulling for him to win. Readers stay hooked to the book to see how, in the big blow-out final scene, the protagonist gets his or her hand raised in victory. Just when it seems it could not get any worse, it does, when news arrives about his brother Donald.

Chapter nine reveals the mystery of Donald, as Kerry's father tells him what happened to Donald and why he cannot remember. A year ago Kerry, Donald, and Donald's girlfriend were in a car accident. His father explains that the girlfriend was killed, and Donald became so distraught he was committed to a mental hospital. Kerry learns that his brother has escaped and is probably headed home, and that Donald may be dangerous. Stine replaces one mystery strand (What has happened to Donald?) with another (What will happen with Donald?) and then interjects that mystery into the book's central storyline as Kerry asks his father:

> "The girl who died - Donald's girl friend. Was her name—"
> "Amanda," his father said. (*Blind*, 97)

It is a chilling moment and a great chapter ending.

SURPRISE!

This type of surprise ending to chapters has become a Stine trademark. Stine, as noted, traces his love of this gimmick to his own childhood. His multiple storyline books consisted primarily of cliffhangers at the end of chapters. No wonder it came easy to

Stine when doing YA thrillers. After imagining so many perilous situations in which to leave his characters and readers dangling, coming up with one per chapter perhaps came easy. Stine also credits the influence of science fiction on his later writing style, in particular, *The Twilight Zone:*

> Most sci-fi stories had a wild twist at the end. . . . I liked surprise endings so much when I was a kid, I remembered them when I started writing scary books. I decided I wanted to have a surprise at the end of every book. Then I decided it would be even more fun to have a surprise at the end of every chapter. (*Ohio,* 47)

Stine's use of the word "fun" is significant in his approach to writing. He is deliberately trying to make his books fun for his readers. Stine's books are designed to be like thrill rides at amusement parks, not like conventional YA novels. The way to kick up the fun, he perhaps surmised, was to remember what he found fun as an adolescent, then use it in his own way.

Stine further twists the plot in chapters ten and eleven as Mandy and Kerry go to a school dance. Readers have been led to believe that Mandy is mysterious, yet not a danger to Kerry, but as they are leaning against the wall kissing passionately, Mandy kisses Kerry so hard his lips start to bleed. After Kerry and Mandy leave the dance, they find vandals have attacked his car. It is exactly this type of plotting that has led to Stine's success. There is danger; it is resolved, then there is more danger just over the hill. Like a comic setting up a gag, he lays out a series of straight lines and punch lines. It is also incredibly readable.

But in this first book, Stine's not at that level yet. There are long passages, like those in chapters twelve and thirteen, in which Stine writes about Kerry's feelings. Interestingly, when Kerry is talking with his father, telling him everything that has happened, Stine writes *about* the conversation, not the conversation itself. Later, he would be much more focused on dialogue. Kerry decides not to tell his father about Mandy. "He needed to keep the one good thing happening to him private. He had to keep it separate, and clean" (*Blind*, 135). A typical reaction of a Stine character to the randomness and disorder of the attacks is to attempt to stay innocent and in control.

The father as a policeman is a convention Stine would rarely use again. The police are seldom involved, except in the most intangible way, in any of his books. But Stine was still tied somewhat to conventions of the past due to the influence of his forerunners in YA mystery: Joan Lowery Nixon and Lois Duncan. Another convention is the use of threatening phone calls. Every time a phone rings in *Blind Date* (or any Stine thriller) readers just *know* something bad (which is good) is going to happen. After getting anonymous phone calls, Kerry finally gets one from someone he knows. His brother Donald calls to tell Kerry, "Be careful, I'm coming" (*Blind*, 137). The stuff that kids love in Stine's books isn't so much the action as the anticipation.

Chapter fourteen reveals that Kerry is not the only person being stalked. As they are driving around town, with Mandy behind the wheel, she tells Kerry that his brother Donald has been stalking her, but she refuses to reveal how she knows Donald. It is clear that Mandy is hiding something juicy from Kerry and the reader. As they are talking, Stine is also busy pumping up the action. Mandy is driving too fast and too carelessly. Every other line there is a reference to the obvious accident about to happen. The chapter ends with Kerry staring in the face of oncoming headlights. Stine flashes back to the accident that killed Amanda. "'She's dead,' Kerry said. . . 'She's dead—and it's all my fault'" (*Blind*, 151).

The headlights spur his memory of not just the accident, but his role in it; Kerry was the driver; Kerry killed his brother's girlfriend. Although Stine buries it in the middle of a chapter, it is one of the climaxes of the book. While Stine has been criticized for the shortness of chapters of his books, they work. In *Blind Date*, it is easy to see where he could have made the chapters shorter. They are so overpacked with scenes that sentences that should be punch lines become buried in the middle. Stine's been building to this moment and then doesn't take full advantage of it. In later books, he would rarely make the same mistake.

CHANGING THE QUESTIONS

Another typical Stine hook is to change the questions just when readers think they have all the answers: "Why was Donald the one who was punished?" (*Blind*, 157) Stine doesn't leave it a mystery for long, however, as Kerry's father tells him the *real* reason that Donald was committed wasn't because of the accident, but because he had tried to kill Kerry. That's another Stine angle: everyone lies. It is perhaps a cynical worldview but one that cuts to the truth of many YA lives. In *Blind Date*, the adults lie, as do the kids. The lies not only reflect the reality of his readers' lives, but add another layer to the mystery. Now that Donald has escaped, his father is worried for Kerry's safety. Not worried enough, however, to stay home with his son. Instead, Kerry is home alone in a scene where every noise scares him, especially when the phone rings. Kerry vows not to pick it up. When he does, the roller coaster car starts heading toward another big hill: "Kerry, you've got to help me. I'm so frightened. It's Donald. I think he's here—in the house" (*Blind*, 166). With that, Kerry thinks he has it figured out: Mandy isn't the ghost of Amanda; instead, she is something much worse. She is Donald's revenge. Just as Kerry "killed" Donald's girlfriend, now Donald is going to kill *his* girlfriend. Stine is tying the loose ends together as he heads for the homestretch and the "big final scene" that is a thriller trademark.

THE BIG FINISH

If one of the inspirations for the YA thriller genre was the success of *Friday the 13th* and other teen slasher movies, it is not surprising that some of those elements—the milder ones—come into play in Stine's books. One element borrowed from the films is the setting. These movies usually took place at a summer camp where teens could be free of adults and rule their own world. At the same time, the summer camp setting provided the remoteness to make the impending danger more threatening. Stine, Pike, and the rest would often send their charges to islands, camps, and beaches for those very same reasons. In *Blind Date* Stine sends Kerry and Mandy out in the woods (the woods of Fear Street, no doubt) to hide. It's stupid, but it's familiar and it works. Stine brings out the clichés: a roaring fire, the sounds of animals, and two young people snuggling for warmth and safety.

It turns out that Mandy has slipped a sleeping pill into Kerry's drink and when he awakens, he is tied to a chair. As Kerry tries to escape and to figure out what is happening, Mandy says she will explain it all: "Then in a harsh, distorted voice—a voice Kerry knew well—she said, 'the toe bone's connected to the foot bone'" (*Blind*, 184). Mandy tells Kerry that she intends to keep her "promise" by smashing every bone in his body. This leads to the book's next revelation, which seemingly (once again) ties it all together and makes the situation even more horrifying: Mandy is Amanda's sister and the motive is simple: revenge. This would become a stock Stine move—a final scene where the protagonist is bound and in grave danger. But before the blood can flow, the villain will answer all the questions: who they are, and why and how they have done it.

The book winds down as it begins, with the sound of a breaking bone, only in this case it is Kerry's bone as Mandy smashes a mallet down on his foot. Stine's books often feature such symmetry, as early scenes contain the same elements as later scenes, so that by the time the final scene comes, it is expected yet still exciting. Again, that's the roller coaster phenomenon. You know the big hill is coming, but that still doesn't make it any less frightening; in fact, it makes it even more so. In this final scene, Stine pulls out all the stops. Having used some hard-core violence, he introduces—for the only time in this book—a gross out. It is a little too comic to have the desired effect as Mandy pulls a moosehead off the cabin's wall and stuffs it over Kerry's head. This is a very strong reference from Stine's childhood; he wrote in his autobiography that one of the things that he imagined in the forbidden attic was a moosehead hanging on the wall. While there's a gross-out element—Stine describes the foul odor—it is a silly image. Maybe Stine felt he needed to undercut a pretty horrible scene: his protagonist is tied to a chair with a mallet-swinging crazy woman bent on revenge. Chapter nineteen ends with Kerry expecting to die as Mandy announces she is going to smash in his head.

Almost every Stine book has a "cavalry to the rescue" scene. Despite the criticism leveled at Stine for his cynical vision, almost every book (unless he is setting up a sequel) ends not just happily but heroically. In *Blind Date*, Kerry survives when his brother Donald rushes to the rescue. Strangely, Donald calls the woman swinging the mallet Nancy. Donald explains that Mandy/Amanda/Nancy "has several different identities, none of them her own. . . . She becomes other people. I told her about the accident, when I was in the hospital. . . . She just moved into the story . . . became Amanda's sister" (*Blind*, 196).

This gimmick in *Blind Date* of multiple identities shows up repeatedly in Stine's books as they feature characters that are twins, lost cousins, or using a second name. Other constants are characters who are thought to be dead only to return under a new identity, and characters who pretend to be someone they are not. In addition, almost all characters show off two sides of their personality, both the dark and the light. That Stine should be playing with identity makes good plotting sense. Like the use of such gimmicks on TV soap operas, it provides explanations for what seems to be unexplainable. On another level, identity is a pressing concern for his readers. Teens attempt to establish their own unique personas. One outgrowth of this is that many of Stine's characters are unable to reconcile their identity struggles and so turn to violence or madness. Stine's books, like *Blind Date*, are loaded with characters who feel they are going crazy and have been committed to, and/or released from, a psychiatric hospital. Double identities allow for trick plots, but also reflect issues of readers.

Donald's explanation is cut short when Stine uses another favorite technique, the false finish, as Nancy struggles to her feet and goes after Donald. The "rising from the grave" scene is a sure-fire hit. From the "bogeyman" in the film *Halloween* to Glenn Close popping up from the bathtub in *Fatal Attraction*, few things are scarier than the seemingly dead villain coming back to life. It is as if the roller coaster comes to a rest, then goes into a "demon drop." Nancy/Amanda/Mandy's comeback is cut short as Kerry saves his brother's life. This allows Kerry to emerge as the hero of his own story.

Blind Date ends, as most Stine books do, on a humorous note. Josh tells Kerry his cousin Sarah is coming to town and they should go out on a blind date. Kerry jokingly threatens Josh, then changes his mind, asking, "'How pretty did you say she was?'" (*Blind*, 212). It is Stine's sense of humor that has always set him apart from the other thriller writers. This would be even more true when Stine started writing *Goosebumps,* which succeeded, in part, because "youngsters unanimously proclaim [Stine is] much funnier than other horror writers."[4] Throughout the book Josh provides ample comic relief, not only because Stine perhaps couldn't resist being funny, but because it adds to the pacing. HBO's popular *Tales from the Crypt*, as well as countless horror and suspense entertainments, including Hitchcock, add comedy to the mix for the same reasons. Get people laughing and relaxed, and then scare the hell out of them.

In his first humorous book, *How to Be Funny*, Stine created a model for other books he would write in the same genre. In much the same way, *Blind Date* contains the essential elements of Stine's thrillers: threats disguised as pranks and jokes, ominous and anonymous phone calls, disinterested or absent parents, teen protagonists whose main fear is not being popular, and twisting plots. The devices he uses are the same: red herrings, roller coaster plotting, mixed-up identities, cliffhanger chapter endings, false finishes, mysteries wrapped inside of mysteries, and a final confrontation scene that answers all the questions. The style Stine uses here—lots of short sentences and sentence fragments, heavy use of question marks and exclamation points, and the overall easy-to-read tone—is the trademark of his later thrillers. The characters Stine uses here—an evil cheerleader, a wisecracking best friend, and a normal "I just want to be liked" teen protagonist— would be central casting for his thrillers yet to come. What Stine hit upon was a mix of knowing what works with kids (funny and scary), what matters to them (popularity), how to tell that story (quickly, filled with dialogue, and loaded with tricks), and what scares them (gross outs and threats).

PATTING HIM NICELY ON THE HEAD

The critical response to Stine's opening scary salvo would follow the pattern of patting him nicely on the head, then sending him to bed with no real praise, support, or supper. *Publishers Weekly* called the plot "convoluted and some details are stomach-churning"[5] while *Kliatt* noted that the book should be "for entertainment only."[6] While many authors might take offense at such a statement, it was perhaps exactly what Stine wanted to hear. *Booklist* noted that the book was "not for the squeamish and riddled with contrivances" although admitting that the "story is well paced and has TV-ish flair that is likely to appeal to teens."[7] The *School Library Journal* noted the storyline was "complicated and not too believable" but that the "writing flows enough to keep the reader's attention" and that the whole book was "mindless entertainment."[8] Finally, the *Voice of Youth Advocates* review stated, "The unsophisticated will like this for its dark twists and turns, but mystery buffs will recognize this hoary and convoluted had-I-but-known style and move on to Dick

Francis, Mary Stewart et al."[9]

It seems, as with Stine's humor books, that there's a real failure here among the critics to understand or appreciate what they are reviewing. Stine wasn't interested in writing a standard teen novel or teen detective mystery romp; he was interested in writing a scary book. The criticisms are perhaps justified, yet at the same time are irrelevant. Like most scary fiction the plot is improbable, but it does make sense (with a few exceptions) within the premise of the story. No, this couldn't happen, but then there aren't any vampires either, which doesn't make Annette Curtis Klause's *The Silver Kiss* a bad book. And what may strike one reviewer as a convoluted plot is merely Stine's method of packing a book with climaxes and keeping the pace moving. The storytelling is solid and in the end everything is explained. Is *Blind Date* scary? Is it entertaining? Those are the real questions to ask, since they are the ones the book is posing.

In essence, critics were dismissing Stine, even those admitting the book was entertaining. What seems to be missing from the reviews of *Blind Date* and almost every other Stine title is the recognition of the talent it takes to be entertaining. While it might be called "mindless entertainment" it is obvious that it takes a creative mind, talent, and skill to scare people. The large number of teen horror novels and series that tried to emulate Stine, yet failed, document that. Much the same, there are plenty of writers of adult horror fiction, but no one else comes close to Stephen King. Admittedly in both cases part of the explanation is simply mass psychology at work. They are popular because they are popular. More than that, there should be a recognition of why they are popular. Other horror writers produced scarier books than Stine, others created books that were better written, others wrote with more violence, and still others created ones with more action. But Stine got the formula right.

It didn't come to him overnight. As successful as *Blind Date* was, it is flawed. Stine would take the best elements of the book and build from there. His popularity isn't just because he got there first, but because he "got it right" first. The "overnight" success of *Blind Date* had been in the making since Stine pounded out his first magazine on a portable typewriter at age nine. Steve Martin's tag line for a while was "Comedy is not pretty." Perhaps Stine's should be "Scary is not easy" (or appreciated by reviewers). What scary was, in *Blind Date*'s case, was very successful, and along with the works of Christopher Pike, it helped launch the horror craze that would come to dominate YA book publishing in the midnineties.

BOB/KERRY

One element in *Blind Date* that makes it unique to the later *Fear Street* titles is its male protagonist. While some of the *Fear Streets*, such as *Goodnight Kiss*, would feature male characters in the lead, as a rule Stine uses girls as the primary protagonists or victims. Writing his first thriller, Stine had to know this was the convention. Pike's *Slumber Party* and the example set in films like *Halloween* showed the effectiveness of this choice. It appears that like many first novelists, Stine drew heavily on his own story. The similarities between Kerry and the teenage Bob Stine are numerous. Kerry is at the book's beginning an outsider, not disliked, but not popular. Throughout the book he is called a dork. Writing about his own high school years, Stine recalled, "I never really fit into any of the groups" (*Ohio*, 34). In the incident that opens the book Kerry accidentally injures his team's quarterback; later he imagines a newspaper headline calling him a "bumbling idiot." In much the same way, Stine wrote about his own athletic prowess, or lack thereof: "I was a terribly unathletic kid . . . a total klutz" (*Ohio*, 34). Like Kerry's pal Josh, Stine's best friend Norm was "fast talking and funny" (*Ohio*, 36). An automobile figures prominently in the plot of *Blind Date;* Stine, in writing about his youth, recalled that "cars were so important to us!" (*Ohio*, 41).

The unnamed town in *Blind Date* looks a lot like Shadyside of *Fear Street* fame, which, not coincidentally, looks a lot like

Stine's description of his hometown of Bexley, which was filled with "enormous mansions" (*Ohio*, 42). While it was a wealthy community, Stine's family was not rich, and he recalled that "sometimes I felt like a real outsider" (*Ohio*, 43). That notion seems to have inspired the creation of the protagonist for his first novel, and many since.

In writing his first book, Stine dug deep into his memory for images and feelings from his own high school years. That feeling of being an outsider obviously stuck with Bob Stine—and the stark terror which it brings in a teenager's life. When everything is about fitting in and being liked, the most horrifying thing to a teenager is, as Kerry says "not being liked." What Kerry and a couple of hundred other Stine teen protagonists would learn, however, is that while not being liked might be their deepest fear, it would not be their only one. *Blind Date* started Stine's and young adults' romance with thrillers.

NOTES

1. *Authors and Artists for Young Adults*, vol. 13, ed. Kevin S. Hile and E.A. DesChenes (Detroit: Gale Research, 1994): 214; hereafter cited in text as *Authors*.

2. R.L. Stine, *Blind Date* (New York: Scholastic, 1986): 1; hereafter cited in text as *Blind*.

3. Jan Harold Brunvand, *The Vanishing Hitchhiker: American Urban Legends & Their Meanings* (New York: Norton, 1981): 24-40; hereafter cited in text as Brunvand.

4. Sally Lodge, "Life After Goosebumps: Kids' Horror Genre Assumes Monstrous Proportions," *Publishers Weekly* (2 December 1996): 271; hereafter cited in text as Lodge.

5. *Publishers Weekly* (22 August 1986): 102.

6. *Kliatt Young Adult Paperback Book Guide* (September 1986): 18.

7. *ALA Booklist* (15 September 1986): 121.

8. *School Library Journal* (November 1986): 108-9.

9. *Voice of Youth Advocates* (April 1987): 33-34.

CHAPTER FIVE
THRILLS, CHILLS, AND SPILLS

The history of fiction designed to scare readers is a long one. There are plenty of books explaining the appeal of horror to readers (and viewers) of all ages, taking in all sorts of psychological, sociological, and cultural viewpoints.[1-3] There is no sense in recounting those arguments in detail here other than stating that horror fiction, as well as horror in all other forms of entertainment, plays an important part in American popular culture. Nor is this attraction new. Annette Curtis Klause, author of the YA horror novels *The Silver Kiss* and *Blood and Chocolate,* reminds us that "since the infancy of humankind we have been afraid of the dark, and that fear still lingers. . . . To cope with these fears, humankind invented stories to put order to them and to be prepared for what might be out there."[4]

That teenagers should be attracted to horror is also no surprise, and again nothing new. Klause explains that "modern children thrill to urban folktales told around a campfire, or consume library copies of R.L. Stine . . . with the same delight that I'm sure ancient cave children felt when huddled around the clan fire listening to the shaman's tales of ghosts" (Klause, 38). Horror is dark, forbidden, and scary—elements which naturally appeal to the rebellious and independent streak in adolescents, perhaps best demonstrated by the Goth movement of the late 1990s. Horror is exciting, and given the rapid physical and emotional changes occurring in a teenager's life, the seeking out of thrills, chills, and spills as an escape valve is quite common.

Psychologists like Dr. Jerome Singer advance that horror serves an important function by allowing kids a "healthy way to explore their feelings and let off steam at a time when they are learning how to control their emotions and behave appropriately."[5] Horror on the page or on the screen taps into something deep in the audience, causing them to have physical reactions to the work. They scream; they shiver. There is really nothing, as Stine noted, quite like sitting in a dark, crowded theater screaming from fright, screaming just for fun.

THE FUN OF FRIGHT

And horror *is* fun. It is fun to yell in terror at a movie theater or feel shivers from reading a terrifying scene in a book. YA horror expert Dr. Cosette Kies writes:

> Horror scares us, and the relief following the realization that the horror is not real brings pleasure. Horror is fun just because it is scary and shocking. Not only does it scare and shock those of us who read horror, but it has the benefit of scaring and shocking those who wonder how anyone could read the stuff in the first place. It is especially fun . . . to shock . . . parents, teachers, and librarians.[6]

That's a critical point: some people just don't get it. They don't like to be scared or grossed out. Others choose to be scared, a fact often forgotten by critics. The violence in *Fear Street* is random, but it is also expected because that is what draws readers to a thriller in the first place—knowing scares are forthcoming. Readers of horror are readers with intent: they know what they want and they read the books that give it to them. The prevalence of horror in culture, from the ancient myths right up to the heavy horror presence on television and in books in the 1990s, demonstrates the fun of fright.

The emergence of horror fiction in the mass media is directly related to the overwhelming success of Stephen King. The King phenomenon, as with the whole horror genre, has inspired many a volume of analysis.[7-10] One of the best came from King himself:

> Novels, movies. TV and radio programs—even comic books—dealing with horror always work on two levels. On top is the "gross out" level.
> . . . The gross out can be done with varying degrees of artistic finesse, but it's always there. But on another, more potent level, the work of horror really is a dance—a moving, rhythmic dance. And what it's looking for is the place where you, the viewer or the reader, live at your most primitive level. . . . The good horror tale will dance its way to the center of your life and find the secret door to the room you believed no one but you knew of.[11]

While talking about all horror, King has made a salient point about the appeal of horror to teens—the appeal to the "secret door." Most adolescents have two sides of their personality. There is the side they show to the world, and a secret side where they do bad things, dream, fantasize, and think dark thoughts. It is not nice, not pretty, but it is normal. The horror novel, as Stine demonstrates, pulls us from our comfort zone and makes us dwell for a while in that secret room. But Stine could only take teens there if he could involve readers in the story by using characters whose lives are similar to their own, thus allowing readers to welcome him warmly. As King and Stine also discovered, nothing is as scary as horror emerging, not from some monster or alien force, but right in our own backyard. Stine's decision to set his YA stories in suburbia rather than Transylvania demonstrates that "the most effective horror is that which takes place in the everyday world. The juxtaposition of the banal with the gruesome makes the story more believable" (Klause, 39).

BOY HORROR

The success of both *Fear Street* and *Goosebumps* emerges from the appeal of horror to teen and pre-teen boys. Reaching that age group, as Stine knew from years of trying, was always difficult, but he said, "These series are the first ones ever to have equal numbers of girls and boys reading them. We got boys to read. That's the difference" (*Alderdice*, 208). This has been a double-edged sword for Stine as "the fact that horror appeals more to boys may account for horror series being less accepted than series novels aimed at girls."[12] The reasons for this appeal are varied. Boys often tend to like books focusing on action rather than emotion, in particular books containing risk-taking, bravado, and facing down fright. This "fact" is not news to anyone as:

> Any high school teacher of English will tell you that horror has been the favorite reading genre of YAs for a long time. Witness the perennial popularity of Edgar Allan Poe in junior and senior high school English classes—an assignment that invariably sent boys scurrying to the library for more. This unaccustomed male enthusiasm for [horror] literature always made English teachers and librarians smile. But, until recently, until Stine, that is, there was little more in the genre . . . to fan this flicker of interest into a white-hot flame.[13]

Stine's thrillers certainly sparked a whole new interest among boys for reading.

Almost all previous series books for teenagers were easily identifiable as to the gender of their target audience. The gender of the protagonists would match that of the audience. Horror is a genre that

> affects all readers alike, male or female. What they all have in common is terror before the unknown, the unthinkable, or the unspeakable. The way that horror fiction has swept all other fiction genres . . . proves what a powerful thing literature can be when the subject matter appeals to both males and females alike. (*Makowski 1998*, 74)

MONSTERS SHAMBLING OUT OF THE DARKNESS

Stephen King's success, like Stine's, was also a matter of timing. King burst onto the scene in the post-Watergate era. The country was a mess: people's trust was shattered and they were not sure what to believe. King explains:

> The horror genre has been able to find national phobic pits, and those
> books and films which have been most successful almost always seem
> to play upon and express fears which exist across a wide spectrum of
> people. Such fears, which are often political, economic, and psycho-
> logical rather than supernatural, give the best work of horror a pleasing
> allegorical feel . . . if the shit starts getting too thick, they can always
> bring the monsters shambling out of the darkness. (*King*, 18)

That pleasing allegorical feel also points to Stine. His readers
are afraid not so much of violence in their schools or gangs, but
of this new life they've been thrust into without any choice, a
life filled with challenges, decisions, and responsibility. With
responsibilities come anxiety, with anxiety comes the need for
release, the need for a monster emerging from the darkness. By
reading a scary book, young people can "project their everyday
fears into a monster and confront them in an environment they
control. This power gives them strength, especially when characters in books for younger readers defeat evil all by themselves.
This is a reassuring message" (Klause, 39).

The monster emerging from within teens is developing
sexuality. Horror serves as an outlet for this turmoil; as teens:

> undergo hormonal changes, youngsters may be frightened by the in-
> tensity of their newly awakened sexual urges. Their changed bodies
> might feel freakish to them, and their emotions alien. As they struggle
> for independence, their feeling toward their parents might swing be-
> tween love and anger, at times even murderous (and guilt ridden) fan-
> tasies....Young people feel they can relate with monsters....They fear
> they have shameful, monstrous impulses, and seeing these films helps
> them sort out their ambivalence.[14]

While most YA paperback horror authors, with the exception of
Christopher Pike and L.J. Smith (and Stine in *Blind Date*),
would avoid discussing sexuality, it is always hovering in the
background. Stine's books are usually about crushes and unre-
quited love. Filled with romance and rejection, these books paint

both sides of the fence. It could just be a coincidence, but the timing of the popularity of these books lines up with the beginning of national awareness of the AIDS crisis. I am not suggesting that Stine or other authors consciously made the connection, but perhaps the readers realized that not only were these new feelings about sex scary, but that acting on them could be deadly. Teens' lives were also becoming scarier for other reasons during the 1980s. The number of kids "home alone" continued to rise, as did the homicide rate among teenagers. Violence filled movies and TV, and naturally would eventually appear in books. This overdose of violence, according to YA literature critic Michael Cart, is the evil root of YA horror:

> Such ubiquitous violence ultimately does have a numbing, almost dehumanizing effect on our emotional selves, impairing our capacity to empathize and forcing authors to . . . work harder to involve the reader's emotions. Jaded, numbed and dehumanized, viewers and readers seem to need ever more visceral doses of violence to jump-start their numbed emotions and sensibilities. This is one reason, I think, for the phenomenal popularity in the eighties of . . . horror novels.[15]

The question becomes a chicken-and-egg thing: does mass media cause violence or merely reflect it? This question of impact surrounds the controversy regarding R.L. Stine.

Given that teenagers live in a culture of violence, why do teens want to take the paranoia of violence with them to bed at night, to study hall at school, or to the beach in the form of scary paperbacks? Stephen King provides the best summation of why people want, and even need, to be scared:

> We make up horrors to help us cope with the real ones. With the endless inventiveness of humankind, we grasp at the very elements which are so diverse and destructive and turn them into tools—to dismantle themselves. The term catharsis is as old as Greek drama . . . but it still has its limited uses here. The dream of horror is in itself an out-letting and a lance . . . and it may well be that . . . horror sometimes becomes the national analyst's couch. (*King,* 26)

King's success, like that of Stine, resides in each author's understanding of the audience's real fears.

Unlike King, however, Stine and Pike didn't originally write monster books or what might be considered classic horror. The secret door didn't contain a monster; it contained teenagers' own fears and doubts. In making this change, Stine and Pike (and novelists like Thomas Harris in the adult field) are redefining horror. They are moving it away from "a reliance upon an outside force of evil (for example, a vampire) to be a more understandable, manageable, threat (for example, your neighborhood psychopath). The mysterious malevolence in Stephen King's *It*. . . . is replaced, in many current horror novels for young people, by something which can be more readily explained."[16] Teenagers were about to meet the monsters, and they were them.

THE MONSTER AWAKES

In the years just before *Blind Date*, Stine was writing joke books and *G.I. Joe* adventures, and Christopher Pike was writing series fiction, as was Richie Tankersley Cusick, who even penned some titles in the failed YA horror series *Twilight* in the mid- 1980s. The breakthrough was Pike's *Slumber Party* in 1985, which more or less invented the teen thriller genre. Stine's *Blind Date* followed the next year and *The Baby Sitter* followed in 1989. Also that year, Scholastic published *The Lifeguard* by Cusick. Stine and Cusick's books, while different in some ways from Pike's, shared many qualities. YA commentator Audrey Eaglen noted their popularity and place in YA collections, writing, "the YA librarian who really wants to meet the recreational needs of young patrons may groan at the thought of another series or a host of watered down attempts to imitate Stephen King, et al, but will have to consider these (Stine, Pike, et al) for their browsing collections and in quantity."[17] In addition to identifying this new field for the library audience and noting its key components, Eaglen named this genre horror/mystery novels. A

better term, however, might have been thriller, as the most important thing in the books is just that—thrills. Those thrills may
come through using the techniques of horror, hard suspense, or
mystery, but the desire is the same: to elicit shock, to cause
screams, and to satisfy.

People other than Eaglen, however, took a look at the covers
and titles, then dubbed these books horror fiction, in particular
comparing them to Stephen King, when they more closely re-
sembled adult thrillers by Mary Higgins Clark or hard suspense
novels by John Sanford than King. Either way, certain elements
make up these titles and explain their appeal to teenagers.

1. The readers of these books are the characters of these titles.
    Most center around a group of well-scrubbed kids with the
    normal set of fears. The fears are not about monsters, but
    about grades, being liked, and fitting in. Most of the charac-
    ters in the books are white, live in the suburbs, hang out in
    malls, and they will do incredibly stupid things, like every
    other bright likable kid.

2. Another part of the mix is the supernatural. Although it
    doesn't always play out, the books all seem to suggest that
    the danger is caused by something unspeakable and unex-
    plainable. Later, many titles would revert to straight horror
    and the supernatural, in particular, vampires. And while there
    are the trappings of black magic, there is no hard-core satanic
    activity in these books. These thrillers aim for the soft middle
    of the teen market, not the edge. Further, while there are
    shocking things in all of these books, everyone is pulling
    punches. If the desire was really to be nothing but shock fic-
    tion, then perhaps these books would include ritualistic kill-
    ings, animal sacrifices, blood bonding, and other files from
    the fringe, but they do not.

3. The format itself is a winner—paperback, about 200 pages.
    The chapters are short; most run about ten pages. There are
    usually between twenty and thirty per book. Good readers
    can polish them off in just over an hour. The reading level is

low, normally around sixth grade. The vocabulary is fairly simple, as is sentence structure. Except for use of flashbacks and dream sequences, most are told in a straightforward way. Certainly trying to figure out "who done it" is part of the thrill, but getting scared is the real appeal and "because stories of the supernatural often make fewer demands on the intellect than on the sensibility they are more accessible to average readers" (Klause, 39).

4. The normalcy of horror. While there are deaths in these books, with exceptions the body count is not high. While critics say the murders are described in detail, they certainly are not, especially in Stine. He'll give you the murder weapon, a glimpse at the body, and show you the blood, but there are few lingering close-ups. The killings rarely go unpunished. The police rush in or the folks from the mental hospital emerge to cart away the villain to just rewards. While "bad things do happen to good people," worse things happen to bad people. These books usually end with the main character saying something like "The horror is over," signifying a return to normalcy. Unless there's a sequel—if so, then right after that line is spoken the phone rings.

5. The secret. Almost all of these books involve one or more of the kids having a secret. Sometimes it is a secret past or repressed memory; other times a secret identity. Few things are as quintessentially teenage as the notion of secrets. Teenagers are developing private lives away from their parents, lives they feel they can't share with everyone. So issues like trust and betrayal figure heavily in these books, just as they do in real YA life. Almost every book has a character who ponders—"Whom do I trust?"

In many ways, most of these attributes (save the last) could be used to describe YA mystery series like Nancy Drew. The YA mysteries of Lois Duncan and Joan Lowery Nixon also fit the bill, including the use of the supernatural. It is interesting that Dell re-released Duncan's and Nixon's mysteries as thrillers with new cover art and new blurbs. Nixon's books, in particular, sound like YA thrillers, with titles like *The Stalker* and *The Seance*. Duncan's *Don't Look Back* and *Summer of Fear* ring the same bell, as do works by Jay Bennett, like *The Executioner* and *The Haunted One*. Also in the 1980s there were original horror paperback series like *Twilight*. Some titles in these series were penned by writers who would be latter-day thriller and middle school horror authors, like Diane Hoh. While popular, these series didn't have the same impact, stir the controversy, or make as much money.

Making money, however, did little to raise the respectability of horror series despite (or perhaps because of) reader enthusiasm and strong sales. This literary blindness stems perhaps from the prejudice many have against paperbacks, as well as horror. Pike, Stine, and Cusick all wrote series paperback fiction, which also is not held in high regard in the library world. Moreover, even "serious YA writers" like Gary Paulsen are criticized when they write sequels or series, so Stine's desire to write only for commercial and not artistic reasons rubs many the wrong way.

Moreover, it is fairly well known that the creative juices behind many of these titles are the editors at the various paperback houses. Along with book packagers, the editors develop concepts and line up the authors to write them. This isn't anything new in YA publishing, but the thrillers seemed to inspire a ruthlessness to it all. Like the vampires in the books, publishers went for the jugular. Sometimes the editor will provide only a title; other times they will pitch an idea—maybe something like "I see a broken-down bus full of teen ballet dancers, a thunderstorm, and a claw hammer. See what you can do with that." In addition, marketing research and savvy drive these books. This market-driven approach, which would escalate to new heights with *Goosebumps,* shocks librarians, teachers, and critics more than the latest knife driven into a (papier mache) head.

STALKING PROFITS

Thrillers were also the outgrowth of slasher movies like *Halloween* and *Friday the 13th*, which had their heyday in the early 1980s. One has to assume that publishers saw the simple formula of "teens plus terror equals profit" and set to work incorporating many of the same elements into fiction. On the surface, thrillers do resemble horror movies more than they resemble other teenage mystery novels. The covers and titles reflect movie promotion tricks, and the books themselves often read like PG-13 novelizations for unmade slasher films. Bold use of black, blue, and blood-red dominate the covers, which feature illustrations of teenagers in danger or graphic emblems such as a bloody knife. There's the same bizarre fascination in inventing new methods of gruesome death. Yet, in many of these films, in particular the *Nightmare on Elm Street* series, there is plenty of humor and black comedy to dull the blade.

In writing about teen slasher films, Vera Dika attempted to define "the underlying structures that distinguish the stalker film from the greater body of horror."[18] YA horror authors like Stine and Pike (the name of whose first book resembles the slasher film *Slumber Party Massacre)* used these films as building blocks. The point of view is important, a technique adopted by Stine. In the films, there are always shots from the villain's point of view as he/she/it lurks behind the next victim. The use of this perspective, Dika noted, creates a new level of audience participation:

> We know the killer will definitely strike and that the victim will not get away . . . the questions of when? where? and, ultimately, how? become those posed by the viewer . . . these conditions involve the viewer in a play of expectations with the film. The viewer's involvement is participatory, as he tries to guess the outcome and eagerly awaits the final jolt supplied by the inflicted wound." (Dika, 54)

Stine captures this perspective with devices like notes, phone calls, and first-person chapters. The constant threats are the print equivalent of film shots from the villain's point of view. Both make the audience aware the villain is dangerous and present.

There are huge similarities in the characters found in both the slasher films and the works of the YA horror authors. In addition to the use of a girl as the protagonist, the surrounding crew came from the same central casting. Dika observes that the characters in the films have a "quality of being undistinguished and non-specific. They are dressed in clothes that do not distinguish by a particular style or trend . . . and most all the characters in the film are white, middle-class Americans. . . . As ordinary, active, youthful characters, they are primarily involved in enjoying themselves and each other" (Dika, 55-56). That's a very strong parallel. In particular the egocentric nature of the teens in these books is dramatized—bodies are falling yet they still manage to go to parties, on dates, and the like. Similarly, Dika noted that "the entire action takes place in a single setting. Not only is the setting a singular one, but it is also exclusionary, in that it separates the young community from the rest of society. . . . The stalker film is usually positioned in a middle-class American setting, one that fosters the greatest degree of 'likeness' to the members of the film-viewing audience" (Dika, 58-59). While Stine wouldn't always make the physical setting exclusionary, the lack of adults, institutions, and rules make a virtual setting of teenville the most common venue.

One of the hallmarks of YA horror is the twist at the end where the readers learn not just *who* the villain is but the motives behind the mayhem. Often the reason is similar to that found in slasher films, where the villain's past explains actions in the present. Dika noted that the villain was spurred on by some past trauma caused by "his viewing of, his knowledge of, or his participation in a wrongful action perpetrated by one or more members of a young community. Because of this event, the killer experiences a loss. The killer responds with rage" (Dika, 59). In some of the films this rage was channeled into violent acts, although as Dika points out, in the movie that started the trend, "explicit violence was almost completely absent in *Hal-*

loween" (Dika, 62). Yet movies grew increasingly violent, which, along with the proliferation of sequels that were really reruns, saw the genre stop raking in profits about the time the YA thriller books emerged. They're back, as a new generation of teenagers, weaned on Freddie videos and Stine's and Pike's thrillers, as a fresh audience for a new era of teen horror films led by *Scream* in 1996.

PIKE'S PEAK

Christopher Pike's *Slumber Party* established the ground rules that make thrillers different from mysteries: to wit, if a mystery is about "Who done it?" then thrillers ask "Who—or what—done it?" The "who done it" aspect remains, but thrillers incorporate elements of horror and the supernatural. Rather than responding to a crime with detective work, the teenage protagonists encounter acts of violence coupled with threats which seem to be the work of a supernatural force. Rather than one character, Pike decided to focus on a group, a small clique of friends. Not surprisingly he used girls, as they have been the traditional victims in scary films and also the primary readers of fiction. He then chose a deserted yet exotic location—a ski lodge (Stine moved *Fear Street* to the slopes in *Truth or Dare* and *Ski Weekend*). Pike mixed in strange happenings (melting snowmen), and disappearances (a character is missing). While it could be supernatural, Pike also throws in some real suspects and potential villains. To add a supernatural flavor, the girls play with a Ouija Board. Finally, the element that gave Pike's early books a very distinct flavor: the secret.

In later books, Pike would refine his formula, sometimes going way over the edge in terms of supernatural content (*Remember Me*). Perhaps his best 1980s book was *Chain Letter*. What is most interesting is that there is nothing the least bit new about the plot—a bunch of kids accidentally kill someone (see Duncan's *I Know What You Did Last Summer*). Again, Pike's vision is sharper, wittier, and darker. The 1997 movie version of

I *Know What You Did Last Summer* (which Lois Duncan disa-
vowed), while keeping the bare bones of the book, seems in
sensibility to be closer to Pike and Stine. In Pike, the kids are
"good kids," but they're not. They drink, they get horny, and
they betray each other. The cliffhangers are often not about violence, but are either a gross out or humiliation. The revenges in
Duncan are meant to terrify the character and the reader; the
retributions in Pike are meant to gross out the reader and not just
scare, but often humiliate the character. Pike has characters who
wake up in the middle of the night to a room filled with cock-
roaches. Whereas Duncan's books take place in the real world,
the YA thrillers seem to occur in a uniquely teen world with its
own set of rules. The motives of the characters are self-
ish—jealousy and envy. Teenagers feel these emotions in-
tensely. Given YA concerns about appearance and identity, to
many YAs the types of psychological violence listed in *Chain
Letter* might be scarier than the threats of physical violence.

Pike continued to churn out thrillers set in this world, some
of them excellent (*Gimme A Kiss* and its cousin, the wonderful
Fall into Darkness), but having invented the genre, he appar-
ently grew bored with it. His books ventured off into time travel,
science fiction, religious parables, New Age ghost stories, and
even Greek myths (*The Immortal*). He wrote several adult novels (*Sati*) and started a middle school scary series called
Spooksville. As the thriller genre evolved and allowed for more
"straight" horror, Pike got liberated by producing the *Last
Vampire* series which was very good and very popular. Pike's
best book of the 1990s was undoubtedly *Monster*. It too serves
as an example of what is right (and what many feel is wrong)
with the genre as it developed.

Monster begins with a bang, literally. A girl crashes a high
school party and shotguns down two classmates "because they
were monsters." It's startling. Normally knives are the weapons
of choice; very few guns show up in these books. The book then
kicks in; it's a rave up, all red eyes and raw meat. *Monster* is

one of the better books to capture the essence of puberty and the physical horrors and changes wrought by adolescence. The characters feel their bodies changing; they can't seem to control them or their hormones and they don't recognize themselves in the mirror. Are they monsters? Or just "good kids?"

A MONSTER SUCCESS

Thrillers became in a very short time a monster success for a variety of reasons. First, they became popular because something has to be. As Pat MacDonald, the editor at Pocket Books who brought *Fear Street* to life, said, "Teen interests go in cycles. . . . In the '70s, it was problem novels, the disease of the week. Then it was romance novels, soap operas like *Sweet Valley High* and *Sweet Dreams*. In the '90s, it's the thrillers."[19] The time was ripe: the romance genre had mutated and become exhausted. The same things that would later plague thrillers (don't these publishers ever learn?) would befall romances: too many titles that were too similar, too many series, and too little attention to what makes quality in series fiction. As the hundreds of failed romance, mystery, action, and thriller series demonstrate, just sticking a number on the spine of a book won't sell it. Part of the thrillers' success was that they didn't start as a series and that there was a void to fill. Thrillers quickly snowballed. Soon scary was cool because these books were engaging, exciting, edgy, and rarely boring for any length of time. Plots moved quickly with lots of twists and turns, using gross-out or shock scenes at regular intervals to keep the reader constantly stimulated and wired to the text. The mystery elements fascinated some readers, but that's not the hook. It is not the brain, but the jugular Stine and the others aimed for, knowing that "the appeal of horror is not the intellect" (Klause, 39).

When a teen picks up one of these thrillers, they're thinking, "This is going to be one wild ride." Thrillers are easy to read, they are fun, and they are funny. While the everyday life of high school reads real, the far-out stuff is the draw. After a while they become repetitious, predictable, and not as shocking. Why do they keep reading them? Do you remember riding a roller coaster when you were in high school? Same short ride, the same every time, but a great ride nonetheless. You know what is coming around the bend, or in the books in the next chapter, and that is part of the fun. The scary parts allow teenagers to enjoy the excitement of being terrified while still feeling in control. The violence puts teenagers out on the edge of danger without pushing them over. Like roller coaster rides, thrillers provide an enticing mix of danger and fun and keep readers coming back for more.

VIOLENCE IN YOUTH FICTION

While violence in youth fiction always draws attention from concerned adults, the popularity of these titles, coinciding with a rapid increase in the public perception of teen violence, perhaps explains the high profile hatchet jobs on the genre. Some stories try to link violence with teen series fiction. There seems to be a critical flaw in that theory. Are we assuming the same group of kids who read *Fear Streets* are the ones in gangs wreaking general havoc? That seems a stretch. Thrillers seem more a reaction to violence than the cause. Any teen can experience more violent acts during an hour of watching television, a movie on cable, or the nightly news, than polishing off a *Fear Street* title.

While there is no getting around the significant amount of research about the correlation between television violence and violent behavior among children, there is no corollary research, that I am aware of, connecting violence in books to behavior. The differences between visual media and reading are intense. Reading demands activity while viewing requires passivity. Reading sparks the imagination and viewing often dulls it. For example, there is a huge difference between a child watching violent acts on TV and reading about them in a classic book like "Grimm's Fairy Tales" because "unlike violent movies, which leave no doubt about death and destruction, fairy tales play out in the reader's imagination. . . . Even the grimmest story gives parents and kids a chance to talk about what is going on in the child's mind."[20] Finally, the very act of reading, of touching and turning pages, always allows the reader to know, no matter how gross and gory the action gets in front of them, that *it is just a book* and they are in control.

A related argument is that such books reinforce kids' "siege mentality," convincing them that there is danger around every corner, and that thrillers desensitize kids to violence. These are the most troubling arguments and in many ways most persuasive. Yet both hinge on the idea that scary paperback books— not great YA literature, but "junk" food reading—can warp the mind of young readers. It assumes a far greater lasting influence than I believe these books have upon kids. The whole notion of these books is that they are throwaways—read this month's scare, forget it, and wait for the next. While thrillers are engaging, entertaining, and involving, most readers can maintain a distance because the books don't have "enough stuff" to stick. Finally, I believe most kids can separate what is real and unreal.

Kids are a work in progress. They are learning every day, not just their academic subjects, but how to be a person in the world. Some will grow out of reading thrillers, some won't. But when they are in junior high and they stop reading, then there is a problem. They'll move on when the books no longer meet their needs. Maybe they'll read Stephen King, which will lead them to read his nonfiction book *Dance Macabre*, which will take them to "classic horror" by Lovecraft. Or if they want real violence, we can introduce them to the bloody mayhem of Shakespeare's plays.

Thrillers are a microcosm of how libraries do and don't react to teenagers. There has been a tremendous surge in thriller popularity since 1985, but as late as 1997 librarians are still wringing hands about spending money on thrillers for kids. The objection, cloaked in the guise of violence, is really about popular reading. The violence in fairy tales for much younger children is certainly grimmer, yet because those books are classics and not pulp fiction they are accepted easily. If YA thrillers are not available in the library, then library collections are clearly unresponsive to teens. The message is: "We don't respect their reading choices, we don't react to changes in the literature, and finally we place our needs over those of the customers." Unresponsive collections, lack of respect, and ignoring customers—now, there's a real horror story.

IS THE MONSTER DEAD?

The success of Stine, Pike, and Cusick unleashed a gusher of gross outs. At first, there were individual titles, but soon the series explosion occurred. Writing in 1994, Cosette Kies noted "There are many series considered YA horror. . . . Most publishers . . . have announced their intentions of increasing their number of YA horror novels."[21] Some of these new series were blatant copycats of *Fear Street,* like *Horror High,* while others, like L.J. Smith's *Vampire Diaries,* were more original. Many of the series died out immediately, as YA readers could obviously separate the wheat from the chaff. Stine's most serious challenger was Diane Hoh's *Nightmare Hall* series. It lasted the longest of any of the competitors, which is not surprising given Hoh's history of writing YA series and scary fiction.

After a decade of dominance, the YA thriller seems to be dying out. While *Fear Street* is still strong (although not selling as it has in the past, according to bookstore managers) most of the competition is drying up. Comparing a jobber catalog's YA section from 1993 with one in 1997 demonstrates in hard numbers that thrillers are starting to fade. To this fact many— librarians, teachers, and even some teens—are happy to exclaim "Rest in peace!" The death of thrillers should come as no surprise. Like most products aimed at teenagers, its success was its eventual downfall. The success in the teen market led to the expansion of horror, often by the same authors, into the children's market. That was the kiss of death. As Nancy Pines of Archway Books observed, "As soon as your little brother picks

up your book, that's it. The older kids don't want it any more"
(Gellene, A1).

The classic definition of an adolescent is a person who no
longer thinks of himself as a child, yet is not considered by others to be an adult. When teen fads become co-opted by children,
the writing is on the wall. YA marketing guru Peter Zollo, in
writing about the quick rise and fall of rap star MC Hammer,
traced how his teen idol role fell as he became involved in massive mainstream product endorsements and Saturday morning
cartoon shows.[22] The same happened here. Suddenly teenagers
who were reading Stine and other scary books caught onto the
fact that their little brothers and sisters were reading them, and
worse than that, fast-food kid's meal prizes were based on
Goosebumps. When the television show started, however, the
real attraction of younger kids to Stine began, followed a few
years later by the exodus of older readers. Stine went from being this "cool guy who wrote cool books" to that guy on the
kiddy TV show. Middle school kids who grew up reading
Goosebumps probably didn't want to read other books by the
same author they read in fourth grade. Finally, the success of the
genre resulted in so many books being pushed on the market,
some of them terrible in the context of the convention, that it
became harder and harder to separate the good stuff from the
dross. There has been only one series that has survived and tri-
umphed over the rest: R.L. Stine's *Fear Street.*

NOTES

1 James B. Twitchell, *Dreadful Pleasures: An Anatomy of Modern Horror.*
(New York: Oxford University Press, 1985).

2. Joseph Grixti, *Terrors of Uncertainty: The Cultural Contexts of Horror
Fiction.* (London and New York: Routledge, 1989).

3. David J. Skal, *The Monster Show: A Cultural History of Horror.* (New
York: Norton, 1993).

4. Annette Curtis Klause, "The Lure of Horror." *School Library Journal*
(November 1997): 38; hereafter cited in text as Klause.

5. Margaret Davidson, "Fright Delights and Tasty Terrors." *Parenting* (October 1996): 170.

6. Cosette Kies, *Presenting Young Adult Horror Fiction*. (Boston: Twayne, 1988): 1-2.

7. Joseph Reino, *Stephen King: the First Decade, Carrie to Pet Sematary*. (Boston: Twayne, 1988).

8. Tony Magistrale, *Stephen King: the Second Decade, Danse Macabre to The Dark Half*. (New York: Twayne, 1992).

9. *Fear Itself: The Horror Fiction of Stephen King*, ed. Tim Underwood and Chuck Miller (San Francisco: Underwood-Miller, 1982).

10. Sharon A Russell, *Stephen King: a Critical Companion*. (Westport CT: Greenwood Press, 1996).

11. Stephen King, *Stephen King's Dance Macabre*. (New York: Everet House, 1991): 18; hereafter cited in text as King.

12. Steven L. Powell, *Fright Light: a Content Analysis of R. L. Stine's "Goosebumps," and Selected Other Juvenile Horror Fiction Series*. (University of North Carolina at Chapel Hill, Library School Thesis, 1995): 9; hereafter cited in text as Powell.

13. Sylvia Makowski, *Serious About Series*. (Lanham MD: Scarecrow Press, forthcoming 1998): 71; hereafter cited in text as Makowski 1998.

14. Barbara Smalley, "Are Horror Movies Too Horrible for Kids?" *Redbook* (October 1990): 37.

15. Michael Cart, *From Romance to Realism: 50 Years of Growth and Change in Young Adult Literature*. (New York: HarperCollins, 1996): 140.

16. Leila Christenbury, *Things That Go Bump in the Night: Recent Developments in Horror Fiction for Young Adults*, ERIC_NO- ED360638. (Syracuse NY: Educational Resources Information Center, 1994): 4.

17. Audrey B Eaglen, "New Blood for Young Readers." *School Library Journal* (December 1989): 49; hereafter cited in text as Eaglen.

18. Vera Dika, *Games of Terror: Halloween, Friday the 13th, and the Films of the Stalker Cycle*. (Rutherford NJ : Farleigh Dickinson University Press, 1990): 54; hereafter cited in text as Dika.

19. Paul Gray, "Carnage: An Open Book." *Time* (2 August 1993): 54; hereafter cited in text as Gray.

20. Michelle Ingrassia, "What if the Three Pigs Tried Conflict Mediation?" *Newsweek* (31 January 1994): 63.

21. Cosette Kies, "EEEK! They Just Keep Coming! YA Horror Series." *Voice of Youth Advocates* (April 1994): 17; hereafter cited in text as Kies 1994.

22. Peter Zollo, *Wise Up to Teens* (Ithaca NY: New Strategist Press, 1995): 54 ; hereafter cited in text as Zollo.

CHAPTER SIX

HORROR MASTER

The success of Stine's early thrillers, as well as those of Pike and Cusick, showed there was a market for scary books for teenagers. It wasn't long before someone would attempt to bottle that success using the familiar series formula. Series have always been the mainstay of many YA paperback publishers and the folks at Parachute Press soon asked Stine to deliver a thriller series. As usual, it wasn't until he came up with the title that he was ready to begin work.

> I decided I'd like to try writing some scary novels. "What could I call it?" I wondered. I sat down and started to think about a title for the series—and the words *Fear Street* just popped into my head. I didn't even have to think about it. There it was. I took the rest of the day off. (*Speaking*, 204)

The Stines got their proposal to Pat MacDonald, the editorial director for Pocket Book's youth paperbacks. MacDonald knew the genre, as she had worked in the past with Christopher Pike. It seemed perfect, but as MacDonald noted, "Some people in the business weren't at all convinced that the series would work, but I was willing to take a chance" (*Lodge*, 24). That chance resulted in the publication of *The New Girl* in the summer of 1989.

FEAR STREET STARTS IN A DIFFERENT DIRECTION

Fear Street represented a shift in direction for series fiction. The most successful series for teens have contained reoccurring characters—Nancy Drew, the Hardy Boys, the Wakefield twins— or a defining gimmick, such as *Choose Your Own Adventure*. The individual titles of the previous teen horror series, *Twilight* and *Dark Forces,* and also many 1980s romance series, were held together only by the series name, similar to adult romance series like *Harlequin.* Yet since part of the whole series notion is to provide repeated enjoyable reading experiences because readers are "visiting" old friends, most series require something other than just the brand name. Jane Stine noted:

> The prevailing wisdom at that time was that one couldn't publish horror as a series. . . . It was hard to imagine how one could craft a whole series, since it was thought that a series needed to have the same characters reappearing. Then we came up with the idea of setting the stories on *Fear Street.. . .* which gave the books a continuity and a basis for the series. (*Alderdice,* 208)

In doing so, the setting itself—Fear Street and Shadyside— became characters in the books. They were always hovering in the background and set the series tone. Stine said that "it was the first time that someone decided to do horror novels as a series, to use one location, and keep coming back to it" (*Alderdice*, 208). Like the *Nightmare on Elm Street* films, the location provided a solid foundation to start building a house of horror.

Later, more details were added in the *Fear Street Saga* trilogy to broaden the character of the town. While the setting wouldn't always be on Fear Street itself, someone in the books has usually just moved there, or at least to the town of Shadyside. The school—Shadyside High—reoccurs, although students normally don't. Stine noted, "There's a very high mortality rate at Shadyside High School" (*Alderdice*, 208). The treatment of *Fear Street* appears in the frontispiece of the very first book:

Are you sure you want to turn down Fear Street?
The most horrifying things seem to happen to those who live on Fear
Street.
The town of Shadyside is nice enough. And the students at Shadyside
seem to be an average group of kids.
So why does everyone tell such stories about Fear Street?
About unspeakable terror, troubled cries in the night, twisted night-
mares. . . .
About strange cries late at night from the old Simon Fear mansion—a
house that's been deserted for fifty years.
About lost teenagers, mysterious fires, brutal crimes, unsolved myster-
ies. . . .
About normal people—people just like you—who turn down Fear
Street...and are never quite normal again.
Go ahead. Take a walk down Fear Street. Those stories couldn't be
true. No way. There couldn't be that much terror awaiting you on one
narrow, old street—could there?[1]

It is interesting that Stine, MacDonald, or the copywriter chose
to use the word "you," since the books, in their construction,
would resemble those multiple storyline "you-directed" titles.
Also this introduction almost dares kids to read the book—"you
think you can't be scared? Well, try this." This intro lays out all
the key elements of the series, from the first book in 1989 up to
those still being published in 1998.

THE NEW GIRL

The first *Fear Street, The New Girl*, resembles *Blind Date* in
many ways. Again, the teen protagonist (Corey) develops a
crush on a girl (Anna) who, like Amanda in *Blind Date*, doesn't
seem to exist. Trying to solve the mystery, Corey visits Anna's
house only to find "she's dead." Mostly the book is about
Corey's obsession with Anna—obsession with knowing her and
knowing *about* her. It is the same kind of obsession that Kerry
had for a mysterious girl, and Stine probably hoped readers
would share it. The book ends with the revelation that Anna is
indeed dead, but the girl is very real—it is Anna's "evil twin"
who killed Anna, then took her place. If this all sounds familiar,

it should—it's really a reworking of *Blind Date*. The names barely change: Kerry becomes Corey and Amanda becomes Anna. But Corey is less interesting, in part because unlike Kerry, Corey is a guy who "has it all," and Anna is less enticing, less frightening, and much less overtly sexual. The book is, however, in some ways far more terrifying as Stine's style continues to improve. The pacing is quicker, the cliffhangers set up wonderfully, and few scenes are wasted: everything matters. Still, *The New Girl* was anything but new.

It begins, like many that would follow, with a strange prologue written in first person. Here, some unknown person is describing the death of Anna and even giving away the motive:

> Bye Anna.
> Good-bye.
> Look at her down there, all crumpled. Her dress all crumpled.
> She wouldn't like that. She was always so neat.
> She wouldn't like the blood, so dark and messy.
> You were always so perfect, Anna. You were always so bright and shiny, as if you were sparkly new every day. . . .
> Who was I while you were Little Miss Perfect?   Well, you're perfect now. You're perfectly dead, ha ha. (*New Girl*, 1)

That mean-spirited nature would really mark the difference between Stine's books and mysteries by Duncan and Nixon. This unknown character is spiteful, resentful, bitter, and ultimately vengeful. Jealousy and envy are intense emotions that Stine invokes repeatedly. Most of the *Fear Street*s would announce similar motives for what is about to happen: the outsider feeling slighted and wanting to get both attention and revenge. Those are normal emotions for humans, and perhaps more pronounced in the teen years when issues such as identity and acceptance reign supreme.

The New Girl, like *Blind Date*, follows the pattern of the Stine playbook, but also expands it. Although Stine would certainly add (and subtract) some elements, all the building blocks are in place in the first *Fear Street*. The evil of *Fear Street*, the cliffhanger chapter endings, the constant threats and pranks, the mix of fake scares with real ones, the red herrings, the twisting relationships between teenagers, the groups of teens who share a job or a certain setting, cars and phones as major props, a sense of paranoia and danger, obsessive thoughts and actions, quick dramatic action told in short one-sentence paragraphs, simple vocabulary, lots of sentence fragments, lots of teen dialogue that sounds authentic without being laced with slang, lots of recognizable settings like pizza places, some violence but more "gross outs" than "gore outs," and finally the trick ending involving a confused identity to explain what seems unexplainable. Every *Fear Street* book is different—yet they are all the same because they work from this formula.

That is true of all series fiction. One reason series books have been popular is because of their predictability. Consumers know exactly what they are getting and they expect it. You go to an action movie and you expect things to blow up; you don't read a scary novel unless you are expecting (and wanting) to scream. Writers like Stine obviously understand what the audience wants and are not ashamed about delivering it repeatedly. One way to do this, as Stine demonstrates, is to develop a repertoire of gimmicks. A Stine reader knows those gimmicks, waits for them, and gets a pay off when they deliver. A *Fear Street* book without a prank phone call, a threatening note, or blood on the floor wouldn't be a *Fear Street* book.

The second book, *The Surprise Party*, contains a definitive *Fear Street* chapter ending:

Meg sat miserably staring at the door of the lunchroom. . . . where was Tony? Why was he being so stubborn? Didn't he know that she needed him now?
She . . . lifted the brown paper bag from her lap. . . .
She started to unwrap the bag.
That's funny, she thought. There's something leaking in here.
Leaking? How could it be leaking? She had only packed a sandwich and an apple. It must be—
She reached her hand in. She felt something wet and sticky. And thick.

"OH!"

She pulled her hand out fast, tipping over the bag. A dark red liquid oozed out, spilling down her white blouse, onto her skirt. Meg pulled up her hand. It was covered with the warm liquid. It dripped down her wrist and onto her arm and puddled on the lunch tray.

"It's blood!" she cried. "My lunch bag is filled with *blood*!"[2]

It's all there: the short sentences, the questions about another character's behavior, the public humiliation, the necessary amount of detail and description, the surprise, the gross-out use of blood, and the cliffhanger chapter ending. Stine takes these stock scenes and characters and sprinkles them throughout the book. There will be a variation on the details, but not on the punch such scenes deliver. Stine is not writing for himself or a small audience; he is writing for a mass audience accustomed, due perhaps to the influence of movies and TV, to entertainment that delivers in a very predictable way.

THE FRANCHISE

After *The New Girl*, Stine would produce at least twelve *Fear Streets* a year. He would (as we'll see in the next two chapters) juice up the franchise with super chillers and trilogies. He's also done a two-part book, *Fear Hall*, and is planning a 1998 spin-off called *Fear Street Seniors*. From the first title, *The New Girl*, up to *Trapped*, Stine has published fifty one "regular" *Fear Streets* as of December 1997. Within that number, there have been sequels, with *The Wrong Number, The Stepsister*, and most recently *The Best Friend* getting encores. Titles would co-incide with the calendar: *Sunburn* coming out in July, *Truth or Dare* (set in a ski lodge) in February, and *Halloween Party* in October. All of the covers would feature a teenager looking afraid. Sometimes the teens are in groups (*The Overnight*), often in pairs (*Missing*), and occasionally alone (*One Evil Summer*). The covers usually contain at least one female; only a few fea-ture a boy. In those cases, he appears as a ghostly figure (*Haunted*), a stalker (*The Boy Next Door*), as a corpse (*The*

Confession), or as a face in a picture with a knife jammed into it
(*Killer's Kiss*). Although the illustrations are different for each
book, every other aspect of the cover looks the same. "*Fear
Street*" is at the top, followed by Stine's name, the illustration,
and the title of the book at the bottom. The type is stylized and
used throughout the series. The back cover features a close-up of
the front cover and a tagline that is the book's main hook, such
as "It's just a bad dream—but it seemed so real" from *Bad
Dreams* or "Five close friends . . . one murderer" from *The
Confession*. The blurb is always, always excellent—and normally features the words "murder" or "die." Finally, each book
hypes next month's offering.

While Stine would change the names and the details, some
general story lines remained consistent. In the normal Fear
Streets—not sequels, trilogies, or super chillers—Stine would
revisit about six main story lines. While not all of these books fit
neatly into one of these categories, they represent a summation
of the *Fear Street* formula. What is impressive about Stine is that
he can take these basic ideas and cut and paste them to make
each book familiar; each is not just a rewrite of a previous book.

1. The confused identity: *The New Girl, Haunted, Switched,
   College Weekend, The Stepsister, Runaway.* This story line
   revolves around one character pretending to be someone else
   or who is just plain mysterious. In *The Best Friend,* Becka
   Norwoods' life is ruined when a girl, Honey, claims to be
   Becka's best friend although Becka swears she has never
   seen her before. These identity novels are also usually about
   obsession.
2. The practical joke gone horribly wrong: *The Fire Game,
   Lights Out, The Wrong Number, The Thrill Club, What
   Holly Heard.* The idea here is that a group of teenagers play
   jokes or pull a prank, only to have it blow up in their faces. In
   The Fire Game they dare each other to set fires, egged on by
   the new kid in school, with a predictable catastrophe.

3. The "pay-the-price" hook: *The Overnight, Dead End, Final Grade, The Prom Queen.* This is the best known hook and Stine went to it early with *The Overnight.* A group of teens goes camping without adult supervision. In the woods, an accident happens in which the teens kill a man, then cover his body with leaves. Soon after, the members of the group start getting notes saying, more or less, "I know what you did last fall." Pay back is the root of all Stine books, although when he was asked why all his books concerned revenge, Stine denied it and responded, "Not all—only some" *(AOL).*

4. The recreational setting hook: *Halloween Party, The Surprise Party, Ski Weekend, Sunburn, Truth or Dare, All Night Party. The Overnight* could fit here as well. In *Sunburn,* a group of teens goes to a "remote ocean view mansion" and the terror soon begins. A direct descendent of Pike's *Slumber Party, Sunburn* concludes with the revelation that "Marla" is really "Allison" who the group thought died the year before.

5. The romance/love triangle hook: *First Date, The Cheater, The New Boy, The Dare, Double Date, Killer's Kiss, The Perfect Date, The Boy Next Door.* While romance is part of every Fear Street, these titles move the conflict to the forefront. In a book like *The Dare,* a girl has a crush on a popular boy and will do anything—including killing a teacher on a dare—to get him to notice her.

6. The "unexplained occurrence" hook: *Missing, The Sleepwalker, The Secret Bedroom, The Mind Reader, Bad Dreams, The Face, Night Games.* In this plot, a character will be confronted with a situation that seems supernatural, such as the dreams of murder Maggie has in *Bad Dreams,* or the visions which lead Ellie to discover a corpse in *The Mind Reader.* Usually more eerie than scary, these titles are among the most chilling, in particular the paranoia of *Missing* and the ghost story of *The Secret Bedroom.*

Stine overlaps these ideas, so that a book like *Halloween Party* has a confused identity, a recreational setting, a series of practical jokes—including ones that end in a murder, and the motive for the villain is revenge.

THE MONSTERS ARE REAL

The similarity between all these books is the setting—not just Fear Street and Shadyside, but the real landscape of teen life. One of the failures of the earlier scary book series like *Twilight* was that the teen protagonists seemed incidental. They really were just props for pushing through the plot and their "teenageness" didn't play a big part in what or why things happened. In *Fear Street*, everything happens because teenagers act like teenagers: they get jealous, they get rejected, and sometimes they want to get even. People in *Fear Street*s rarely die from supernatural phenomena, but because of all-too-natural deadly sins. The monsters are real—the monsters are the fears that every kid has about fitting in and being popular. Teens want to be popular and be the center of attention, and it is by becoming a victim that Stine's characters get that attention.

But not everyone is a good guy. One major way Stine (and Pike) differ from Nixon and Duncan is the unlikability of their characters. The teens in their books argue with their parents, fight with their brothers and sisters, and are often at odds with their classmates. They steal boyfriends or girlfriends from friends, they betray each other, but mostly they bear deep-seated grudges. They blackmail and challenge one another in books like *The Dare*. Insecurity and jealousy complicate their dating relationships. There is economic envy in these books, as the poor outsider attempts to bond with the rich in-crowd with terrifying results in books like *The Cheater*. Stine's characters are competitive and they want to succeed, but sometimes that is the problem in books like *The Prom Queen*. Like characters in Hitchcock movies, they have accidentally found themselves in the middle of something they can't escape—nice metaphor for adolescence.

Fear is what makes *Fear Street* work. Each book is loaded with the things that cause fear. The characters don't feel safe; they feel threatened and in danger. They feel afraid for their lives. They are unsure whom to trust or what to do. They do the best they can and sometimes that doesn't work out. Yet they are also—in the great duality of adolescence—strong, smart, and unafraid, especially the female characters. They care about their friends and family deeply and try to protect them. They are afraid because people are playing jokes on them, or "grossing them out," or because people around them are dying. For all the talk of death and murder, very few *Fear Street*s feature more than one or two deaths. Attractive serial killers, psychopaths, or random killers don't live on *Fear Street*. There is always a motive; it is (almost) always explained. Stine doesn't need to write "It's wrong to kill people or stalk them"—he knows his readers know it's wrong. The killers are caught, punished, and sent away to an institution, either a prison or mental hospital. Stine is showing kids with intense yet twisted emotions, then showing the consequences of acting on emotions turned to obsession.

As he learned in his joke book and multiple storyline days, Stine writes action to create a reaction. Just as comics tell jokes to get a laugh, horror writers want to hear screams. They want a physical reaction. In order to get that reaction, the action needs to keep coming. Stine's books have been called "unmade TV movies," which is meant as a slur, but in another sense seems to be a compliment. It means he can tell a dramatic story, make it reach his readers, and make it readable. The pacing is fast— there's something coming around every corner. Most *Fear Streets* alternate between real and fake scares, where the "bony hands" for instance turn out to be that of a little brother. Something happens in a *Fear Street* book, the character reacts to it, guesses why it happens, then moves toward the next incident. That pace may be jolting, but the constant motion seems to mirror the pace of the lives of Stine's teen readers.

While Stine's books are often touted as material for reluctant readers, my experience is that good readers gobble up *Fear Street*s as well—kids who not only like to read, but have good reading skills, kids who do well in school, are involved in activities, and popular within their peer groups. The late *Sassy* magazine used to claim "we are our readers," and the same might be said of Stine. While there are lots of female characters and most of the books feature a girl as the main character in peril, Stine is also writing many male characters, most of them not psychopaths. Call it market research or responding to your readers, but Stine read his mail and reacted. He commented, "When *Fear Street* started, we assumed it would be all girls, because no one has ever been able to sell a series to boys. Boys aren't readers. Then the mail started coming in and it was 50 percent boys, so I started changing the focus a little" (Gilson 1994, 8G).

Not only can readers relate, but the books are ultimately relaxing. Like a thrill ride, there is a tremendous rush, followed by a period of release. As readers read more of the books another type of awareness develops—recognition of the repeated experience. Another part of the delight is similar to that experienced by viewers of slasher movies, as Vika pointed out. Inevitably, characters will do the stupidest things: go into dark rooms, open the door to a guy wearing a hockey mask and carrying a big knife, etc. Everyone in the audience knows the characters are about to meet a grisly fate, except the characters themselves:

The fact that something evil inhabits *Fear Street* and that this force hates teenagers is, of course, a delicious secret shared only by reader and writer. The luckless teen, who lives on *Fear Street* or happens to move there with unimaginative families, never seems to put two and two together when they are, one by one, maimed, crippled or driven insane by forces beyond their comprehension. Meanwhile, the omniscient reader watches with fascinated horror and sometimes a macabre kind of humor as . . . protagonists stumble blindly and inexorably toward their destined end—to provide victims for *Fear Street*. It becomes a sort of inside joke for the readers, a 'how are they going to get it, this time' feeling of goosepimply anticipation. (*Makowski 1998*, 76-77)

Anticipation is one of the keys to all good writing, in particular suspense writing. Bodies will fall; that is a given, and Stine keeps his readers guessing as to who, when, where, and most important, how. His readers keep reading, Stine insists, because they "like the fact that there is some kind of jolt at the end of every chapter. They know that if they read to the end of the chapter they're going to have some kind of fun surprise, something scary, something that's going to happen. . . . And force them to keep reading" (*Authors*, 215). Stine keeps a delicate balance between new characters and variations on plots, and the familiar writing style and formula in each new book.

A BUMPY BUT SCARY ROAD

Sometimes keeping this balance is not enough, as not all *Fear Streets* are created equal. The difference among the books isn't just in plot, but in quality, defined within the context of the genre as the book's ability to carry out its goal to be entertaining. Talented entertainers like film director Steven Spielberg or horror author Stephen King have their duds, like *1941* or *Rose Madder*. Given the number of books that Stine pens, the odds are that some will not be as entertaining, because the premise isn't interesting, the characters don't involve the readers, or the plot itself is not constructed correctly. The work also fails if it doesn't deliver the expected punch lines. While some books in the series are bumps in the road, the series as a whole delivers gags, gross outs, and gazillions of thrills.

Stine himself has said he was "never really happy" with *The Knife*,[3] published in January 1992. While none of Stine's stories are pleasant, this one is particularly unpleasant. The plot revolves around Laurie, a high school hospital volunteer, who becomes involved in some nasty goings-on at the hospital, then faces threats and possible death, none of which is presented in a particularly clever way. The secret that Laurie uncovers concerns doctors who kidnap and sell children. There are also strong hints of battered children throughout the book. This is an unpleasant mess, in part, because by dealing, even so slightly, with real issues like child abuse, Stine is out of his, and his readers' comfort zone.

FAVORITES: THE FACE AND SWITCHED

Two other books, *The Face* and *Switched*, are also out of his zone, but with much better results. Stine listed these two as his favorites because "their stories are very different from other *Fear Streets*" (*Scholastic*). That's true, but they are not so different that Stine's readers would be put off by them, as they might be by *The Knife*. *The Face* starts strangely—a first-person prologue relating a dream involving a silver line and a patch of red. The dream causes Martha to wake up screaming. Martha tries to remember something about an accident—another *Blind Date* tie-in. She is under a doctor's care and her friends are instructed not to mention the accident to her. Most of the early part of the book consists of Martha trying to remember with limited success. Martha is an artist who loves to draw, but she finds she keeps drawing the same thing over and over again—a portrait of a boy's face, a boy she doesn't know or can't remember. Stine mixes the obsession element with the repressed memory gambit for a nice blend. The suspense is in figuring out what the dreams and this boy have to do with the unspoken accident. Stine throws in a stalker hook, too. Martha gets a phone call in which a voice says, "You keep drawing him because you killed him."[4]

It is an interesting idea for a mystery. Not only do readers not know who did it, they don't even know *what* was done, just that it was so horrible that Martha can't remember. Eventually the story emerges. It seems Martha, her boyfriend Aaron, and her other friends went on a skiing trip. During the trip, a boy named Sean was horribly killed. Stine echoes his story from the urban legend of the ghost motorcyclist or beheaded snowmobiler. Someone placed a thread of silver wire in Sean's path when he was skiing, thus severing his head. It is one of the more gruesome deaths in a *Fear Street* book, perhaps more so because Martha's memories have increased our expectations of something horrible, and this decapitation doesn't disappoint. The final scene explains it all, as Sean's killer and Martha's tormentor Adrian lets loose:

> "I saw you in the back room of the cabin, Martha. I saw you kissing Sean. And something—something snapped. . . . That's when I knew I had to kill you. You had Aaron. You had a nice family."
> "You—you have everything Martha!" Adrian screamed. "Why did you need Sean too? Why couldn't you leave something for me!" (*The Face*, 145)

In a great final fight scene, as Martha and Adrian are struggling, Adrian has wrapped some wire around Martha's throat and is choking her. The fight ends suddenly when Adrian becomes transfixed by a portrait of Sean that Martha has drawn. Martha escapes with her life because of the dead boy and the picture of *The Face*—"The face that had saved my life" (*The Face*, 150).

Switched is another Stine favorite, perhaps for several reasons. It is much closer to science fiction than any other of his scary books, and also because Stine claims that "my son gave me the ending."[5] It also features a stronger than usual first-person voice that announces itself on page one, sentence one: "My name is Nicole Darwin and I'm a loser."[6] After recounting her catalog of problems, she runs into her best friend Lucy who shares similar woes. The solution is simple and far-fetched: change lives by switching bodies. Because it is *Fear Street*, however, that is possible. Lucy shows Nicole the "Changing Wall" located in the *Fear Street* cemetery. This is not a new premise—body changing is a classic horror, science fiction, and hard suspense staple (movies like *Seconds* and *Face/Off* are prime examples and it has been played for laughs in films like *Switch* and *Freaky Friday*). What's new and different for Stine is that rather than saving the revelation of the switch until the end, he gives it away near the beginning. Nicole soon realizes she has made a mistake, as it looks as if Lucy traded bodies with her to escape arrest for murdering her parents. It is one of the scariest of thoughts—that because of mistaken identity an innocent person will be punished.

While *The Face* is about Martha tracking down her memories, *Switched* is about Nicole trying to track down her actual self because Lucy has disappeared. Both books are about the power of memory and imagination. The action is as much in the characters' minds as it is on the page. Both books switch the convention of the genre; rather than being chased themselves, Martha and Nicole are both trying to chase down someone else— someone to make them whole and give them back their lost identity. Finally, *Switched* and *The Face* are about obsession, a common theme in *Fear Street*. Stine has a way of getting readers caught up in his characters' obsessions, intensity, and curiosity. By using the *Fear Street* horror setting and trappings, Stine always lets readers think that something evil or supernatural could be the answer.

After the first few *Fear Street*s, Stine seems to have worked out a formula. Formula is a dirty word in some circles, but with few exceptions almost all books for teenagers follow a core formula. The character is confronted with a problem and the book is that person's journey to find a solution and to change into a better person. Looking at the works of some of the most honored writers in YA literature, one will find a fairly strict adherence to this pattern. Stine's books also follow this formula. His characters face a problem—to stay alive in the face of an unknown danger. In the end, the character, not the police or any other adult, finds a solution to that problem. They emerge demonstrating traits of loyalty, compassion, and courage. The climax of almost every *Fear Street* is a confrontation between the book's protagonist and antagonist, in which the good guy comes out on top. This basic formula is used in literature, films, television, and even in professional wrestling: good guy gets "beat up" then makes a comeback and triumphs over evil. It is a formula that was first demonstrated in *Blind Date* and has not changed because it always works.

SECRET ADMIRER

Stine published *Blind Date* in 1986. Ten years later he published a *Fear Street* called *Secret Admirer*. Both hang from the same pegs as all *Fear Street* plots—the anonymous threat, followed by scares, ending with a confrontation. While *Blind Date* began with action, *Secret Admirer* kicks off with a warning:

> Dear Selena
> Your name means "moon." Like the moon, you are pale, beautiful, and mysterious. Your blond hair is silvery like the moon's rays. Every one admires you. Everyone applauds you. I'm in your audience too, Selena. Though I see you every day, you don't see me. But someday that will change. Someday I will be the only person in your audience. It will be just you and me, Selena. Someday. Someday very soon.[7]

The note is signed "The Sun." Stine has used the anonymous note before in books like *The Overnight* or in the form of the demented Valentine's Day cards in *Broken Hearts*, but he hauls it out here again, knowing it is a real grabber that will hook readers. Stine digs this hook deep: a person has written a note demonstrating obsession ("I will be the only one") and impending danger ("someday very soon"). The writer is probably someone Selena knows ("I see you every day") and knows something about her ("your name means moon"). By naming his protagonist "Moon" and his antagonist "Sun," Stine sets up one of many opposite pairs.

Per usual, the first sentence of the first chapter is an attention grabber: "He'll never hurt you again," but as often happens, the words are not what they seem. Here, they are merely dialogue from a play. Stine has used the play setting many times in his books (*Curtains* is the most obvious example) and it is easy to see why. It allows him to blur the mix between what is real and unreal, as Pike did in *Last Act*. A gun goes off—is it a prop or a real gun? A character is bloody—the result of an injury or by applying stage blood? The stage gives Stine a chance to work with a set of teenagers who want attention. Theater provides chances for teens to be successful and noticed; therefore, it is also competitive. That competitive nature anchors the rivalries that make up *Fear Street* and exaggerates these natural teen conflicts. Two students at a high school might be competing for something: a scholarship, an award, to be *The Prom Queen*, etc. Most feel some negative emotions toward their competition. Stine grounds his story in that emotion, then inflates it into exciting action sequences. If readers couldn't understand that core motive, then the action wouldn't be involving or interesting. The realness of the characters' emotions allow the reader to relate to and ultimately care about even Stine's characters.

It is noteworthy that Stine's critics constantly bring up the lack of character development in his books. It would be interesting, however, to note their reaction if he were taking the time to develop full characters, only to kill them. With all their concern about Stine's effect upon his readers, surely they would find this more devastating. Stine can kill off his characters with ease because they rarely rise above being characters, and his readers recognize this. They know they are reading a thriller, and they know someone is going to get hurt. You can't have a thriller without thrills and in most thrillers that comes through violence. While his characters might be plot props in many cases, they have enough flesh, and or course blood, to get that job done.

RED HERRINGS ABOUND

Stine seems to give away the identity of the villain when Selena's fellow cast member Jake calls her "Moon." Jake is described as looking distracted and preoccupied, as if he is hiding something. This will be one of the many red herrings introduced in the book; it is not the only one in the chapter. Stine has said he reads "a lot of Agatha Christie" (*AOL*) and it is easy to see that influence. Like Christie's *Murder on The Orient Express*,

Stine gathers his characters and gives each of them opportunity, means, and motive to commit the book's crimes. In *Secret Admirer* it is up to Selena to play the role of detective, and along with readers, evaluate each suspect's guilt or innocence. No sooner than Jake is introduced as a suspect, Stine provides another foil in Danny, Selena's ex-boyfriend: "We meant something to each other . . . but it lasted six months" (*Secret Admirer*, 4). A nice Stine touch here. It shows his insightfulness into teenagers as Selena comments about the six-month courtship: "I can't believe I went out with him as long as I did" (*Secret Admirer*, 4). To a teenager, lacking perspective, a six-month relationship is a major one. Any Stine reader knows "ex's" are certainly included among the usual suspects. It is revealed in a few pages that Jake and Danny are rivals. Stine not only sets up two suspects, but he also sets up a second conflict.

Next, the best friend is introduced. Katy is also Selena's opposite: she has short black hair; Selena has long blond curls. She works backstage; Selena acts. Katy is fearless (she runs lights from a catwalk); Selena is fearful, in particular of heights. The catwalk, as any thriller reader knows, is going to be important. It presents a perfect place for things to occur. Katy is Selena's best friend since childhood and is very supportive—too supportive. Selena thinks: "Why does Katy always have to exaggerate?" (*Secret Admirer*, 5). A third suspect and another set of opposites have been introduced, all in the five pages of chapter one.

HERE COMES THE SUN

The first chapter ends with a cliffhanger. This one is typical: Selena discovers a bouquet of flowers only to gasp "in open-mouth horror" (*Secret Admirer*, 8). The scene reads much the same as the passage quoted earlier from *The Surprise Party*, serving the same dual purpose: a clue in the mystery story and a gross out in the horror story. There are three variations on Stine's cliffhangers: the first, demonstrated here, is a character screaming at something that has really happened. Sometimes it is an object that has been left for them with some sort of grue-some twist (blood is often involved); other times it is some act of violence. The next is the pretend scare where the character screams only to find someone was just playing a joke. Finally, there are the dream sequences which Stine uses to allow the most gruesome acts to occur to his characters. *The Sleepwalker* and *Bad Dreams* are the best examples of the blurring of dream and reality.

In the first eight pages, Stine demonstrates the economy of his style. He introduces his main suspects for the crime: a male friend, a female best friend, and an ex-boyfriend. He does noth-ing more than describe them physically, establish their relation-ship with Selena, and drop some clues as to their guilt. Stine foreshadows the ending (it occurs on the catwalk), establishes what the characters are fighting for (a scholarship), and provides one scare.

Actually, the scare turns out to be rather tame, a bouquet of dead black roses, but accompanying it is another note. The un-signed note merely contains a child's sticker: a large yellow cir-cle, like the sun. As Stine's characters often do (don't they read his books?), Selena dismisses it as "a dumb joke." This is a common theme in the *Fear Street* books: the protagonist thinks someone is playing a joke and so ignores the pranks and threats, which leads to escalation. Like a comic building a routine, Stine's gags become more gruesome as the plot unfolds. The protagonist begins to develop an idea—which is always wrong—about who is playing the jokes. In this case Selena as-sumes it is Jake.

An overriding concern with Stine's characters is popularity. While that may seem shallow, it is what teenagers are worried about, according to Peter Zollo (Zollo, 70). Stine's characters thus normally have two fears: getting killed and getting asked out on a date. This theme is developed immediately in *Secret Admirer* as Katy asks Selena, "Did you ever think you'd grow up to be so popular?" (*Secret Admirer*, 20). Working in oppo-

sites as he often does, Stine makes the asker of the question unpopular. As they talk, readers learn more about Selena and
Katy's friendship, in particular about Katy's envy of her best
friend. Again, Stine is hitting a teen chord perfectly in this section.

The habitual scare that ends chapter two is the "someone is at
the window watching us" gag. It turns out at first the girls think
it is just the wind blowing leaves against the window, only to
then discover a ladder on the ground below Selena's second-
floor bedroom. After seeing the ladder, Katy asks her friend if
she thinks someone is stalking her. Stine then does what he does
best and delivers a good scary punch line to the scene. They go
downstairs and look at the ladder and find at the bottom another
round yellow sun sticker. Stine used something like this before:
in *Lights Out,* a red feather was found at the scene of each
crime.

Next, Stine introduces another favorite gimmick: "the new
boy." Lots of Stine's novels concern a new kid at school
(including *The New Girl, The New Boy,* and *The Best Friend*).
The new person brings with them a mix of danger and excitement. Eddy is no exception. This is not a red herring—it is a red
whale. Eddy's introduction to Selena makes him seem like a
stalker poster boy as he rattles off facts about her and Selena
realizes she's seen him before. Yet, he is cute, and that fact
alone seems to block Selena's reservations about him out of her
mind.

THE GROSS OUT

Throughout his books, Stine uses the gross out to great effect.
He always brings in a scene designed to make his readers feel
queasy or embarrassed. Stine is certainly not alone in this pref-
erence according to Dr. Robert J. Thompson, who notes "for
better or worse, there's a growing presence of gross stuff in our
popular culture."[8] Stine gives enough disgusting detail, but not
so much as to be nauseating. This may originate in his comedy

writing and his training in prompting a physical response from his readers, but it is also Stine knowing his audience. When YAs talk about books they've read or movies they've seen, the gross-out image gets remembered and retold. As usual, the gross out ends a chapter:

> Selena breathed in the foul odor. . . .
> And then—when she saw what she held—she dropped it to the kitchen floor. . . . .And went running to the sink, gagging, covering her mouth, unable to hold down her disgust. (*Secret Admirer*, 54)

The next chapter reveals the source of the odor is a dead rat. Small furry animals are always showing up as props in Stine's books, usually in the gross-out scenes. Stine has used snakes, bats, worms, and a variety of other creepy crawlies to get a response. He escalates here. Not only is the rat dead, but it is already half decayed. The "gift" comes accompanied by another note from the Sun, telling her "Don't be a rat."

One reason Stine's characters are easy to scare is something the teen horror moviemakers of the 1980s realized: more teens are spending more time alone. With single-parent families and working parents, teens more and more are coming home to a house without an adult. In *Secret Admirer*, Selena's mom works in the evening, setting up another stock scene: the teen protagonist home alone, in bed, when:

> She heard something over the noise of the storm. The thud of heavy footsteps.
> Footsteps in her house.
> Selena's breath caught in her throat. . . . The footsteps came closer.
> Someone was on the stairway. (*Secret Admirer*, 60)

The someone turns out to be her mother, in an example of the Stine pattern of alternating real scare (the dead rat) with imagined ones, like this scene. In writing it, Stine uses short, punchy, one-sentence paragraphs to build suspense. This not only allows the reader to concentrate on one image at a time but also helps with the pacing. The description is perfunctory so readers can spend time concentrating on the terror of the character rather than the color of the drapes. If the action is gripping enough, they will read on. More than that, Stine uses cliché scenes: anyone who has seen a scary movie *knows* this scene, so Stine taps into that.

AND THE KILLER IS?

The next few scenes of the book, involving Eddy and Danny, seem to implicate both of them. Eddy goes "psycho," forcing Selena to suspect him, then to find that she and Eddy have been followed by Danny. Then Eddy seems to push her in front of a car, but that is another misunderstanding. This flipping back and forth mirrors the reader's confusion over whom Selena can and can't trust. After these scenes, Selena thinks, "I can't trust anyone" (*Secret Admirer*, 85). Trust is a key element on *Fear Street*.

Mainly Selena is trying to figure out who The Sun is. Another tried and true Stine technique is to solve the mystery halfway through—or at least appear to. Selena is convinced it is Danny and she decides to prove it. When Selena gets ready to open Danny's locker, she accidentally opens the one that belongs to Jake. There she finds a sheet of sun stickers. When she goes to confront Jake, she finds that he is dead. He's been pushed off the catwalk. In *Secret Admirer*, not surprisingly, it is decided, after Jake's death, that the show must go on. Selena debates dropping out of the play momentarily but then says, in wonderful Stine-like irony, "It won't kill me to do the play" (*Secret Admirer*, 109).

That decision, of course, leads to more notes, more threats. This Stine plotting demonstrates the debt he owes to his multiple storyline experience. Each chapter requires the protagonist to decide something. Sometimes the decision is to ignore the threats, sometimes it is to take an action. The notes, again used often by Stine, get not only more threatening, but more personal.

The notes, like the phone calls all the way back to *Blind Date*, serve to scare the protagonist, deepen the mystery, drive the plot, and finally create suspense. Who is doing this, and will they carry out their threats? Threats, not violence, are Stine's real stock in trade. In *Secret Admirer*, there's a nice variation. Selena finds another note from The Sun in her backpack. This one says that another friend has been killed; the gimmick is that Selena found the note by accident and too early. So not only have the threats escalated, now it is very specific: someone will die. Who?

Stine also excels in writing stock scary scenes: characters roaming around in the darkness with the threat of danger lurking about them. Selena goes to the school to try to prevent the murder that is yet to happen, but the stage area is dark and empty. Stine conveys the mood in just a few clipped sentences. These scenes are hardly original, but that is why they work so well. Selena walks into a darkened auditorium and hears a sound coming from up high, up on the catwalk. Stine adds to the excitement by reminding us that Selena fears heights, and makes an already scary scene doubly frightening.

Another gimmick Stine uses is the trick ending he loved from *The Twilight Zone*. He employs a variation of that in *Secret Admirer* as Selena's scaling of the catwalk brings her face to face with Danny Morris, who she now is convinced is The Sun. Everything seems tied up, but it turns out the only thing actually tied up (a la *Blind Date*) is Danny, who has been attacked and is bleeding. If The Sun is not Danny, then who is it?

> The footsteps moved closer. Right below them.
> Selena switched off the flashlight. She felt sick with fear.
> The steps continued up the ladder. Steady, confident footsteps.
> Then a long silence.
> The door creaked open.
> In the doorway . . . stood a large figure.
> The stalker. (*Secret Admirer*, 129)

The stalker turns out to be the best friend Katy.

This type of betrayal is used often by Stine and usually with the same motivation—envy. Two teens who are lifelong friends grow apart during high school, which for many teens is a real and emotional experience. Katy explains this as her motive:

> You're so conceited, Selena. It was so easy to convince you that a stalker was following you around . . . . Do you have any idea how I've felt the past two years, Selena? Do you know how it feels to have your best friend treat you like a servant? (*Secret Admirer*, 134)

Stine's villains usually get this chance at truth telling, to explain how they did it, and why. In many cases, as in *Secret Admirer*, they point out a flaw in the major characters. Readers of *Secret Admirer* have witnessed Selena's ego and probably know kids just like that in their schools. While the readers won't agree with Katy's actions, they can understand her motive.

The big final scene is typical. It takes place in an interesting setting (the catwalk), it contains violence (Katy smashes Danny with a flashlight), and then the troops rush in. In this case, as is true with *Blind Date*, the rescuer turns out to be the person readers assumed was the bad guy—Eddy. From his first introduction to Selena, he seemed like a stalker, only to turn out to be the one who makes the save. But, again, Stine lets the hero make her own comeback. Eddy bursts in and saves Selena, but then Katy turns her attention to him, bashing him with the flashlight, causing him to lose his balance high on the catwalk. As he is hanging by his fingertips, Katy smashes his hands, as Selena lies prone on the catwalk:

> She knew he couldn't hold on much longer. . . . She couldn't be careful any more. . . . She forced herself to stand. Without looking down, she dove toward Katy. (*Secret Admirer*, 144).

The book ends with the villain subdued and a romance blooming between Eddy and Selena. Selena has demonstrated to herself that she is strong, brave, and that she can conquer her fears.

PERFECT

The Secret Admirer stands as a perfect example of R.L. Stine's thriller writing. Beginning with a threatening note, all the way to the final scene, Stine delivers thrills repeatedly, chapter after chapter. But more than that—because after all there are other thriller writers out there—Stine is writing about some of the emotional truths in YA lives. By shining a light on the everydayness of YA life, Stine casts the shadows of the darker side of teen feelings. *Fear Street*s work because they are exciting, action-filled, often funny, but mainly because they are scary. Not scary just because of what the reader might think is "behind the door," but because, as King writes, "Horror does not horrify unless the reader or viewer has been personally touched. . . . Horror in real life is an emotion that one grapples with . . . all alone. It is a combat waged in the secret recesses of the heart" (*King*, 25). Stine has pried open those secret recesses and let the blood spill on *Fear Street* every month. Although the blood will now be spilling for a different publisher, as in late 1997 Golden Books secured the rights to publish Stine's teen thrillers. With a contract worth a rumored $13 million, Stine and Parachute Press signed to produce sixty-five more *Fear Street*s.[9] Given his track record, his winning formula, and his endless capacity to entertain, it looks as if *Fear Street* will remain open for business for sometime.

NOTES

1. R.L. Stine. *The New Girl* (New York: Archway Books, 1989): i; hereafter cited in text as *New Girl.*

2. R.L. Stine, *The Surprise Party* (New York: Archway Books, 1989): 54-55.

3. "A Live Chat with R.L. Stine," *America Online* (conducted 10/31/94); hereafter cited in text as *AOL.*

4. R.L. Stine, *The Face* (New York: Archway Books, 1995): 101; hereafter cited in text as *The Face.*

5. "Exclusive TBR Interview with R.L. Stine," *The Book Report* http://steamship.bookwire.com/TBR/transcripts.article$4178 (19 December 1997); hereafter cited in text as *TBR*.

6. R.L. Stine, *Switched* (New York: Archway Books, 1995): 3; hereafter cited in text as *Switched*.

7. R.L. Stine, *Secret Admirer* (New York: Archway Books, 1996): i; hereafter cited in text as *Secret Admirer*.

8. Thomas Haung, "Oh that's Gross! Pop Culture has Developed a Taste for the Tasteless." *Dallas Morning News* (7 January 1998): C1+.

9. Calvin Reid, "Golden to Publish New Series by R.L. Stine," *Publishers Weekly* (18 August 1997): 10-12.

CHAPTER SEVEN

TWICE THE THRILLS
TWICE A YEAR

While in many ways *Fear Street* broke new ground for YA series fiction, it also followed the marketing formulas established by series romances. One example is the super edition—in this case *Super Chillers*. *Sweet Valley High* and a few other romance series have used super or special editions. The idea is simple: a longer book, often released to coincide with a holiday or time of year. Stine's *Super Chillers* fit that category with a summer book as well as one released in the winter; the timing is planned to coincide with school breaks and vacation reading. Archway's motto—"twice a year, twice the terror"—has the ring of truth because several of the chillers are more terrifying in the classic sense of the word. While most *Fear Street*s promise horror but deliver mainly suspense, the *Super Chillers* honor their word. They are longer than Stine's other books—around 220 pages compared to the normal 150 pages, but there are few other departures in writing style, structure, and plot. One difference is that the chapters are named, and there are a lot of them. For example, *Dead Lifeguard* has forty-three chapters, while the normal *Fear Street* weighs in the high twenties. Another change is the division of the books into sections. Most of the *Super Chill-*

ers have four parts, some framed by prologues and epilogues. But perhaps the main difference in the *Super Chillers* is in the content, not the format.

The first two *Super Chillers, Party Summer* and *Broken Hearts,* would stay very close to the format. *Party Summer,* from the summer of 1992, moves from the darkness of *Fear Street* to an exciting summer place, in this case an island hotel where a group of teens has come together because of a common job. *Broken Hearts* was released to coincide with Valentine's Day in 1993. That makes good marketing sense, since Stine's books replaced the series romances as the reading choice of many teenage girls. Almost all of his books involve a romance, or more than one. While all the mayhem is breaking loose, there is usually a boy and girl trying to get together. The villains are motivated by their bitterness that no such relationship exists for them. Stine's books are filled with the revenge fantasies of the rejected, acted out. Sometimes rejection comes from a member of the opposite sex, sometimes from the peer group, or as in *Secret Admirer,* a jilted best friend. In some cases, it is not so much rejection as feelings of inferiority, often within families. Most of Stine's characters have brothers and sisters, and all his families have rivalries where slights are not forgiven or forgotten. When jealousy meets rage, violence ensues, as in *Broken Hearts* when the villain Erica explains her motive for mayhem: "Rachel is the best one. . . . Josie was the popular one. And me. It was poor Erica; so plain, so shy, so ordinary."[1] Perhaps one reason Stine strikes such a chord is that there is rarely a teenager who has not felt ordinary or plain by comparison. Stine's villain characters dramatize the sharp edges of teenage hurt. Rarely are the teens who are being terrorized totally good nor is the villain all evil. Stine is also not afraid to throw in unlikable characters who are even "bitchy."

SILENT NIGHTS

The prime example of this is Reva Dalby of the *Silent Night Super Chillers*. Stine said, "My favorite *Fear Streets* are *Silent Night* and *Silent Night II*. That's because they have my favorite character in them—Reva Dalby. I loved writing Reva because she's so rich and mean and nasty to everyone. She's really fun to write" (*Scholastic*). Stine makes his lead character, his stalkee, almost totally unsympathetic. Reva seems to have earned the bad things happening to her, as payback for all the mean things she's done.   There is a sublime wonderfulness to watching this character—so accustomed to being in control and dishing it out—having to take it. Stine gives us a secondary character—Pam—to care about. Pam has gotten herself involved in a plan to rob Reva's father's store, with the usual unhappy results. The book is a tale of these two teenagers' payment for their sins. When Reva escapes death at the end (she's being hunted by Santa Claus, the villain in disguise), she promises to be "nicer."

Reva breaks that promise and returns to her old ways in *Silent Night II*. Here she is the object of a kidnapping plot. The motives of the kidnappers, Pres and Diane, are simple. Reva's father fired Pres, and Pres wants to get back at the older man by taking his most precious possession. They decide they need a third person and so involve Pres's brother Danny, which turns out to be a mistake. There is no real mystery here—just a series of complications. For example, they accidentally kidnap Pam instead of Reva. The ending sequence allows Pam to save her cousin again, and there is a sudden appearance by FBI agents to wrap up the loose ends.

Silent Night III brings Reva and Pam back again. Stine adds a new character, Grace Morton—Reva's college roommate—to the mix as a new victim. Grace is being stalked by her ex-boyfriend Rory as mystery number one, while Pam has a new boyfriend, Willow, who takes an instant dislike to Reva. There is a subplot which underlines Reva's evilness as she takes credit for some clothing Pam and Willow have designed. Soon Reva starts getting threatening phone calls; acquaintances start dying, and more new characters are introduced. In the end, all is re-solved (the line "the horror is over" is repeated) and Reva seems to have reformed—that is, until *Silent Night IV,* no doubt.

GOODNIGHT KISSES

The limitation of thrillers, even more evident in the first *Super Chillers,* is that they involve people; horror novels, because they involve monsters, offer more variations. In a thriller, if you kill a villain off, they need to stay dead; in a horror movie, the monster can keep returning. We saw this in the slasher films as Jason keeps digging his psycho self out of the grave for another *Friday the 13th* romp. But this series was not the first to do this: the monster dies at the end of *Frankenstein* but producers brought him back (and back and back). While horror used to equate with the Gothic tradition, the breakthrough success of the Universal films of the 1930s brought a new definition of horror: monsters.

Goodnight Kiss was Stine's first monster book: chapter one ends with Gabriel plunging his fangs into Jessica's throat. The gag, however, is that not only is Gabriel a vampire, or an Eternal One, but so is Jessica. It's a goofy scene—two teenage vampires talking about blood being "nectar." Gabriel reacts by challeng-ing Jessica to a contest over which one of them can get a human under his or her power by drinking three sips of the victim's blood on three evenings. This is Stine's twist on the vampire legend and a nice gimmick, the familiar Stine ploy of a bet that establishes the goals of the character. There is no mystery: we know who the monsters are. What we do not know is the identity of their victims. It's a departure from the thriller in premise, even if the execution is similar.

Stine introduces the protagonist (or is it antagonist—are the monsters villains?) immediately. Her name is April and she is happy to be visiting the beach so she can spend time with her boyfriend Matt (which is Stine's son's name). In another inside joke, April complains,   "Why does everything have to be scary?"[2] Stine then goes on to quickly introduce several potential victims, including Matt's pal Todd. Gabriel and Jessica try to line up victims, with mixed success. Stine's having some punny fun here with chapter titles like "A Quick Bite in Town" and "No Time for Reflection." He's also pared down his style drastically. Every neck-biting scene is just a string of sentence-fragment paragraphs:

> Her fangs lowered, and her face pressed against Todd's throat and she bit deeply.
> Deeply,
> And drank.
> The bat fluttered lower. Lower. But he was too late.
> Too late.
> The race was lost.
> Jessica drank. More and more.
> Then, as Todd uttered a loud moan of pain, of helplessness, of ecstasy, Jessica pulled her face back.
> The color faded from Todd's eyes as they rolled up into his head.
> (*Goodnight*, 113-114)

Jessica tries to disguise Todd's death as a drowning, but Matt thinks he knows the truth, and shares it with April. Thus, when the second part begins, the plot shifts slightly—the monsters are now becoming the prey.

In the final chapters, Matt destroys the vampires by burning them and their coffins. The book seems to end with a typical Stine ironical punch line when April tells Matt: "I'll never make fun of your horror movies again!" (*Goodnight*, 211). But the irony is just beginning as the last chapter, "A Happy Ending," has a surprise—April is a vampire.

> "But April—." He [Matt] insisted, panic gripping his throat.
> "It—you—can't be. Back on the island you—you saved my life!"
> "I know," April said softly, smiling at him behind her ivory like fangs.
> "Why should Jessica have all the nectar. I was saving you for me."
> (*Goodnight*, 216)

It's a doubly shocking ending, not just because the villain wins, but because Stine trips up his readers' expectations of a happy ending. Instead Stine surprised his readers and set up a sequel.

Goodnight Kiss II answered their questions, four years later. It is a mirror image of the first book. Stine is reworking the same plot and structure—same use of division into parts, four this time instead of three, same punny chapter headings ("Hammer Time" or "A Pain in the Neck"), and same basic plot set-up: vampires competing against each other: "First one to turn one of those three boys into an immortal wins."[3] This time, however, there are three vampires, one of them April. The main human character is Billy. His girlfriend was killed by vampires and he is out for revenge. Stine grafts a play onto this structure, as the characters take part in a drama called "Night of the Vampire." With Billy pursuing the vampires, and the vampires pursuing his friends, every chapter contains an attack or attempted attack.

The final confrontation, like that in *Goodnight Kiss*, is a long one and takes place on Vampire Island. Again, the female protagonist—Diane—is in danger when Billy comes to the rescue. Stine is using about every vampire movie cliché available, including a sequence where Billy is about to pound a stake through the vampire's heart: "And Kylie opened her eyes. . . .Kylie sat up, instantly alert. Her eyes narrowed on Billy. An angry hiss escaped her throat" (*Goodnight II*, 202). Diana saves Billy, who he thought was April, who he thought was a vampire, as Stine again acts as the Grand Marshal of the mistaken identity parade. Diana saving Billy turns out to be a huge mistake, as this trick ending has Billy (the vampire slayer) as the vampire:

> "If you're a vampire," Diana demanded, "Why did you kill the two others?"
> "To pay back the vampires. To pay them back for turning me into one of them." . . . Billy whispered. "Now I have no secrets. And I'm so hungry. So terribly hungry." (*Goodnight II*, 213)

With that ending, *Goodnight Kiss III* must be a given.

THE DEAD LIFEGUARD

In Stine's first *Super Chiller* he took his teen characters away from *Fear Street*, gave them fun jobs, and then used double identity as the hook. Stine has been using the false identity hook since *Blind Date*. In *The Dead Lifeguard* he goes one better by giving us two characters who are not who they think or say they are. Adding to the confusion are multiple narrators. Point of view has never been Stine's strong point; here he toys with different narrators for various chapters. Each chapter is named for the narrator, although the characters don't have distinctive voices, with one exception—Mouse:

> I know I'm talking to a dial tone here. I can hear the buzzing you know.
> . . . I know you're dead, Terry. And I know why you're dead.
> Because of the lifeguards.
> That's why I'm going to kill them. One by one. [4]

Per usual, Stine has laid out the hook. Lifeguards are going to die, and it is a matter of waiting for the next one to fall and figuring out who Mouse is. Stine quickly adds the mystery of Lindsay, who thinks she is a ghost and sees other ghosts. The book differs from the usual *Fear Street* in the high body count: three die and Terry kills himself, a rarity in Stine. Stine comes close to a supernatural twist, but pulls back with the usual repressed memory/false identity/final fight scene conclusion.

CHEERLEADERS: THE NEW EVIL

Stine shows no such restraint in his *Cheerleaders* trilogy (to be discussed in the next chapter), or in its *Super Chiller* coda. Like the trilogy which precedes it, *Cheerleaders: the New Evil* is not about stalkers, but about an evil spirit. Released in December 1994, the cover features a young woman menaced by someone in a Santa Claus suit. Unlike some *Fear Street* covers, this is an actual scene in the book and one of the many fake scares. But the big scare in this book is that "the evil" returns to Shadyside and starts killing off cheerleaders again. Despite being a retread of the books in the trilogy, *Cheerleaders* is a quick and gory read:

> Blackish brown water poured out of their open mouths and dribbled down their chins. They moved their swollen lips silently, spewing a steady stream of murky water. . . . His dead eyes glowed at her from across the floor. He had a deep purple gash down the side of his face, but no blood spilled from it. . . . One of his eyes had sunken in its socket. The other squinted at Corky. [5]

Stine, here, as is the case with most of the *Super Chillers*, is edging toward the extreme. The violence is often more graphic and there is certainly more of it, with more gross-out scenes. But, again, we are back to the dilemma: should books for teen-agers be gross?   If you accept that that is permissible, then scenes like this one demonstrate Stine's talent; if not, then they demonstrate his "evilness." But there is no dilemma about the fact that Stine's readers like this stuff. A "bad" Stine book to most of his readers would be one without a gross-out scene or two. Other than saying that kids like gross stuff, Stine has never explained his fondness for such scenes. Perhaps it is similar to the reason stated by Stephen King: "I recognize terror as the fin-est emotion. . . .and so I try to terrorize the reader. But if I find I cannot terrify him/her, I will try to horrify; and if I find I cannot horrify, I'll go for the gross-out. I'm not proud" (*King,* 37). Given Stine's creed that "All I really want to do is entertain kids," *(TBR)* no doubt he would agree with King The gross out shows horror authors at their shameless best, or worst, depend-ing upon your point of view.

This scene, like many of the worst ones, turns out to be a dream, even more gruesome than usual. In the regular *Fear Street* titles, the dream sequences provide scares and action that could not possibly happen. If it is possible for evil to overtake people's spirits, then it is just as possible for characters to rise from the dead spewing water out of "open purple maws." Since there are no loose ends to tie up—unnamed evils have no motives—Stine opted for an unbelievable crowd-pleasing finish. The ending of *The New Evil* is particularly confused because of the blurring between dream and reality, although it seems that "The Evil" has been eliminated. And it was, until Stine added another volume with 1998's *Cheerleaders: The Evil Lives!*

BAD MOONLIGHT

Confusion reigns in his next *Super Chiller, Bad Moonlight*. Each time out Stine seems to top himself. If *The New Evil* had a few scenes between dream and reality, this confusion between fantasy and actuality makes up the crux of *Bad Moonlight* as the main character, Danielle, thinks she is a werewolf. Not only does she have vivid fantasies, she occasionally acts them out, including an opening sequence where her brother catches her munching on a pack of raw meat, reminiscent of a scene in Pike's *Monster*. Stine also builds on the fantasy element as he gives his group of teen protagonists "dream" jobs better than cheerleaders or lifeguards. The characters make up a rock band. But like the lifeguards and cheerleaders, this group contains bickering, rivalries, and eventually murder.

When two band members die—both of them ripped to shreds by "wild animals"—it seems obvious that Danielle is to blame. Unlike other *Fear Street*s, in this book there is only one plausible explanation because the two people who were murdered—Dee and Joey—were the only ones with motives. It soon becomes apparent that Danielle is the only character who is *not* a werewolf. If Stine has played around with horror before, he takes a big bite out of it this time in the book's concluding scenes. Almost all the characters turn into wolves and all pretense of reality disappears. A pack of wolves traps Danielle, while her two boyfriends both claim they can save her, and each accuses the other of being a monster. Danielle wonders, "What should I do?. . .Who can I trust? Who?"[6] It's basic and it works because it pulls this plot that was spinning out of control with an overload of horror back into a real life situation: whom to trust.

The final scene covers several chapters and is quite long (almost forty pages) as Stine packs in lots of action, false finishes, and the necessary explanation of why everything occurred.

NEW YEAR'S PARTY

His next *Super Chiller, The New Year's Party,* would also have a lengthy final sequence with several false finishes. The book starts in 1965 with two teenagers attending a party. Stine gets to throw in lots of 1960s images—Beatles, a Ford Mustang. Someone plays a practical joke on Jeremy, and he leaves the party with Beth. Driving home, they hit something—Jeremy thinks it is a person, while Beth insists it was just an animal. As they argue about it, they are involved in a car accident that ends with the usual Stine cliffhanger of a character announcing that he or she has been killed. The next part of the book jerks forward to the present to tell a parallel story about another party, another joke and its consequences. In this one, the shy PJ (who has a bad heart) is tricked into thinking he has killed someone, which leads to his death, much to the horror of his friend Liz.

This might seem like a standard Stine thriller until midway through, when the action flashes back to Jeremy and Beth. They emerge from the wreck and go looking for the thing they hit. Unsuccessful, they return to their mangled car to find two bodies—one boy, one girl.

> "Jeremy," she whispered. "The dead boy and girl in there. I recognize them. . . "
> "Beth, who are they?" Jeremy repeated angrily.
> "They're. . . .us." [7]

With that, Stine pulls the reality rug out, as he did in *Bad Moonlight,* and plunges into a horror story. Having done vampires, werewolves, and unnamed evils, he gets back to basics with a simple ghost story.

The action jumps to the present as PJ's death has had tragic consequences. The character, March, who planned the joke, is killed, quite horribly by Stine standards. When Stine veers off into the supernatural, so does the violence. It becomes more outlandish—for example, March's neck is broken and his head turned around. Sandi, who played the joke on PJ, is killed in the same way. No one knows who the killer could be since the most likely suspect, PJ, is dead, although his body has vanished. All is revealed at the big New Year's Eve party that Liz plans. It's quite a finish. Liz announces she is killing everyone in revenge for PJ's death. Just then, PJ shows up, not to save the day, but to assist. One of the teens, Sean, stabs Liz, but

> Liz laughed. . . ."But you can't kill me. Know why?"
> "Why?" Sean managed to choke out.
> "Because I am already dead." (*New Year's*, 184)

Liz shows them the yearbook from 1965 and the story of how Elizabeth (Liz) and Philip Jeremy (PJ) died in an auto accident. Since the accident was the result of a practical joke at a New Year's Eve party, they have come back to seek revenge for another practical joke. It seems all is lost when Ty jumps in. He is the ghost of the boy that Beth and Jeremy ran over that New Year's Eve back in 1965. When the clock strikes twelve, however, all the ghosts disappear. The cross-cutting between the past and present works well in this story and would be the cornerstone on which Stine's trilogies would be built.

One problem with Stine's books being so plot heavy and full of trick endings is that once the finale happens, the book limps home for the last paragraph or two. There is the normal "the horror is over" line and a dumb joke. The sign on the marquee says "thrills," and once those are over, there really is nothing more to say. The solution to that problem was simple: have the ending of one book lead to the beginning of the next, just as the cliffhanger chapter endings pull readers into the next chapter. Stine's narrator in the *Fear Street Saga* triology announces at the end of the book, more or less, that "if you thought that was scary, you ain't seen nothing yet" and the final words are simply "to be continued." Once Stine doubled the fun and the fright, tripling it would be next on his agenda.

NOTES

1. R.L. Stine, *Broken Hearts* (New York: Archway Books, 1993): 210.

2. R.L. Stine, *Goodnight Kiss* (New York: Archway Books, 1992): 38; hereafter cited in text as *Goodnight*.

3. R.L. Stine, *Goodnight Kiss II* (New York: Archway Books, 1996): 35; hereafter cited in text as *Goodnight II*.

4. R.L. Stine, *The Dead Lifeguard* (New York: Archway Books, 1994): 4.

5. R.L. Stine, *Cheerleaders: The New Evil* (New York: Archway Books, 1994): 186-7.

6. R.L. Stine, *Bad Moonlight* (New York: Archway Books, 1995): 156.

7. R.L. Stine, *The New Year's Party* (New York: Archway Books, 1995): 112; hereafter cited in text as *New Year's*.

CHAPTER EIGHT

THRILLOGIES

Despite the many disparaging comments people have made about R.L. Stine as a writer, the one thing you cannot say about him, his wife, or Parachute Press is that they are not shrewd business people. They must have known that no matter how good the *Fear Street* books or how popular, something more could be added to the product line. After the success of the *Super Chillers* which boasted "twice the terror," Stine decided to triple it. Trilogies would give readers a change from the normal structure, hook them for three books. *Fear Streets* are not a numbered series nor do the plots carry over between books. If readers miss one volume, that is all they have missed; they may choose or not choose to buy another book. The triple book format, as Pike discovered in his *Final Friends* trilogy, locks the reader in for three titles. They can't (well, okay, in Stine's case they probably could) understand the second book if they have not read the first. Bringing back the same character repeatedly probably wouldn't work—that was the original roadblock to YA horror series—yet if there was no unity between books, they wouldn't hold together as a trilogy.

Stine's solution was to use the Gothic tradition of timeless horrors, an interesting mix of the eternal evil supernatural force with historical fiction. Most *Fear Streets* happen in the present. In most of the trilogies he would use events in the past. In *Fear Park, 99 Fear Street,* and the *Cataluna Chronicles*, Stine would set one story in the present, but have it parallel events in the past, while the *Fear Street Saga* would be set entirely in the past. Only the *Cheerleaders* would have each story set in the present, although "The Evil" is from the past. This arrangement gave Stine the flexibility and focus he needed to write three books and preserve an internal unity. We'll look at three of these trilogies—*Cheerleaders* (the first), *Fear Street Saga* (the best), and *Fear Park* (the latest) and skip over *Cataluna Chronicles* and *99 Fear Street*. While these two have their good points, it is in the other three thrillogies that Stine's talents and weaknesses stand out.

One drawback, for example, concerns characters. In books where the characters span more than one title, most don't stretch: they remain more plot props than real people. A horror series or even trilogy with the same reality-based character set also requires a huge suspension of belief. Unlike series like the *Hardy Boys* where the action occurs because the characters are crime fighters, the action in Stine occurs because the characters are victims. A monthly victimization of the exact same character seemed unlikely. The *Cheerleader* tried to get around this roadblock by overloading on the supernatural, focusing on a group situation, and keeping one main character throughout. The *Fear Street Saga* solves it by using the same families and spanning the action over time, while *Fear Park* mixes both of these solutions.

While the plots of each book are not interchangeable, they are very similar in many ways. *Cheerleaders* does at times seem like the same book replayed with new characters cropped in. Stine's a formula writer and his formula usually works. In the trilogies, the flaws in that formula appear. Sylvia Makowski noted these were

Stine . . . at his worst. And it usually happens when he forsakes the single novel, where he can formulate a single plot with black humor and a twist . . . as he did in the truly awful *Cheerleaders* trilogy, or the world of Gothic horror, as he did with the *Fear Street Saga* which was also a trilogy. I am not saying, mind you, that these were not popular with teenagers. I am simply saying that, by Stine standards, they were awful. (*Makowski 1998*, 80-82)

While I don't agree totally with Makowski, because I think some of Stine's "best stuff" is in the trilogies, she is certainly correct about their popularity. The *Cheerleaders* trilogy spawned a *Super Chiller*, and the *Fear Street Saga* spawned a sequel subseries called *Fear Street Sagas*. They also served their purpose: giving readers something new which was really more of the same.

CHEERLEADERS

One key to Stine's success is his ability to tap into the world of teen fear and loathing. In looking for a premise to explore the dark side of the teen psyche, choosing cheerleaders was genius. The cheerleader clique is powerful and intimidating. It is a source for many girls, and boys, of both envy and admiration. The cheerleader's image is perfection: the two main characters, Corky and Bobbi are hated for "your perfect faces. Your perfect bodies. Your perfect lives."[1] This makes cheerleaders not only perfect targets, but great Stine characters: competitive, prone to screaming, and unlikable. Stine seems to be having fun writing these books—they are filled with some great gags. For example, the first book begins: "'You are evil,' Corky said (*First Evil*, 3). Given what is to come (an evil spirit killer), it's a great opening.

In the first book readers met Corky and Bobbi, new girls at Shadyside who just happen to live on Fear Street. Their arrival sets off a chain of events on the cheerleading squad, as these outsiders break up the group. Jennifer, the best cheerleader, feels threatened; Ronnie gets dropped from the squad; while Kimmy and Debra fall in hate with them at first sight. Without anything supernatural, Stine's already put his two main characters in harm's way. They will be threatened because they threaten others, because they are outsiders, and because they are "perfect." Given these natural rivalries and rampant backbiting, Stine seems content with letting it happen. Most of the first book is breathing life into the cheerleaders before the "evil" kills them off.

The first death is truly an accident, as the cheerleaders' bus crashes on Fear Street. Jennifer is thrown from the bus and her body is found in the Fear Cemetery, lying directly over the grave of Sarah Fear (here it says she lived 1875-1899, but her birth date, according to the *Fear Street Saga*, is 1878). It appears that Jennifer is dead, but then, miraculously, she comes back to life. Her body has been possessed by "The Evil" that had possessed Sarah Fear. The graveyard scene is filled with gross outs, mostly involving worms and corpses, as well as this image:

> The girls gaped in silent horror. Jennifer's skin dried and crumpled, flaking off in chunks. Her long hair fell out, strands blowing away in the breeze. Her eyes snaked back into her skull, then rotted to dark pits. Her cheerleader costume appeared to grow larger as her flesh decayed underneath it. (*First Evil*, 164)

Corky manages to shove Jennifer/Sarah/The Evil back into the grave for the fake happy ending, but in the next scene Corky discovers to her horror (and the delight of Stine's fans) that while Jennifer/Sarah might be in the grave, The Evil has escaped.

Which sets up *Cheerleaders: The Second Evil* nicely. As he would do in all the trilogies, Stine adds a new character, Sarah, who is said to be related to her late namesake,and some new variations on old tricks. Corky is obsessed with her sister's death and killing off The Evil. This is another Stine hook: the death of a sibling or best friend driving a main character to find an answer and to seek revenge. But as in the first book, all that Corky finds are more strange accidents and mysterious deaths, including that of her boyfriend. It seems obvious that Sarah is responsible, but that's just a misdirection because the real evil is within

Kimmy. In the final scene, Corky and Kimmy battle in one of Stine's more perverse choices for the final showdown—a bathtub. It appears that The Evil is gone, but again Corky learns at the end of the book that that is not the case.

The Third Evil adds a cheerleader from another school, a person so good she's bad. Stine moves the action from the high school to a cheerleading camp, but there are still the same accidents that pervaded the first book. Stine is writing up a storm here—there is really nothing new to add to the plot line, so he kicks into overdrive with gimmicks. There are plenty of gross outs, like a severed head found in a bed (it's a fake), and a cliffhanger ending in every chapter, a feature which was missing from the first two volumes. The book ends, as did the others, with a confrontation between Corky and The Evil, with Corky winning the battle, but not the war. Those final grudge matches were so big they had to be put into the *Super Chiller* format. *The Cheerleaders* is Stine unleashed. Even more than the regular titles, these books capture some of the downright nastiness and pettiness of teen life. Just as teens say they want to be popular, many would probably confess to resentment toward those who are the most popular: cheerleaders. In this first trilogy, Stine was establishing the model for later three-book efforts in gross outs and terror. Perhaps too much so, because Stine's critics always seem to choose an excerpt from this series to demonstrate his shock fiction techniques. Cutting loose in the world of supernatural phenomena allowed Stine more latitude than the "it was just a dream" wrap-ups. Stine also thought the three-book format would provide latitude, commenting that since the books are about cheerleaders they'll have "a new squad every year, because so few of them survive."[2] Makowski, however, thought the latitude inspired lameness:

> The action becomes simply unbelievable, the characters are too thin and uninteresting to sustain the readers' interest across the span of three books. . . . Had Stine stayed with his familiar and trusted format, one book and a surprise ending with a twist, this saga of a cheerleading

squad gone berserk could have been suspenseful, taut and interesting. By spreading it needlessly over three volumes, he succeeded in thinning down the action and the characters to the point that you just want it to end already. (*Makowski* 1998, 81-82)

I, on the other hand, really liked this trilogy. It is filled with great gross outs and it builds heat through the books: it really cooks."[3]

THE FEAR STREET SAGA

Before R.L. Stine, teenagers wanting scary books had to choose titles written for adults. One of the most popular authors for teens was and is V.C. Andrews. Her novel *Flowers in the Attic* was a sensation, for some of the same reasons that Stine's books would be. The conflicts of the characters are quite real to the readers and each chapter seems to contain a new shock, each more gruesome than the last. When Andrews was looking for a way to expand the *Flowers* franchise, instead of just writing sequels she wrote prequels by going back before the first book to provide a history of the characters and their families. Perhaps it was that, or the growing demand from his readers for more information about *Fear Street*, or his introduction of Sarah Fear in the *Cheerleaders* trilogy, but Stine went retro with the *Fear Street Saga*. These three books—they are also sold as one volume complete with a genealogy chart—lay out the history of the Fear family. They are not historical fiction: there is little attention paid to period details. Instead they are Gothic family horror stories tracing the bloody war between the Fier (a.k.a. Fear) and Goode families.

The first book begins in 1900 with the fire that is destroying the Fear mansion. Since *The New Girl*, the burned-out mansion has been part of the series scenery, so no doubt longtime readers were curious. Stine shows the fire right off the bat, but then spends three novels explaining why it happened. Only Nora Goode has escaped the fire and thus is free to tell the story.

Throughout the first two books, short chapters of Nora's story are interspersed to provide transitions between time periods and between the books. The books cover from 1692 up to the fire of 1900. The trilogy starts during the witch hysteria and it ends with the naming of Fear Street. There is a large cast of characters, Simon Fear being the most interesting and evil. All of the characters are either members of the Fear or the Goode families. The main leitmotif is that a pair of teenagers from the opposing families fall in love and plan to marry, believing this will end the curse on each family and the feud. They are always wrong.

Although Stine had used the supernatural before, that element is more pronounced here, especially in the use of black magic by both the Goodes and the Fears. Throughout the book, an amulet with black magic powers is used—in particular by Simon Fear—as is the phrase "dominatio per malum" (power through evil). What makes this trilogy stand out is the building of suspense toward the fire. The setting of these books is radically different—no malls, no pizza place hangouts. Most of the action takes place on farms, in the woods, or in mansions. Stine's not concerned with the details, lifestyles, or artifacts of his characters' lives in the historical period, nor does he do much to adapt the dialogue. These historical characters sound very contemporary. He's using history as a backdrop to paint a bloody Gothic.

The horror is similar to Stine's other books, yet different in a few important ways. Some of his usual stuff is out—no threatening phone calls in the 1600s. But the cliffhanger endings are in, though fewer. Again, working not with the realistic world of the thriller, but with Gothic horror, Stine can stretch his imagination and credibility, in particular toward tricky demises. The deaths here are grisly: characters buried alive, impaled on a wood stick, stabbed to death with swords and knitting needles, and burned to death. The gruesomeness of the deaths serves to underscore the hatred and violence between the two families. Rather than being about threats to one somewhat likable character, these stories are about two evil and accursed families wreaking havoc on each other through the generations. It is not the same level of suspense: there's no mystery and there is really no character to cheer for. Instead there is only the anticipation of the next discovery that a Goode and a Fear have fallen in love, only to bring on bloody vengeance. Most of Stine's books revolve around someone seeking revenge—here, someone is everyone.

Each book tells the story of one generation. In each generation the story is different, yet very much the same. The first book, *The Betrayal,* covers the years 1692 through 1737. Edward Fier is the son of Benjamin Fier, the village magistrate, who has been instrumental in the witch trials. Susan Goode has fallen in love with Edward Fier and they want to marry. Benjamin Fier is furious. He plans for Edward to marry the daughter of a wealthy businessman and solves the problem by accusing Susan and her mother of being witches. Distraught, Susan's father, William, bribes Benjamin's brother Matthew to allow the women to live. Goode is swindled, as the Fiers take his money but leave Susan and her mother to die at the stake, without protest from Edward (hence the title, *The Betrayal*). It is revealed that although the women were not witches, William Goode does practice the black arts and vows that "my hatred will live for generations. . . . The fire that burned today will not be quenched—until revenge is mine and the Fiers burn forever in the fire of my curse."[4] The rest of *The Betrayal* shows Goode tracking down the Fiers to seek his vengeance, climaxing with the demise of Matthew Fier in a wicked twist by Stine—he laughs himself to death.

The second book (*The Secret*) covers the years 1737-1843. Prominent here are hidden identities, as characters keep their names secret in order to seek vengeance. The book ends with the death of Frank Goode, poisoned by Elizabeth Fier. Simon Fear shows up as a character, and is soon to be family leader. He vows that "goodness is weakness" and the only way to battle evil is with evil. He declares that he is powerful enough to beat the curse and attempts to trick them by changing his name to Fear.

The third book (*The Burning*) suffers from the same problems as the other trilogies when it starts to spin out of control. The supernatural elements are more pronounced, the violence more evident, as in a scene where Simon kills a mugger using the amulet.

Simon stared in helpless horror as the man's face darkened more. Then blistered. The blisters popped open and began to seep.
The man's eyes rolled around. His hands flailed. . . . as the blistered skin burned away.
Chunks of skin melted off, revealing gray bone underneath. Gasping in agony, the man continued to whisper until no skin remained. A gray skull, locked in a hideous grin of horror, stared pitifully at Simon.[5]

The book starts with Simon Fear boldly declaring his love for a woman he meets at a party and continues with the subsequent death of her two other suitors. Simon Fear thinks he killed them. But his love, Angelica, is responsible, as she too has evil magical powers. The book tells the story of Simon Fear's family, their move to the town of Shadyside, and the various accidents which befall them, including one daughter who is buried alive and another who is accidentally killed by Simon.

The Burning is a catalog of horror, ending with the most horrible scene of all. Simon's daughter Nora has married Daniel Goode. When she brings him to the Fear mansion to meet her father, the man screams in horror, then the house starts to burn, making good on William Goode's curse of over 200 years ago. Nora escapes, but looks back inside the house to see images of all the horrible deaths in the books floating by. The book ends with the revelation that Nora has been writing the story from an insane asylum because everyone assumes her story is quite mad. The hospital staff tries to cheer her up by telling her a road near the ruins is being built. It is going to be called Fear Street.

All of the *Fear Street* books refer to the curse on this road and the burnt-out mansion as a constant backdrop. This trilogy answers readers' natural curiosity—how did things get this way? Stine knows his readers are smart, have good imaginations, and

are curious. That's why readers read. Historical fiction this is
not. No teacher will allow *The Betrayal* to take the place of *The
Witch of Blackbird Pond*—but for Stine fans, these books are
required reading.

FEAR PARK

The best elements of *Cheerleaders* and *Fear Street Saga*
would be used to greater effect in *Fear Park*. He provides the
three books with one of his better villains—Robin Fear. The
Fear family feud with the Bradley family spans generations, as
does Robin. Stine's books have been described, often by Stine
himself, as roller coaster rides. An amusement park was the setting for two of his rare non-Goosebumps juvenile titles (*The
Beast* and *The Beast II*), so it is no surprise he's revisited this
setting for a *Fear Street* book. An amusement park or carnival is
a wonderful setting for horror (Diane Hoh's teen thriller *The
Funhouse*) or for the climactic scene of a suspense tale
(Hitchcock's *Strangers on a Train,* for example) because of the
props available, like the Ferris wheel, merry-go-round, or other
rides that suddenly go out of control. There's a wonderful mix of
fun and fright—it is a place where people go to be entertained.
There's lots of screaming, but on purpose. Again, the analogy
with Stine's books is clear—if people didn't want to be scared,
they wouldn't choose his books. One could look at Stine's *Fear
Street* as an amusement park sometimes mixing in a little humor
with horror.

There is also a little history. *Fear Park* is like the other trilogies in that it mixes "historical" incidents (the building of Fear
Park) with the supernatural. Robin Fear, a direct descendent of
the Fear Family, has learned the black arts and manages to stay
seventeen forever for the purpose of destroying Fear Park and
the family (the Bradleys) who constructed it. *The First Scream*
begins in 1935. Robin Fear is a high school student at
Shadyside. He's a shy, awkward, lonely teenager who has devel-

oped a crush on Meghan Fairwood. In a familiar Stine triangle, Meghan is dating Richard Bradley, the local BMOC. When the book opens, Nicholas Fear has been approached by some town leaders from Shadyside about giving up land for the town to build an amusement park. The leader of the delegation is Jack Bradley, Richard's father. With rivalries and conflicts among the Bradleys and the Fears established, Stine is ready to crank up the scare machine.

Most of *The First Scream* is set in 1935 as the Bradleys and the Fears feud. There are the usual false deaths, chapter-ending screamers, and the like. There are some great gross outs that Stine achieves when using this supernatural riff. Nicholas Fear has conjured up the spirit of his dead wife for his son Robin to see:

> Robin saw his mother's face.
> Saw the gray-green bone of her mold-spotted skull.
> Saw the black, gaping pits where the eyes had once been.
> Saw her hollow, gap-toothed grin. Her jawbone hanging slack. Bits of dried black skin clinging to the hole where her lips had at one time smiled. . . . No lips now. No mouth at all. Just rotting chunks of meat and bone. . . . He saw the fat brown worm twist its way out of his mother's gaping left nostril. [6]

Just as Stine knew words that were funny to make readers laugh in his joke books, he repeatedly shows he knows the vocabulary of gross out to make his readers squirm—worms, rats, and snakes are part and parcel of his writing and a key to his success. A similar image is presented later when Richard Bradley finds his father's dead body. Jack Bradley's death would be the first of many gruesome deaths to come. When Stine writes horror of the "no way this could happen" variety, filling it with supernatural elements, the violence is more gruesome, more fantastic. The best example is the "ax" scene in *The First Scream*, the most horrific scene Stine has put on paper in a YA novel. The town has taken a part of the Fears' land to build an amusement park and they have hired teens to clear the tree stumps. But something goes wrong:

> Meghan . . . saw another boy swing his hatchet, a two-handed blow.
> The blade sank into Richard's back. . . . He uttered a hoarse bleat as
> another blade cut into his side.
> She couldn't move. She couldn't take her eyes off the scene of horror
> all around her.
> As hatchets swung. And kids cried out.
> Startled shrieks of pain.
> A blade sliced off a girl's arm at the shoulder. Meghan watched the arm
> slide over the blood-soaked dirt like some kind of snake. (*First Scream*,
> 105-106)

The carnage continues, due to a spell that Robin Fear used on the teenagers to ensure that the amusement park would never be built.

The last two-thirds of the book takes place in the present. The action focuses on a new triangle: Deirdre Bradley, her boyfriend Paul Malone (another BMOC), and a mysterious teenager named Rob. This part of the book concerns the opening of Fear Park sixty years after its planning, and the realization of the dream of the Bradley family. One of the main attractions is a stage presentation called "The Hatchet Show," which re-enacts the tragic events of 1935. Another is the Ferris wheel, which Paul Malone is hired to run. Not surprisingly, Rob's rival ends up dead in yet another accident: "Paul's head had been neatly sliced off. It lay on its side on the pavement, wide-eyed, light brown hair matted down, the open throat emptying." (*First Scream*, 147). Stine cranks up the terror, revealing that the mysterious Rob is really Robin Fear, although he denies that he is anything more than a distant cousin to the evil Fear family.

The Loudest Scream starts with a joke, then quickly recaps the events of the first book. Deirdre suspects that Nicholas Fear has put a curse on the land where the park was built, which would explain all the accidents and deaths. Stine kicks his triangle back into shape by introducing Paul's brother Jared. He also re-introduces Meghan Fairwood, whom Robin Fear has brought with him into immortality. *The Loudest Scream* is a strange book with lots of twists and turns and unappealing characters. Jared runs with a group who wreak havoc, including causing a gruesome death by forcing a teenager literally into a lion's den where his body is ripped to shreds. Jared and his friends meet a grisly end as Robin uses his supernatural powers against them:

> Deirdre . . . stared in horror at the thick purple smoke, snarling around the shed.
> Wrapping itself around Jared. Around his friends.
> All of them grabbed at their faces, moaning and crying.
> Their skin is stretching.
> Tighter and tighter against their skulls! . . .
> With a loud pop, the skin cracked on Jared's forehead, revealing white shiny bone. . .
> Jared's neck stretched high and higher—until his head broke off.[7]

Like the first book, *The Loudest Scream* ends with Robin's evil sarcasm, as he tells Deirdre he will take care of her.

The Final Scream completes the trilogy. In many ways, the book is more of the same, with gruesome deaths and terrible accidents befalling workers and visitors to Fear Park as Robin proceeds with his plan to close it. Stine also throws in a variation on a usual ploy—Deirdre gets phone calls, but they do not threaten her, but warn her away from Robin. There is also ample retelling of incidents from the first books, in particular the disgusting parts. The most gruesome sequence is a mirror of a scene from the first book—during the "The Hatchet Show" Robin again places a curse that causes real carnage. This sequence involves a twist; instead of attacking each other, the ax-wielding teens are zombies of those killed back in 1935, and they attack Robin. Robin's evil is thwarted by the other immortal, Meghan. In *The Loudest Scream*, Meghan has grown jealous of Robin and Deirdre and decides that Robin is evil and must be destroyed. At the end of *The Final Scream*, she saves the park and Deirdre's life by destroying Robin and herself.

Fear Park, like most of these trilogies, represents the best of Stine and also some of the worst, which are often one and the same. The "hatchet frenzy" scene is horrific, but when it appears in the last book, it is the third time he has used it. Many of the deaths are gruesome, but whatever the means, the end result is the same—an image of corpses, the flesh rotting, chewed, or exploding. Stine keeps things fresh by introducing new characters into the mix while keeping the old ones, although some characters, like Jared, don't really fit into the flow of the story. In general, the second volume of all of these trilogies is the weakest. The first provides the rush of the new story while the third gives the payoff. Despite these flaws, the trilogies deliver the goods—lots of chills, great gross outs, memorable evil characters, and more thrills than even the rides at *Fear Park*.

NOTES

    1. R.L. Stine, *Cheerleaders: The First Evil* (New York: Archway Books, 1992): 156; hereafter cited in text as *First Evil*.
    2. R.L. Stine, "Ghost Writer," *Life* (December 1994): 112.
    3. *Kliatt Young Adult Paperback Book Guide* (January 1993): 13.
    4. R.L. Stine, *The Betrayal* (New York: Archway Books, 1993): 74.
    5. R.L. Stine, *The Burning* (New York: Archway Books, 1993): 27.
    6. R.L. Stine, *The First Scream* (New York: Archway Books, 1995): 50-51; hereafter cited in text as *First Scream*.
    7. R.L. Stine, *The Loudest Scream* (New York: Archway Books, 1995): 145-46.

CHAPTER NINE
OFF FEAR STREET

During his *Fear Street* years Stine penned several other books. He continued to write joke books as late as 1990 and even promoted a series of three books called *Space Camp*, published in 1991 and 1992. In 1992, Stine started the megasuccessful *Goosebumps* series (to be discussed in the next chapter). In the years between 1989 and 1998 Stine published several other thrillers, two comic novels, and a horror novel for adults. While none of these except *Goosebumps* achieved the same level of success as his *Fear Street* titles, they are an important part of Stine's writing career. His comic novels show him attempting to use many of his thriller gimmicks in a different vein. The adult book is important mainly because it exposed him to a new audience with different reactions than those of his teenage fans. Finally, the non-*Fear Street* thrillers demonstrate Stine's productivity and serve as an interesting complement to his Shadyside screamers.

Stine followed his first novel, *Blind Date*, in 1987 with *Twisted*—another great title whose plot is indeed quite twisted. It is a story about Abby, who is pledging a college sorority, the Tri Gammas. The initiation ritual is to rob a store. During the robbery, the owner dies of a heart attack. Some of the sorority sisters want to report the incident to the police, while others think it is a hoax. In the end, the explanation emerges: the deaths were hoaxes to test Abby, which leads to her getting taken away by the men in white coats.

In many ways, there is more than a vague resemblance to Christopher Pike's *Slumber Party* here. There is the same deserted setting, a group of girls—some of them with secrets—and strange happenings. It is also very similar to *Blind Date* not only in style but even in the major plot devices. There are "double" characters—just as "Mandy" was really Nancy, in *Twisted* "Abby" is really Gabriella. The reaction in the reviews was also similar to the reception given *Blind Date*. *Publishers Weekly* wrote, "For shock value, this book adds up to a lot of cheap tricks,"[1] while *Voice of Youth Advocates* noted that

> Stine's plot could have made a story that would cause teens to consider the consequences of succumbing to peer pressure. By populating the novel with stereotyped characters and by not taking full advantage of the opportunities presented by the plot, Stine has provided what appears to be a summary of a movie script or an outline of a more detailed novel to come later.[2]

English Journal while noting problems—in particular, shifting points of view—said it was a "well-written . . . thrilling story."[3]

Stine's next scary effort was anything but thrilling. *Broken Date*, written as part of a romance series called *Crosswinds*, was very traditional. The emphasis in the book is on Jamie and Tom, a couple who are very much in love. Complications ensue when Jamie thinks she observes Tom holding up a jewelry store and killing the owner. Soon afterwards, a series of strange incidents occur: Tom cancels a date, refuses to talk to her, gives her a piece of jewelry, and acts strange. In the end, however, we learn that it was not Tom, but a hardened criminal who robbed the store and just happens to look like Tom. Tom and Jamie, in the final scene, are tied up in a cabin in the woods, but manage to escape. This final scene is more than a tip of the hat to *Blind Date*. But it seems that Stine was reined in by doing a book for a romance series. There is no gross out, no stalking, and no real scares. That changed when Stine began clubbing baby sitters.

BABY SITTER CLUBBING

Stine continued to turn out other thrillers for Scholastic. Perhaps the most successful was *The Baby Sitter*, his third scary book. It spawned three sequels (as of this writing). *The Baby Sitter* drew on Stine's teen emotional memories. In his autobiography he tells a story about how he and his brother used to baby-sit for their cousins, and from that experience came his notion that "baby-sitting was a very scary job" (*Ohio*, 131-132). In addition to using his own experience, Stine perhaps knew a little about pop teen culture. Movies like *Halloween*, the film that revitalized the teen horror film in the late 1970s, featured terrorized baby sitters, as do many other films from the same time period. More than that, the story of a baby sitter who gets threatening phone calls is a classic urban legend, a tale so ingrained in the teen culture that adolescents who tell it swear not only that it is true, but that it happened to someone they know. The "baby sitter and the man upstairs" is the most well-known variant:

> Adolescents played up the spookiness of the situation—details that would be familiar to anyone who has ever baby-sat—a strange house, a television, an unexpected phone call, frightening sounds, the abrupt orders from the operator, and finally the shocking realization at the end that the caller has been there in the house. (Brunvand, 55)

When Stine wrote *The Baby Sitter* he took those details and put his spin on them: lots of phone calls, lots of strange occurrences, characters who seem nice enough, but you never can tell. The first book, *The Baby Sitter*, tells the story of Jenny, a prototypical teen baby sitter character. The book is made up of a series of threatening acts designed to terrorize Jenny and the reader. It ends with seemingly little ambiguity. Jenny survives and her tormentor, the father of her charges, Mr. Hagan, dies when he falls—or was he pushed?—to his death.

The sequel came a few years later, and given the ending of the first book, probably hadn't been planned. But the first book was popular not only because it was a good quick scary read, but because baby-sitting is a job many of Stine's readers do. *The Baby Sitter II* is more of the same: Jenny decides to go back to baby-sitting at the suggestion of her psychiatrist, in part to help her deal with her guilt over the death of Mr. Hagan. Any adult figure in a Stine book is suspect, but the guilty party turns out not to be the doctor but the doctor's assistant, who taunts Jenny because "she was jealous."[4] There is an interesting, if sometimes confusing, mix of reality and nightmare in this book. Stine, having subjected Jenny to so much in the first book, escalates the scare as she imagines great horrors. This mix would soon become cast in stone in *Fear Streets*. Stine is also buzz-cutting through his books by this point—short sentences, more sentence fragments, shorter paragraphs, shortest chapters. *Baby Sitter II* is loaded, in particular in the dream sequences, with paragraphs of nothing but one sentence, many of them questions.

What else can Stine do to Jenny in *The Baby Sitter III*? Even within the large suspension of disbelief Stine's readers allow him, no one would buy Jenny ever taking another baby-sitting job. Solution—ship her off to a relative, usually a cousin, so they are the same age, and make the cousin a baby sitter. The cousin, Debra, runs the same horror gauntlet as Jenny did in books one and two. Although Jenny changes scenery, it doesn't change her emotional state, and she is still obsessed, and becoming more so, about Mr. Hagan. Every time she sees someone with a baby she imagines it to be Mr. Hagan.

Soon after Debra takes a baby-sitting job, the calls start. Jenny is convinced it could only be Mr. Hagan rising from the grave to make the phone calls. In addition, there are pranks, in particular a cruel one involving a baby doll. There is also a reference to "the baby sitter and the man upstairs" urban legend:

> The hideous howl rose . . . a terrifying signal, a call from beyond the grave. "It's—it's in the house," Debra said aloud.
> Her heart pounding, the howl piercing through the room.
> It's here. In the house, she realized, gripped with fear.
> It's—it's upstairs.[5]

The hideous howl, of course, turns out only to be the baby crying, but the next shock (one up, one down) is real, if farfetched, as Debra encounters Maggie—"the evil baby sitter." The book's climax comes when both the baby and Jenny are missing and a phone caller taunts Debra, saying, "Now do you believe I'm really back?" (*Baby III*, 169).

The final scene takes place in a riding stable as the police converge, searching for Jenny and the missing baby. Suddenly a figure riding a horse emerges, carrying a baby, screaming "I'm alive! I'm alive!" The rider on the horse is not Mr. Hagan; it is Jenny. It's a nice plot twist, although given no other good suspects or non-supernatural explanations, it was the only possible one. It seems Jenny became so obsessed with Mr. Hagan that she became him. Stine is again using an identity confusion as his no-fail fallback. The book ends with a realization that "this . . . is the end of the nightmare" (*Baby III*, 183).

Well, not exactly. Stine drags poor Jenny out of the psychiatric hospital for another round of terror in *The Baby Sitter IV*. The book kicks off with a prologue in which Jenny is beating Mr. Hagan to death. Actually she is taking a baseball bat to a dummy her psychiatrist, Dr. Morton, created for her to release her anger and fear and to rid herself of Mr. Hagan forever. This is another Stine repeated set piece: a character seemingly doing great bodily harm to another person, only to discover it is not a person, but a doll or some other inanimate object. This type of scare allows Stine to use what seems to be horrible and scary violence, yet have his characters emerge unscathed.

By this time, Stine not only had the story but the storytelling down to an art. Almost every chapter has a cliffhanger. For example: "Jenny saw a dark figure come out from the shadows at the side of the house,"[6] or: "The phone rang again. . . . Jenny reached for the receiver. She hesitated. Should she pick it up?" (*Baby IV*, 18), or: "Jenny shivered. 'What's making that cry?' she wondered out loud. She tiptoed to the window" (*Baby IV*, 21).

In between the scares are scenes of Jenny baby-sitting Mr. Warsaw's twins, Seth and Sean, and his daughter Meredith. Stine throws in a jolt at the end when Jenny learns the Warsaws don't have twins. Instead, the house is haunted by the ghost of the little boy who was killed by a baby sitter years ago. In *The Baby Sitter*, Mr. Hagan wanted revenge because a baby sitter had killed one of his children; here the child wants revenge for being killed. After just hinting at the supernatural for the first three books, Stine goes over the edge in *IV* with two ghosts locked in the attic. In the last scene Jenny must decide which of these ghosts is friendly. Multiple storyline books were loaded with this kind of situation in which the main character has to decide whom to trust and whom to flee. It seems that Stine realized that the only way to continue the series for Scholastic was to bring in the supernatural.

THE OTHER SCHOLASTIC THRILLERS

In his single-title Scholastic thrillers, Stine hints lightly at supernatural elements. The marketing style is also different: rather than an obviously endangered young woman on the cover, most of the Scholastic thrillers feature objects like telephones, jack-o-lanterns, snowmen. The setting isn't *Fear Street*, but it could be. The books themselves are also not as threatening: rarely is there a real death. Even the pranks are few and far between. Both *Halloween Night* and *Call Waiting* feature a younger brother whose sole purpose is to sneak up behind the protagonist and pretend he is dead. Instead of overt violence, the books are heavy with threat. Brenda gets notes with messages like "You're next" in *Halloween Night,* as does Roxie in *I Saw You Last Night*, while Karen in *Call Waiting*, naturally, receives threatening phone calls. Most of the chapters end with another threat rather than a gross out or violent cliffhanger. Most of the cliffhangers are fakes and the books only contain a few gross outs, the best in *Halloween Night* when Brenda finds her bed filled with rotten maggot-covered meat.

The Scholastic thrillers lack an edge. Maybe it is because there's not the *Fear Street* curse to build suspense. Perhaps Scholastic, who use their school book clubs as one of their primary marketing tools, wanted the violence toned down. Many of these books, like *Broken Date*, deal primarily with relationships, with thrills lurking more in the background. *The Boyfriend, The Girlfriend*, and *The Dead Girlfriend* are all similar in that way: the real action centers on the couples and their betrayal of each other. These books do have plenty of unlikable characters— Shannon in *The Girlfriend* and Joanna in *The Boyfriend* are exceptionally cruel and nasty. All the books are full of plot twists and turns but with more bark than bite.

The Hitchhiker shows what happens when teenagers take on adult responsibilities (driving), yet don't heed adults' warnings (about picking up hitchhikers). It has a tightly contained plot, focusing on the question of whether the hitchhiker Christina and Tina have picked up is running from trouble or *is* trouble. Stine counterpoints this by giving Christi and Tina some secrets of their own. The violence here, as in most of the Scholastic thrillers, is more threatened and implied than actual. These titles show, in many ways, Stine's attempt to tone down his act a little, to make his books more accessible. That, of course, is the direction that would take him and Scholastic to the mother lode of writing for children with the *Goosebumps* franchise.

STINE GETS FUNNY AGAIN

One element of Stine's scary books that is often singled out by both his fans and his critics is his sense of humor. *Fear Street*s are loaded with humor, in particular sick black humor and smart-alecky comments from best friends. With *Fear Street's* success Stine returned to comedy with the humorous novels *Phone Calls* and *How I Broke Up With Ernie* (both recently reprinted with new covers). Despite the change of genre, there is little change in technique. Characteristics of Stine's writing such as short sentences, shorter paragraphs, authentic teen dialogue, and complicated teen relationships work for co-medic purposes.

How I Broke Up With Ernie resemble a situation that kicks off many a thriller. The main character, Amy, likes two guys, Colin and Ernie. In a thriller, one would end up dead, while the other (or his cousin who was presumed dead) would be responsible. Rejection plays a huge part in the thriller, as the rejected person stalks the protagonist, but here that situation is played for laughs. Amy breaks up with Ernie to go out with Colin. It is an unexpected decision to everyone around Amy since they all like Ernie; it is especially confusing to the lovable "goof" Ernie who refuses to acknowledge the breakup and go away. Instead, he shows up at her house, tries to go along with her and Colin on a date, and causes other wacky complications. He stalks her like a similar character would in a thriller, but with humorous results. Chapters end with cliffhangers, there are jokes that backfire, and a funny conclusion that seems like a parody of a Stine thriller—Ernie gets a pie in the face rather than a knife in the back. But more than anything else, it is a funny romance written in an easy-to-read, crisp style.

There are several key props from everyday YA life in every Stine book. Telephones are used ad nauseam as characters threaten, react to threats, and talk. That's what teenagers do—talk. *Phone Calls* is almost a thriller: Julie thinks Diane has played a joke on her and seeks revenge by planning her own prank. All of the planning, the gossip, everything in this book occurs in telephone dialogue format. Each chapter begins by announcing who is talking to whom (luckily Stine didn't use conference calls here), and then continues through a few pages of dialogue which advances the plot. The narrative is rapid-fire—forty chapters in under 150 pages, with the longest para-graphs about five sentences long. Like *How I Broke Up With Ernie, Phone Calls* is a comedy of errors in which Stine adapted his successful technique to work in a new, or revisit an old, field. These novels are among the very few Stine books to get positive reviews, reinforcing the idea that a large part of the resistance to Stine is resistance to the horror genre as literature for youth.

SUPERSTITIOUS

It seemed natural that with his success with children and teenagers Stine would soon be asked to recreate the magic for the adult book-buying public. As with most Stine projects, it began with an overture from an outside source. The late Brandon Tartikoff, TV and movie producer and former head honcho at NBC, called Stine and said: "You write an adult horror novel . . . and I'll produce the movie."[7] While the movie has yet to be produced, the book sold well in hardback and gave Stine a chance to do something new while using the same tools. What was new, according to Stine, was that "I could be as scary as I wanted, even brutal. My friends were shocked; my mother was horrified. Also, I didn't have a happy ending. . . . I figured that adults can take it" (*Ermelino*, 32). Many adults, especially those in the book reviewing business, couldn't take it. This is not a syndrome limited to Stine. When YA author Judy Blume attempted to branch out into writing adult fiction, the results were less than successful from both a critical and sales standpoint.

The success of *Superstitious*, published in the fall of 1995, was mixed. Although it sold briskly, Stine commented, "The book is selling pretty well. But I'm very spoiled because I am used to selling over a million books a month. And so when the publisher tells me they're very pleased that *Superstitious* is selling 800 copies a week, it doesn't seem that much to me" (*Webchat*). *People* gave the book a good review, but *USA Today*, who helped make Stine famous, panned it. But Stine must have expected no less. He has read negative reviews of his work since college. He probably realized reviews didn't really matter because he wasn't writing for people who wrote reviews, he was writing for people who wanted entertainment and escape.

Stine's YA readers would recognize a lot of his gimmicks in

Superstitious, like the cliffhanger endings, even a chapter ending in which "the creature attacked" but is revealed to be merely a dog. They would recognize the main character—a young woman involved in a romance who is making poor decisions and getting threatening calls. They would recognize the style— instead of thirty or so chapters packed into 150 pages, this contains 390 pages covering sixty chapters. The sentence structure, the pacing, and other elements of Stine's style are quite recognizable. What is new here is graphic sex and horrific violence.

Stine announces this early: the prologue starts with a man and woman in bed. They are strangers and she can't recall his name. The woman, Charlotte, asks herself: "Why do I hang out in these campus bars after work? Why do I let myself get picked up by these guys?" [8] The book is filled with several sexual encounters, most described in some detail. The sex isn't passionate or erotic: it is filler. But it is certainly further than Stine had gone before: the term "blow job" is mentioned in the first five pages. His characters, in particular the main character Sara, are adults but they still talk and carry on like teenagers. The difference is that now Stine can write about it using graphic language and description.

The violence, as Stine noted, is more brutal. The killer is some sort of beast that cracks the backs of its victims and makes their entrails look like sausage. The violent attacks in *Superstitious,* even more than in his YA supernatural books, are not just gross, they are gory. Deliberately so. Yet the details surrounding the killings are similar to *Fear Street. Superstitious* is loaded with suspects; it is like a gory game of *Clue.* Was it Dean Milton using his knives? Was it the charming Professor O'Connor? Was it the angry ex-boyfriend Chip? The police are ineffectual to the point of providing comic relief.

The other business of the book is a whirlwind romance between Sara and Dr. Liam O'Connor, easily the world's most superstitious man. As the book progresses it becomes increasingly clear that O'Connor, rather than being the dashing hero of the piece, is actually the villain.

> Liam heard the door close behind him.
> Then he opened his mouth wide—as far as it would open—and let out
> a long painful howl. His hands shot up and he tore at his hair, tore
> wildly, frantically, pounding the sides of his head, ripping hair, beat-
> ing himself, slapping himself, his eyes shut. . . .
> The fat purple tongue coiled from his mouth. It made a wet splat as it
> slapped the mirror. (*Superstitious*, 263)

Liam's evil is just warming up. The book climaxes when Sarah
returns home to find her husband Liam in bed with another
woman—his sister Margaret. Then things get really strange and
gruesome. Margaret is quickly killed—impaled on the shower
nozzle—and Dean Milton is torn open, his blood and guts spilling. Sara runs from Liam but he catches her, so "all may be revealed." Liam explains that Margaret was not his sister but his
wife and they were unable to have children. Thus he had to
marry Sarah. The reason to have a child, Liam explains, was to
free himself from the demon living inside him. When Sarah tries
to kill Liam, he turns from his human form into a wild demon
beast. These final scenes are well done—Stine's honed his skills
on writing not just horror, but action sequences. Like the final
scene in the last volume of *The Cataluna Chronicles* (*The
Deadly Fire*, coincidentally published at the same time as *Superstitious*), a swarm of demons kills off another demon. Also like
that book, *Superstitious* ends with the same twist; Sarah discovers she is pregnant, and therefore "the evil" will continue to
live.

Superstitious demonstrates many of Stine's writing talents
and his endless capacity to entertain. *Superstitious* further
shows how difficult it is to take success in one field and apply it
to another. Stine did that once—devising, revising, and honing a
formula to build *Fear Street* after *Fear Street* around his own
hybrid style. If *Superstitious* is a failure, it is not that the formula doesn't work, but that the characters themselves don't
work even as plot carriers. Other problems were that Stine had

not written for adult characters before nor had he attempted anything of this length. Skinny scary books, not adult horror novels, would make Stine a household name.

NOTES

1. *Publishers Weekly* (10 July 1987): 71.
2. *Voice of Youth Advocates* (December 1987): 238.
3. *English Journal* (March 1988): 86.
4. R.L. Stine, *The Baby Sitter II* (New York: Scholastic, 1991): 125.
5. R.L. Stine, *The Baby Sitter III* (New York: Scholastic, 1993): 120-21; hereafter cited in text as *Baby III*.
6. R.L. Stine, *The Baby Sitter IV* (New York: Scholastic, 1995): 13; hereafter cited in text as *Baby IV*.
7. Louis Ermelino, "Talking with . . . R.L. Stine," *People Weekly* (9 October 1995): 32; hereafter cited in text as Ermelino.
8. R.L. Stine, *Superstitious* (New York: Warner Books, 1995): 3; hereafter cited in text as *Superstitious*.

CHAPTER TEN
NUMBER ONE WITHOUT A BULLET

While Stine wasn't such a hit writing for adults—after all, he had no experience in that area—his writing for children has been almost indescribably successful. *Fear Street* made him popular, but *Goosebumps* made him famous. *Goosebumps* doesn't just describe a series of books, but an entertainment juggernaut in publishing, television, videos, multimedia, and especially merchandising. In many ways the stories themselves began to lose importance, as what made kids "cool" was owning the books, being part of the trend, not necessarily reading them. That is the approach here as well—to look more at the phenomenon of *Goosebumps* rather than looking at the books themselves. But what is more important, our concern in this book is not with Stine the children's writer, but with Stine as a writer for teenagers. We'll compare and contrast *Goosebumps* with *Fear Street* rather than focus on the children's series for itself.

JUST THE FACTS

Goosebumps is "the best popular children's book series of all time."[1] In a recent listing of all-time best-selling children's paperbacks, every *Goosebumps* title shows up—almost all of them with sales near one million copies, some as high as 1.2 million.[2] There are 180 *Goosebumps* books in print in over thirty languages. The numbers for the *Goosebumps* by-products are just as impressive. The *Goosebumps* TV show has been a top-rated show since its debut in 1995 and remains a centerpiece in the Saturday morning schedule of the Fox network. *Goosebumps* prime-time and after-school specials are rating winners as well. Videos based on the shows have sold over a million copies, while the first CD-ROM based on the books, *Escape from Horrorland,* was a big seller. The World Wide Web overflows with kids' personal *Goosebumps* pages, not to mention Scholastic's official site. A movie is in the works with Fox Family Films, while Disney has cashed in with a *Goosebumps* Horror Land at its MGM Studios site in Florida. It should be of no surprise that the roller coaster plot twister is tied in with an amusement park with an attraction featuring "a live *Goosebumps* show . . . performed five times a day and a *Goosebumps* Fun House with a scary hall of mirrors and a place to have your photo taken on a *Goosebumps* cover." Disney also sponsored a *Goosebumps* parade and signed Stine for a *Goosebumps* cruise on the Disney Cruise ships (*TBR*).

Before there was *Fear Street,* the most successful YA series was *Sweet Valley High.* It wasn't just a series; it was an institution. It wasn't long before the publishing industry decided to cash in on the "brand name" recognition and expand the market by launching a series aimed at middle school readers, *Sweet Valley Twins,* then at younger children, *Sweet Valley Kids,* then trying to recapture the older teen market with *Sweet Valley University.* Publishers, like movie producers, know the value of "franchise" and the profits to be made by spinning off into new money-making ventures with a different product for each youth marketing segment. Not only do they sell more books, but they also get kids hooked on series—in particular, their series—at an earlier age.   As publishers become part of large entertainment conglomerates, "packages" and "synergy" become the watchwords for expanding a book into other moneymaking avenues. With *Goosebumps,* given Stine's writing style, television was the natural first step, thereby creating a boomerang effect: the books made the TV show popular, which then made the books even more popular.

Parachute Press had watched *Fear Street* become popular among teens, but also among pre-teens. Parachute and Stine developed an idea for another scary series, this one to be aimed at younger kids. There still needed to be scares and dangers, but no blood, no guts, no bullets, no guns. In addition, they could play up the humor—another Stine strength—while playing down the violence. In order for the books to be scary, there would still need to be a threat to the character, but the threats would be different. Most of the *Fear Street*s are not monster stories, and so they have an edge of realism. A new series could be broader— less emphasis on emotional underpinnings, more emphasis on thrills. Also, rather than wallowing in the pit of teen angst, Stine could romp around with the silly pre-teen humor he featured in his own magazine at age nine. Finally, for a younger audience the books could be even simpler in terms of format, style, and vocabulary.

Stine writes in his autobiography that he saw an ad in *TV Guide* to promote horror films which read "It's *GOOSEBUMPS* week" (*Ohio*, 114). With that, he was off and running, turning out the first title, *Welcome to Dead House*, in ten days. Edited by Parachute Press, assisted in the concept development by Jean Feiwel, and published by Scholastic, *Goosebumps* was a go.

It was not an instant success, however. *Welcome to Dead House* sold less than a million copies. Nor did the next book— *Stay Out of the Basement*—set the publishing world afire. Like *Fear Street* before it, *Goosebumps* was a series without a central set of characters, and in this case, not even a central location. *Fear Street* also came out after some seeds had been sown by Stine in books like *Twisted* and by other authors. In contrast, there was nothing even remotely like *Goosebumps* on the market: it was a brand new field. It wasn't until the third book, *Monster Blood*, that the series caught on, mostly due to word of mouth. As kids learned about the books, they told their friends, who told their friends. With the easy availability through Scholastic book clubs, the growing number of megabookstores, and discount stores like Wal-Mart, *Goosebumps* started to climb, then soared. By the sixth title, *Let's Get Invisible, Goosebumps* cracked *Publishers Weekly*'s children's best-seller chart. The books received a boost in visibility when *USA Today* began its own best-seller list in 1994. Unlike other rankings that don't include paperbacks or children's books, or if they do include them, don't compare their sales to adult best-sellers, *USA Today*'s premise was a book is a book is a book. It became obvious that *Goosebumps* was outselling anything else with two covers and pages in between, outselling adult authors like Michael Crichton. While each individual title didn't always rival those by adult authors, the cumulative effect of the series made it clear to all that *Goosebumps* was hot.

In the world of youth marketing (and the best-seller list), the key to having a hot product is to have it perceived as hot. Nothing is so popular among kids as something that is popular. The more popular *Goosebumps* became, the wider the market. The books were originally aimed at eight to twelve-year-olds, but soon children as young as first grade wanted *Goosebumps*. They couldn't read them—but that wasn't the point. Like *Power Rangers* and every other youth fad before it, *Goosebumps* was "it." *Goosebumps* domination took everyone by surprise, including Stine, who said that the success "is thrilling in a way, and totally surprising. . . . Nobody is more amazed than me."[3] Similarly, Joan Waricha of Parachute Press said, "It became much bigger than anyone, myself included, would have predicted."[4]

MAGIC IN HIS NAME

Soon other publishers followed suit, just as they had with the young adult series. They were everywhere—filling the bookstore shelves with titles like *Graveyard School, Doomsday Mall, Bone Chillers*, and the like. All of them were imitators, some more blatant than others. They took the ideas that made *Goosebumps* a success—from cover art to style to promotion tactics—and went into competition. Some attempted to take *Goosebumps* head-on, while others looked for niches and variations. While some series did well, most didn't, and even those that achieved some success didn't come close to *Goosebumps* in sales.

The reason for this had something to do with quality, but also a lot to do with brand loyalty. According to one bookstore manager, "It's the *Goosebumps* name that has hooked them, not the genre. . . . Kids head right for the *Goosebumps* display and don't turn to the right or the left at any other series" (*Lodge*, 26). According to another bookseller, the reason for this was simple: "When you look at the sale of *Goosebumps* and *Fear Street*, you realize that R.L. Stine has magic in his name" (*Lodge*, 26). Some small stores didn't even carry the other series. Although many publishers were getting beaten badly by *Goosebumps*, they realized it was for good reason. An editor for Harper said, "As much as we're competing with *Goosebumps*, we owe its creators special thanks for making the middle grade horror genre easier to classify and to market" (*Lodge*, 24). Nor did the folks at Parachute Press mind the competition. Jane Stine said, "If *Goosebumps* and *Fear Street* have inspired other series this means that kids have even more reason to go into a bookstore and greater incentive to develop the habit of reading" (*Lodge*, 27).

Interestingly, the most popular and successful of all the Goosebumpian titles are *Animorphs*, also published by Scholastic. The basic premise of the series is characters who can transform ("morph") into different animals to fight an evil force. With more emphasis on science fiction, no doubt due to the popularity among kids of *The X-Files* and movies like *Men in Black*, *Animorphs* has over two million copies in print. During the summer of 1997, it took over from *Goosebumps* as the hot series. Like Stine, *Animorphs* author K.A. Applegate found herself listed with John Grisham and Mary Higgins Clark on the *USA Today* best-seller list in June 1997.[5] That success is perhaps due to the fact that Scholastic sought not to imitate *Goosebumps*, instead opting to be inspired more by the look and mood of the series. Although lacking Stine's humor, *Animorphs* made up for it with the clever kid-friendly premise, a mix of horror and science fiction, plenty of twisting plots and the notion, according to Scholastic's Jean Feiwel that "anything can happen—and it does" (*Lodge*, 25).

Other publishers, however, are looking to repeat the rationale behind *Goosebumps*, increasing market share by expanding the age range. Jean Feiwel had known a middle school series would work because of the fan mail Stine was getting for his YA thrillers. She observed, "When the kids who are writing you letters about one series are younger than the target age, you have a pretty good hunch there's a new market out there."[6] Publishers are aiming new horror series not at middle school students, but elementary kids, who became a core of *Goosebumps'* readership. The trick is to make the books more humorous so as not to "send seven year olds screaming into the night" (*Lodge*, 26).

While Stine's competitors, imitators, and undercutters have all developed books attempting to capture Stine's lightning in a bottle, "none is even in the same field as *Goosebumps* in terms of sales" according to an executive at Borders bookstore chain (*Lodge*, 27). Part of the explanation is that Stine got there first, part is brand loyalty, but most of it is simply that the other series are missing the most important ingredient—R.L. Stine. According to Jean Feiwel, "The key thing . . . is to marry it to the right person . . . . Then you have the right package and the right timing . . . . [A single author] means someone behind it who has a vision, a kind of commitment, and creative involvement" (*Dunleavey 1993*, 30-31). Those three descriptors sum up Stine nicely.

Stine's desire to mix humor with horror might be one cause for declining *Goosebumps* sales. This sales drop, coupled with the increased competition, have led Scholastic and Stine to make a drastic change in *Goosebumps*. According to Stine:

> We are changing the name of *Goosebumps* to *Goosebumps 2000*. And we are starting all over again with number one. These books are much scarier. Kids have been writing to me asking me to make the books scarier, and that's what we're going to do with *Goosebumps 2000*. *(TBR)*

This is a very risky move considering the attack *Goosebumps* has been under from parents for being too scary. In fact, *Goosebumps* topped the American Library Association's 1997 Banned Books Week list of most challenged titles. In school libraries across the country, Stine's *Goosebumps* were under fire. Despite their declining sales and popularity, parents ripped into Stine with a vengeance claming, "These books are from the devil."[7] According to one parent, Stine's books "spell out formulas for witchcraft and occultism" (Stepp). It will be interesting to see if this direction results in more sales or more censors, or perhaps both.

WELCOME TO DEAD HOUSE

Stine's particular style shows through from the very first book—*Welcome to Dead House*. As usual, he tells you everything you need to know in the first line: "Josh and I hated our new house."[8] Many of the *Goosebumps* would be written in first person and all would begin with a bang. Stine chooses to write as Amanda, who is twelve. Her brother Josh has just turned eleven. At first it seems Stine is trying to set up another Shadyside with a description of the town of Dead Falls. Much as his adult novel announced its differentness from the beginning, *Welcome to Dead House* just sounds like a children's book:

> Sure, it was big. It looked like a mansion compared to our old house. It was a tall red brick house with a sloping roof and rows of windows framed by black shutters.

It's so dark, I thought, studying it from the street. The whole house was
covered in darkness. . . .
Tall weeds poked up everywhere through the dead leaves. Thick
clumps of weeds had completely overgrown an old flower bed beside
the front porch.
This house is creepy, I thought unhappily.
Josh must have been thinking the same thing. Looking up at the house,
we both groaned loudly. (*Dead*, 1)

Although *Welcome to Dead House* has spooky atmosphere, it is
much more spooky and creepy than it is scary and gory.
Throughout, Stine uses more humor and less horror because, as
he said, "I try to give readers SHIVERS—not NIGHTMARES"
(*AOL*). Although this first book featured death, most of the others would not. Perhaps this is one reason that even though *Welcome to Dead House* wasn't translated to TV until the summer of
1997, it was then shown in prime time rather than on Saturday
morning.

The story follows the scary things that happen to Josh and
Amanda in their new house and town. There is a strange adult
character—Mr. Dawes—who readers should know is trouble
right away because the dog, Petey, barks at him. The first couple
of kids Josh and Amanda meet surprise them by saying they had
also lived in the house. Obviously, something is up. Josh and
Amanda discover the secret when walking in the cemetery,
where they come across the names of all the kids they have met
on gravestones. Soon Josh and Amanda are confronted by one of
the kids, Ray, who tells them he and the others are "the living
dead." They've killed Josh and Amanda's dog because "dogs
always recognize the living dead" (*Dead*, 93). Any child who
has ever watched a horror movie or a show like *The X-Files*
knows that when the dog starts barking at someone, that person
is not of this world. These conventions seem to both increase
the excitement as well as take the edge off it. The readers *know*,
yet they don't.

Josh and Amanda manage to escape from Ray, rushing home
to find their parents, but they have strangely disappeared. Dawes

shows up to help them, but soon Josh and Amanda find his gravestone and realize he is also an undead. They learn, from Dawes, that indeed the population of the whole town consists of the undead. They escape Dawes and manage to rescue their parents. The book ends with Josh, Amanda, and their parents leaving town, only to see a new family moving into the "dead house."

It is interesting that in the first *Goosebumps* Stine chose a female narrator, as one of the greatest successes of *Goosebumps* is its large male readership. Every other middle school success was of the *Baby Sitters Club* variety—stories about girls for girls. The shelves of many bookstores are littered with boys' series that didn't make it. Only the multiple storyline books lasted, but without the impact or sales of the girls' series. *Goosebumps* changed all that. Stine noted this with pride:

> I searched for 25 years for something that boys would read. Everyone in publishing accepted the fact that girls read books and boys do not. And *Goosebumps* is the first series in the history of publishing that has been read equally by boys and girls. And this came as a great shock to me. (*Webchat*)

Not only did boys read them, they bought them. Even more than that, they bragged about reading them, or at least buying them. The books became a status symbol. Teachers report "kids bring these books to school and sort them by subject: mummy, monster blood" (Gellene, A1). Instead of hiding books for fear of teasing, they showed them off at school and traded titles like baseball cards. Books, thanks to R.L. Stine, became "cool" for ten-year-old boys. They were cool for boys because they had weird titles, great covers, and scary stories inside. They were cool because they looked cool, always an important element in youth culture.

THE TOTAL PACKAGE

Goosebumps has a uniform look. Each book has the stylized

logo at the top, an illustration in the middle, and the title at the
bottom. Every book ends with the first chapter of the next book.
Later in the series all sorts of marketing ploys emerged. There
were contests to come up with a title and books shrink-wrapped
with temporary tattoos or packaged with flashlights. There were
sequels (*Night of the Living Dummy, Monster Blood,* and *The
Haunted Mask*) and story collections (*Tales to Give You Goosebumps*). The books were in paperback trade size, although
Stine's autobiography would also be published in hardback. Like
Fear Streets, the copyright of each title was held by Parachute
Press and every book was sure to include a mail order form to
get more titles. Companies like Parachute Press are called book
packagers and it is easy to see why: *Goosebumps* is the "total
package."

Inside, the package was similar to *Fear Street*s in the same
use of cliffhangers, fake-outs, and other Stine tricks. Chapters
were short, usually between five and ten pages, and each book
contained about twenty to twenty-five chapters in its 120-page
format. Stine's ability to write to, rather than at, youth shines
through. The dialogue, including lots and lots of bickering between siblings, is on target. The action sequences move along at
roller coaster ride speed. In *Welcome to Dead House*, the best
and most exciting parts of the book were not the far out stuff,
but action scenes of   Josh and Amanda being chased. Not a
chapter goes by without something happening nor does one end
without a cliffhanger. The plots are simple and unrealistic.
There is no doubt this is make-believe. If the origins of *Fear
Street*s are the slasher movies, then the most obvious source for
Goosebumps were classic monster movies of the 1930s and
1950s, as these books are filled with mummies, werewolves, and
other imaginary beings.

There is humor, tons of chase and action sequences, and lots
of science fiction clichés, including the mad scientist father in
the second book, *Stay Out of the Basement.* But these stories
are still about fright. Stine's formula is simple: put the charac-

ters at risk. Make the characters feel unsafe and afraid. Children's literature expert Dr. Perry Nodelman commented that the books are

> supposed to be terrifying. Adults try to arrange the lives of children so that they will be safe from fear, but in the culture of the school yard, to acknowledge fear is be defined as a weakling, to test one's fearlessness an ongoing activity. Not surprisingly, then, the marketing of *Goosebumps* often implies that books offer such a test. The teaser on the cover of *One Day in Horrorland* does so explicitly; it says, "Enter if you dare."[9]

There is an element of pride in the *Goosebumps* phenomenon— children are able to say they read the books and weren't scared by them. They see themselves as characters in the book; they become involved and feel better when those characters win or survive. They are convinced that the fact that they were able to read a scary book shows that they are strong, able, and smart. The mass consumption of *Goosebumps* allowed kids also to take pride in having read every book as a sign of status and achievement.

Characters in *Goosebumps* are forever saying that they are not afraid of something, or challenging other kids, as in *You Can't Scare Me!* They play jokes on each other, sneak up behind each other. Stine uses monsters for the big scares, but the little and fake scares are kids trying to terrify each other. The fright could come at any moment, but always at the end of a chapter. What the reader doesn't know is whether it is a real scare or a fake. In the *Fear Street* books, characters are afraid because they are stalked, but in *Goosebumps,* the character's fear is of monsters—or even fear that he/she will turn into a monster. That shows up in *Welcome to Dead House* and in later titles like *The Werewolf of Fever Swamp, Let's Get Invisible,* and *My Hairiest Adventure.* The lack of plausible explanation is similar. Just as every *Fear Street* ends with a "why I did it" speech, *Goosebumps* have similar resolutions. The difference is that in the *Fear Street* endings, reality is often stretched but it doesn't break, while in *Goosebumps* the conclusions are as fantastic as the book itself. For example, everyone is dead in *Welcome to Dead House* because of a chemical explosion. Yet somehow there is a school and someone buried all these children and . . . . In *Goosebumps*, Stine isn't interested in logical explanations—he just wants to entertain, and *Welcome to Dead House* with its ghosts, cemetery scenes, missing parents, and spooky house is certainly entertaining.

What is striking here is the tone of these books, which is part of the entertainment. The narrators really do sound like children, just as the teens in *Fear Street* sound like teens. Like *Fear Street*, some (*The Haunted Mask*) are better than others, mainly because the premise is clever and well-executed. Like *Fear Street*, *Goosebumps* works because Stine is a great entertainer who knows the right mix of horror and humor to please his audience. The books are filled with snappy answers and practical jokes, but also slime, worms, and other creepy crawlers that kids love and fear. These books would not work if they didn't elicit fear by putting characters in danger. There is danger and a pervasive sense of threat to create the suspense that generates the thrills that turns the pages.

WHAT IF THIS HAPPENED TO YOU?

When writing for this younger audience, Stine knew he had to tone it down. In part, he did this by changing the question the book poses. The *Fear Street* books ask the teen reader, "What if this happened to you?" The question seems real because all the trappings of the readers' lives—the settings, the relationships, the dialogue, and the characters—are mirrored in these books. The events in most *Fear Street*s are unlikely, but they could happen. There is much less emphasis placed on motivation, and much more on monsters. Thus, in *Goosebumps*, the question becomes: "What if this could happen?" Then, if it could happen, "What if it happened to you?"   In many ways though, Stine is writing juvenile speculative fiction. Because the horror is more imaginative and outrageous, more speculative, less possible, the books are less scary. They hang on the balance between what kids know and what they feel. Fifth graders know there are no such things as monsters, but it doesn't mean they *know* it when confronted with it in a book. That element of doubt coupled with disbelief stirs the *Goosebumps* soup.

As in *Fear Street*, Stine made the outward trappings of the characters very recognizable. They live in the suburbs, usually with Mom and Dad and a brother or sister; they wear all the right things, have kid hobbies and concerns, and are in every way "normal." Part of the normalcy of children is childishness. These kids are not cute or precocious, in fact they are insufferable in their selfishness. These kids are

> decidedly egocentric. They rarely report any feelings about others except in so far as those others' actions affect themselves. They are very conscious of the power of property ownership. They often express envy over someone else's possessions, or enjoy the envy created in others by their own possessions. They are also, and most notably, incredibly competitive. They compete for parental attention and about who will have the best science fair displays. . . . They are less interested in what they might win than in that they have won. . . . All of this is presented without question or comment, as merely being normal—as what children mostly are, and as what readers are invited to identify themselves to be. (*Nodelman,* 8)

For many adults, that might be what is most disturbing in *Goosebumps*. Rather than presenting children in fiction as parents and teachers would like them to be, Stine presents kids as they sometimes can be. Kids may say the funniest things, but they can also say some of the nastiest. And unlike classic characters in children's literature, these little "imps" don't become lovable by the end of the book. As Stine said, "I have no crying, no hugging, and the kids never learn anything" (*People,* 103). To his credit, these negatives are balanced with plenty of positive attributes, mainly the child's intelligence, imagination, ingenuity, and independence. These traits, however, seem overlooked by Stine's critics. Stine's children, flawed as they are, always make it through the book, like characters in fairy tales, by outwitting the villain.

Some have compared *Goosebumps* to fairy tales, folk tales and campfire stories, not only in similar themes, but in the telling of the stories. Folk and fairy tales, as well as urban legends, are primarily oral arts. They are handed down from generation to generation not just through publication, but through the oral tradition. Part of the appeal of Stine's books is that they read like stories that are told rather than written. The easy vocabulary, short sentences, and conversational style give *Goosebumps* a campfire scary story feel. In this way, *Goosebumps* serves an important function by acting as a conduit for children to move from being read to, to independent reading

Another connection is the element of violence. Children's fairy and folk tales are often laden with violent acts, gross-out scenes (Greek myths are big on gross outs), and content similar to that which is objected to in Stine. Yet, few schools are asked by parents to remove folk tales from the shelves. This connection between Stine and fairy tales, coupled with the contradictions of the would-be censors, led one pro-*Goosebumps* parent to comment that "if conservatives want to get really upset about violence in children's books, they should read the Grimm Brothers' fairy tales. There, birds peck young children's eyes out and limbs, toes, fingers and body parts are lopped off with regularity and abandon."[10]

In his thesis *Fright Light: A Content Analysis of R.L. Stine's Goosebumps, and Selected Other Juvenile Horror Fiction Series*, Stephen Powell looks at *Goosebumps* and other middle grade horror fiction in that context. Many of those seeking to explain *Goosebumps* as fairy tales quote from Bruno Bettelheim's *The Uses of Enchantment* to show the connection between the two. Many fairy tales are stories of courage; Stine's

writings are as well. Throughout *Goosebumps*, the main characters are in danger and the stories are about surviving that danger.
Powell argues that

> the characters in these stories are not unlike the heroes and heroines of
> fairy tales. They are brave, curious adventurers who breathe heavily as
> they open one creaky door, but who do not hesitate to go on to the next
> door. . . . These characters also represent a type of brave, heroic per-
> son that the readers of these stories want and imagine themselves to be.
> (Powell)

Like most successful works of entertainment, *Goosebumps*
achieves its greatness from providing readers with an escape to a
different reality. But at the same time, the characters are real
enough to the readers: the books are both smoke and mirrors.

GOOSEBUMPS INC.

Whatever *Goosebumps* is—horror, adventure, fairy tale, or
wish fulfillment—mainly *Goosebumps* is successful. Not just the
book, but a whole cottage industry sprang up around the series.
This was nothing new—the idea of licensing popular names as
brand names had been around the entertainment industry a long
time, but by the 1990s it had become a well-oiled machine. Soon
Goosebumps was everywhere, in exactly the same places as the
earlier megasuccess, *Mighty Morphin Power Rangers*. Interestingly, one of the reasons *Goosebumps* was, for many, a welcome
relief from the senseless kicking and fighting of *Power Rangers*
was because it was less violent—scary, but not violent.   That's
a point that those writing critically about the violence in *Goosebumps* often forget to mention. Although the age range of the
books is middle school, it was obvious from the products and the
real audience of the books that *Goosebumps* mania was highest
among six to ten-year-olds. The great advantage that *Goosebumps* held over every previous juvenile brand name was its
appeal to both boys and girls, a rare phenomenon in kiddyland.
By 1996, Scholastic/Parachute Press had granted more than

forty licensees to use the *Goosebumps* name on products ranging from clothing to stationery to board games. All the products bear the *Goosebumps* logo, colors, and "feel." Scholastic graphic designer Sharon Lisman developed the blood-splattered typeface and the stylized "G." She "keeps a bible of designs to keep the look consistent—and to make the brand instantly recogniz-able."[11] Every product featured that look and the *Goosebumps* colors of bright day-glow green and purple—green being the hue of monster blood. By contrast, the colors most used in the *Fear Street* product line are darker reds and blues. The *Goosebumps* look had to be scary, yet not seem too edgy or violent.

One drawback in marketing *Goosebumps* merchandise was that while the books were hot, there were no marketable charac-ters. This made the folks on Madison Avenue think very crea-tively about pushing *Goosebumps* products. Eventually, they had to invent a feature character, Curly, to be the product mas-cot, even though he doesn't appear in any of the books. Unlike product tie-ins associated with movies that stay hot for a season, the products associated with an ongoing series could stay hot for a longer period of time. With Scholastic's official fan club and newsletter, *The Scream*, with store shelves decorated with *Goosebumps* logos and colors, with bookstores sponsoring *Goosebumps* clubs, everyone was cashing in by getting into the act.

Business Week dubbed *Goosebumps* the "Thing that Ate the Kids' Market," noting it was "a wake-up call for the children's book industry who saw, for the first time, how to expand a brand. While books were often involved with entertainment packages, the required novelization of almost every film, books—until *Goosebumps*—never had been leading the way" (*Dugan*, 195). *Goosebumps* was the focus of another business article about "a billion dollar bonanza."[12] When it reaches that level, it would be up there with brands like the *Teenage Mutant Ninja Turtles* or *Mighty Morphin Power Rangers*. What is amazing is that *Goosebumps* would be the only brand on the list

of megasuccessful franchises that began as a book; the rest grew
out of nonprint media. But like those other brands, *Goosebumps*
laid its mark everywhere with the *Goosebumps* logo found on:

- party goods
- school supplies
- walkie-talkies
- stick-on fingernails
- T-shirts and sweat shirts
- hats
- board games
- various Halloween paraphernalia
- fake skulls, dolls, and other toys

During the big push of 1995-1996, it was hard *not* to see children decked out with at least one *Goosebumps* accessory. Although the books were popular, it was the success of the TV
show that put *Goosebumps* on the merchandising map. With the
exception of a few *Sweet Valley High* and *Baby Sitter's Club*
products, mostly standards like board games and calendars, there
was no precedent and therefore a cool reception to merchandising a book. But when it became a TV show and hit big, these
same retailers became not just receptive, but enthusiastic.

In the spring of 1997, a series of "lifestyle products" bearing
the *Goosebumps* logo hit the market. Products included bike ac-
cessories, in-line skating gear, and other sports equipment. It's
an interesting tie-in, choosing sports that are both normal kids'
activities, yet also featured on television as extreme sports. That
mix of safe and scary is familiar to *Goosebumps* readers. The
biggest push for *Goosebumps* products came in the fall of 1996
with a massive tie-in involving Pepsi, Frito-Lay, Hershey, and
Fox TV. This campaign featured TV ads, newspaper inserts,
coupons, contests, ads in kids' magazines, and point-of-purchase
displays. Minibooks were created and stuffed into bags of snack
chips while Hershey featured *Goosebumps* graphics on its prod-

ucts. Taco Bell used *Goosebumps* as giveaways in its kids' meals, putting the series on a par with Hollywood's biggest blockbuster films. While these made lots of money for everyone involved, it was, as noted in chapter five, perhaps the beginning of the end of Stine's decade of dominance, as now his scary books were not just products, they were toys for young children.

Despite the fact that all of these products were based on books, they were met with some resistance. One educator called the merger of books and commercial products "troubling," asking, "Will advertising and literature begin to look the same to kids?"[13] Scholastic countered by using the line "reading is a scream" in its promotional tie-ins and displays. That is another troubling aspect of the *Goosebumps* mania, to educators in particular. Unfamiliar with the books themselves, many adults saw *Goosebumps* everywhere, glanced at the catchy covers and assumed something of such great commercial eminence could have no other value.

Goosebumps wasn't everywhere, although it seemed like it at times. Many pitches for product tie-ins were not approved, including a toothpaste called Tombpaste. Scholastic's director of marketing, Mary Sadeghy, said: "Our strategy from the outset was not to overpromote it or overwhelm it with products."[14] Knowing some of the opposition to the books already out there, Scholastic wanted products that kept within the spirit of *Goosebumps*, knowing they must "walk a fine line with being edgy and cool, but want to make sure that everything is safe, clean fun" (Benezra, 48). In addition, Sadeghy commented, "We've been very careful that our partners share our views and values about the property. We have a very strict approval process and a style guide that our licensing and promotional partners are required to use."[15] In addition to avoiding overexposure and complaints, keeping the brand somewhat restrictive was seen as keeping it still cool for middle school kids. The tie-in with Taco Bell, however, seems to negate that in its appeal to kids much younger than the audience for which the books are written and marketed. Also the flood of *Goosebumps* merchandise in product remainder stores like Big Lots demonstrates that Scholastic either overexposed the brand or vastly overestimated the market. Once *Goosebumps* was through being the "thing that ate the kids' market," it began to cannibalize itself. The products began competing with the books for dollars, and both ended up suffering. Finally, once *Goosebumps* shot into the realm of "fad," its fate was sealed because of ever changing youth tastes. What will be interesting is seeing, now that the bubble has burst, if *Goosebumps*, with the *Goosebumps 2000* makeover, can survive like the *Sweet Valley* franchise.

LITTLE SCREEN AND MORE SCREAMS

When Stine appeared at the top of the *USA Today* bestsellers list, a lot of people took notice, including a television executive at the Fox Network. After reading about Stine, Margaret Loesch, chief executive of the Fox Kids Network, did some research on her own with her six-year-old son. After getting his opinion on *Say Cheese and Die!* (he loved it), Loesch set up a TV deal. The first show (*The Haunted Mask*) debuted in prime time as a special, then moved to a regular time slot on Fridays. The move to Friday was temporary for a good reason. Loesch explained, "I was concerned about the public perception, so we wanted to air it in an appropriate time period where parents were more available."[16]   After the test period, *Goosebumps* moved to a regular kid slot—Saturday mornings—where it has been the ratings champ ever since. A few of the stories that are a little scarier, like *Welcome to Dead House* or *Night of the Living Dummy*, are shown as prime-time specials, again with great success.

To no one's surprise, other scary kids' shows soon followed. There was, however, a precursor. Nickelodeon's *Are You Afraid of the Dark?* ran between 1992 and 1995, although it was much more in the darker *Fear Street* mode than the lighter *Goose-*

bumps style. Other scary book series, like *Bone Chillers*, have also morphed into television shows. The HBO and syndication fright feast—*Tales from the Crypt*—spun-off to a kiddy version called *Secrets of the Crypt Keeper's Haunted House*.   Fox, however, beat the others to the punch by marketing the TV shows as videos, where of course they became best-sellers. The translation to film is due from Fox's Family Film Unit. To be produced by Tim Burton, director of dark, quirky films like *Ed Wood*, it will be interesting to see how Stine's commercial sheen meshes with Burton's artistic intentions.

If the success of *Goosebumps* books increased R.L. Stine's exposure, then the TV show put him into the limelight, not only because it attracted the attention of nonreaders, but because Stine himself appeared on the shows. In what must have been another dream come true, Stine took on the role of the host, much as his idol Rod Serling did with *The Twilight Zone*. Stine didn't write the scripts, but seems to be fairly involved in the productions and admits that he is "happy with the show. I think some of the shows are scarier than the books" (*TBR*).

With the demand high, Parachute Press decided to increase the supply. While Stine continued to crank out one *Goosebumps* and one *Fear Street* a month, new series were launched with the familiar name and title on the cover (to be discussed in the next chapter). *Ghosts of Fear Street* was Pocket Books entry into the fray—an attempt to hook younger readers on the *Fear Street* name. Scholastic added two spin-off series, *Give Yourself Goosebumps* and *Goosebumps Presents*. The first are multiple storyline books bearing the *Goosebumps* name and similar plotting. *Goosebumps Presents* are bizarre creatures—novelizations of television shows based on books, although as Stine noted, sometimes the "TV shows don't follow the books. But I think it's fun to see what other writers do with the stories" (*TBR*). Loaded with pictures from the TV show, they contain fewer pages and are even easier to read. All of these books come through Parachute Press, which retains editorial control.

For those looking for the *Goosebumps* experience without reading, Scholastic licensed the multimedia rights to Dreamworks. Predictably, the first *Goosebumps* CD-ROM, *Escape from Horrorland,* became a best-seller during the 1996 holiday season. Based on the *Goosebumps* title *One Day in Horrorland,* with its amusement park setting, the CD-ROM has levels where users try to outrun monsters, as well as gather clues and solve puzzles. Trying to capture both the spirit and the style of Stine, the CD-ROM mixes humor and horror as users go through a blend of live-action video and computer graphics attempting to help the characters escape from Horrorland. A second CD-ROM, *Attack of the Mutant,* was released in the fall of 1997. One review noted "the beauty of Stine's bad guys. They're disgusting and diabolical, yet ultimately dispatchable. Life should be this much fun."[17]

Goosebumps came along just as the Internet was opening up to everyone, with more and more kids getting on-line. Scholastic maintains the official *Goosebumps* site and keeps it filled with information on new releases in all formats, photos, information on the fan club and its newsletter, information on Stine, plus photos. There are also hundreds of kid-produced sites, ranging from a page where a youngster writes how much he or she likes *Goosebumps,* to very sophisticated sites like *The Bumps.*

Goosebumps are more than books; they are popular culture products. From the movie tie-ins to the Cheetos bags, *Goosebumps* stopped being just books very soon into the series. They also made Stine famous. Almost every major newspaper did a *Goosebumps* article, usually based on an interview with Stine. There was great curiosity. Here was this amazing phenomenon occurring among kids and most adults were clueless. Stine noted, "No one over 14 has ever heard of me" (*Santow,* 116). By 1998, few people with kids or who worked with them in libraries, toy stores, or any retail shop had not heard of R.L. Stine. He was more than a person, more than an author. He is the engine of a merchandising, marketing, and entertainment machine.

NOTES

1. Matthew Flamm, "Between the Lines," *Entertainment Weekly* (9 January 1998): 63.

2. "All-Time Best-Selling Paperback Children's Books," *Publishers Weekly Online Edition,* http://www.bookwire.com/pw/articles/childrens/all-time-paperbacks.html (7 May 1997).

3. "R. L. Stine," *People Weekly* (25 December 1995-1 January 1996): 102-3; hereafter cited in text as *People*.

4. Joyce M. Rosenberg, "Goosebumps Books Take Over the Kids' Section," *Houston Chronicle* (25 October 1996). http://www.chron.com/content/chroncile/business/96/10/27/goosebumps.html (14 February 1996).

5. Cathy Hainer, "Animorphs Evolve into a Kid's Hit," *USA Today* (25 September 1997): 8D.

6. M.P. Dunleavey, "Books That Go Bump in the Night," *Publishers Weekly* (5 July 1993): 30; hereafter cited in text as Dunleavey 1993.

7. Diane R. Stepp, "Panel to Decide Book Ban," *Atlanta Constitution* (14 May 1997); hereafter cited in text as Stepp.

8. R.L. Stine, *Welcome to Dead House* (New York: Scholastic, 1992): 1; hereafter cited in text as *Dead*.

9. Perry Nodelman, "The Ordinary Monstrosity: The World of *Goosebumps*," (unpublished paper, 1997): 4; hereafter cited in text as Nodelman.

10. Bonnie Erbe and Josette Shiner, "Should Schools Ban *Goosebumps*? Pro/Con," *The Journal* http://www.jrnl.com/news/97/February/jrn81130297.html (7 March 1997).

11. Jeanne Dugan, "The Thing That Ate the Kids' Market," *Business Week* (4 November 1996): 175; hereafter cited in text as Dugan.

12. Laurie Freeman, "Searching for the Next Billion Dollar Bonanza," *Advertising Age* (12 February 1996): S4.

13. Bernice Kanner, "Too Much Ado about *Goosebumps*," *Journal of Commerce and Commercial* (31 July 1996): 7A.

14. Karen Benezra, "Scholastic's Cool Ghouls," *Brandweek* (3 June 1996): 47; hereafter cited in text as Benezra.

15. Cyndee Miller, "Scary, but Nice," *Marketing News* (7 October 1996): 2.

16. Michael Mallory, "Scare Fare: Lite Horror Staple of Young Audience," *Variety* (9 December 1996): 47.

17. Nancy Malitz, "CD Romp: *Goosebumps* Scares Up Fun in a New Game," *Detroit News* (2 October 1997): E6.

CHAPTER ELEVEN

THE STINE MACHINE

Perhaps the question R.L. Stine is most asked after "What does R.L. stand for?" is "Do you really write all those books?" It seems a logical query because it is hard to believe that one person has written over 300 books, most of them in a ten-year time span. More impressive is that he writes two titles a month. Each book is a best-seller; every *Goosebumps* title normally sells over a million copies. Some people strive their whole life to write one best seller and Stine does it monthly. Some joke that there is no R.L. Stine, that it is a corporate name or a group of uncredited writers churning out all these titles. There are precedents: *Sweet Valley High*, the various Stratemeyer offerings, and other series in which the "author's" name that appears on the cover is not the actual writer of the books. Until *Goosebumps* took off in 1995, Stine could still say that he wouldn't hire out the writing, joking, "I'm too vain and too greedy for that" (*Authors*, 217). But once the mania hit and the demand called for supplying more books, it was admitted that for the new spin-off series like *Ghosts of Fear Street* that "Stine himself will not actually be writing the books." (*Alderdice*, 209).

Goosebumps Presents, *Ghosts of Fear Street*, and the *Fear Street Sagas* series are credited to someone else either on the title or copyright page. The multiple storyline books, *Give Yourself Goosebumps*, are penned by his sister-in-law Megan.[1] The first two *Fear Street Sagas* (the spin-off series which began in

169

1996, not the trilogy) had Stine's name as the writer, but noted the "editorial assistance" of another writer. Since number three of that series, however, the books are identified on the copyright page as being someone else's work. Still, Stine does turn out, with the help of his editors, one *Fear Street* and one *Goosebumps* each month. How does he do it? According to his son Matt, in a rare interview, the answer is simple. "I would describe my Dad in this one word . . . machine."[2] Is Stine angry at this remark? Well, he really couldn't or shouldn't be because he used that descriptor himself, telling *USA Today*, "I am a machine."[3] Indeed, a highly efficient and productive best-seller machine.

INSIDE THE MACHINE

Stine's creative process starts, as it does with most writers, with a singular idea. He has said that he worries "that one day I'll sit down and I'll have idea block. But so far, I've been lucky. . . . Every time I need a new idea for a book, I get one" (*Webchat*). Stine's success is, however, due perhaps more to perspiration than inspiration. He doesn't wait to write novels when the mood strikes, but churns out two a month because he has to (and he wants to). Stine has said, " I really have no choice—I have to have ideas. I usually just sit down at my desk and don't get up until I have one" (*Speaking*, 204).

Stine got the title for *Goosebumps* from a *TV Guide* ad and now seeks ideas everywhere:

> I was on vacation, lying on the beach, talking to a guy . . . I told him I wrote horror books, and he said, "You should do one on earwigs. Earwigs are scary." . . . Some people send me things like newspaper clippings of stories they found. I actually did a *Fear Street* based on a true story about a girl who planned to murder her teacher. (*Authors*, 213)

Many of his stories, as noted, might trace their origins back to urban legends, such as "The Death Car" legend used as the basis for the three *Cataluna Chronicles* titles.

An "idea" means many things to Stine; sometimes it is an image, but often it is a title. For his first YA novel the title was handed to him, but others he has developed himself and with Parachute Press. The title is more than a starting point; it is a breaking point: no title, no book. According to Stine, "If I have a story idea but I can't think of a good title for it, I don't do the book. Because I know I'll never think of a good title" (*Alderdice*, 209). Obviously that's an exaggeration; coming up with *Wrong Number II* didn't take much, but Stine is thinking in marketing terms. What's the title? What's the hook? The opposite has also happened. Stine said, "I had a *Goosebumps* title—*Legend of the Lost Legend*. But it took me weeks to think of a story to go with it!" (*Scholastic*).

The idea can take the form of an image:

> Sometimes a picture pops in my head and I start to build a book around it. One day, I pictured a boy in a bathtub filled with worms; worms pouring from the faucets and slithering down the walls. I don't know where that picture came from. But it was the start of a *Goosebumps* book called *Go Eat Worms*. Sometimes something in real life gives me an idea. I was walking down the street one day and suddenly smelled a horrible odor. I don't know what it was, but it was pretty bad. It made me think: I haven't written a really smelly book yet. And it started me thinking about smelly ideas—which led to *The Horror of Camp Jelly Jam*. (*Scholastic*)

Normally, Stine does not rely on personal experience for his books, as he has explained frequently:

> One of the questions I am asked most often is: "'Did any of the things in your scary novels ever happen to you in real life?" Kids are always disappointed but I have to tell them no. I've never been . . . haunted by a ghost . . . I did get a very bad papercut once. But that's about the most horrifying thing that has every happened to me. (*Scholastic*)

It is a funny answer, but not entirely correct. Like many writers for children, Stine uses things his own child has experienced. The idea for *Monster Blood,* Stine said, came from a day when "my son had a plastic container of slime. He stuck it to the wall and couldn't get it off" (*Ohio,* 135). Stine also confessed that the idea for *Haunted Mask* came when "one Halloween my son Matt put on a mask and then had trouble pulling it off."[4] In the same title, Stine also used his own childhood memories:

> Halloween was a painful time for me when I was a kid. I wanted to be something scary, but my parents bought me a duck costume. I was so embarrassed! We were very poor and I couldn't buy a new costume every year. So I had to be a duck for years. I remembered this when I wrote *The Haunted Mask* and I gave Carlie Beth a duck costume in that book. (*TBR*)

While titles like *Blind Date* are more directly autobiographical, Stine, like any good writer, looks for the things in his childhood and teen years that made an impact. Those experiences—some comical, some embarrassing, and some scary—are certainly fodder for his writing process.

The title or image leads him to ask questions. For example, Stine explained the process of writing *The Girlfriend:* "The book started out with a simple idea. What would happen if you got a girlfriend you couldn't get rid of? How do you get rid of someone who won't leave you alone? Who is going to ruin your life?" (*AOL*). In asking and answering the questions, he plots the book out. The most important question is "How will it end?" He tries to think about what types of tricks or gimmicks he can use to make each book entertaining. As critics have accused, he's figuring what to use from his bag of tricks: "I try to get the ending first, especially for the *Fear Streets.* I have to know who did it. . . Then I can go back and figure out how to fool the kids. I know right from the start how I'm going to mislead them so they can't guess the ending" (A*lderdice,* 209). Stine enjoys his writing process: "By the time I sit down to write the book, I really

know everything that is going to happen. I can just have fun"
(*Authors*, 217). Saying he's out to "fool the kids" demonstrates
that Stine is not only writing for an audience, but that he under-
stands exactly what they like in his books. He also knows he's
writing formula fiction and is proud of it.

THE SECRET FORMULA

There's also a formula to his writing process. Stine says,
"Every book is outlined in detail. I do maybe a 20-page outline,
chapter by chapter, for every book. I even have all the cliffhanger chapter endings" (*Alderdice*, 209). The outline takes a
couple of days and is all done on a legal pad. Stine commented:

> The strange thing is, at least it's strange to me, that I cannot plot on the
> computer. I do everything else on the computer, I write and I revise,
> but when I outline the stories I have to outline them in longhand on a
> lined pad. I don't know why the plotting process is so different than the
> writing process, but it is. It's a real mystery to me. (*Webchat*)

Before he starts writing Stine explained that "the outline has to
be approved by my editors" (*Webchat*). This outlining process
works for Stine, but he said at first he resisted it, "I started doing it this way kicking and screaming. . . . I didn't want any part
of these outlines, because sometimes you end up revising the
outline, and revising it again until the editor approves it, and it's
an arduous process" (*Authors*, 217). Armed with an outline, an
ending, and a title, Stine begins writing.

The opening of the book will usually present the book's hook
or an image of something scary, real or imagined. Stine said he
begins this way because he wants his audience to "know exactly
what the book is about—in the very first chapter" (*Ohio*, 135).
The main character is usually introduced right away, most of the
time in the first sentence. It is usually a memorable first impres-
sion. This practice extends from his first *Fear Street*, "When
Cory Brooks saw the new girl for the first time, he was standing
on his head in the lunchroom" (*New Girl*, 1). By the first few

chapters, usually the group of teens who figure in the plot will be named, their physical features noted and their relationships to others in the group explained. Names, Stine said, are a sticking point: "I need a lot of names because I have maybe 8 to 10 different kids in every book, and I usually get the names from my son's school directory. Just about everyone in his school has been in a *Goosebumps* or a *Fear Street*" (*Webchat*).

He is, as he and his son both admit, a writing machine with tremendous discipline and stamina. That stems from his attitude toward his work. Stine says:

> I kind of treat writing as a full-time job, with just about the same hours. I sit down at the computer every morning at 9:00. I've very disciplined, partly because I enjoy it so much. And I set a goal for myself every day. I say—today I'm going to write 15 pages or today I'm going to write 20 pages and I don't get up until I do. I work six days a week. (*Webchat*)

In another interview Stine said, "I've never had a day where I couldn't write 15 pages" (*Alderdice*, 209). He further adds that

> people always ask me what I do about writer's block and I have to tell them in all honesty, that I've never had it. . . .That's just luck I think. Some days it feels as if I'm writing uphill. And some days I'm not quite sure what language it's in, but I just keep going because I know I'll go back and fix it. (*Webchat*)

The writing is all done on computer. His friend Joe Arthur claims that Stine still types all his books with "one finger" (*Ohio*, xii), but Stine has never mentioned that in any interview. In addition to working a lot, he works fast. It takes him about two to three days to outline a book, then eight days to write a *Goosebumps* and ten to write a *Fear Street*. It normally takes seven to ten months for Stine to turn an idea into a book on the shelf.

Once he's done the first draft, Stine says, "It goes to my editors and they usually require quite a few revisions. They always insist, for some reason, that the books make sense. Which makes it a lot harder for me" (*Webchat*). His wife Jane still edits the *Fear Street* manuscripts, occasionally handing them back with a note dubbing the work "psychotic ramblings" (Gellene, A1). Making sense is always tough in writing any sort of speculative fiction. Things will happen that can't be explained in reality, yet they need to make sense within the context of the book. That, according to Stine, is not easy: "The plots have to be logical. If they get too scary, they get silly and no one will believe it. But if they're too believable, then they'll be boring" (Santow, 115).

Although all his books are plot driven, the characters still matter. As noted, the characters are Stine's readers; they have the same emotional underpinning, the same worries, but also the same appearance. Not only do Stine's characters look and feel like the readers, they sound like them. Stine insists it is "very important to these books. . . . that the kids sound and look like real kids, suddenly trapped in something horrible"(*Authors*, 216). That's always been one of the selling points of Stine's books: they sound like kids talking. Getting the voice right is vital, Stine said, because "I don't want to sound like some middle-aged guy who doesn't know what he's doing" (*Authors*, 216).

Stine credits a great deal of his ability to keep in touch with teens to his son Matt. Although Stine wrote thrillers and started *Fear Street* before Matt reached adolescence, Stine declares his son is a big influence: "I work very hard at staying in touch with young people. . . . I spend a lot of time with my son and his friends" (*AOL*). Another way he keeps up with kids is via the letters from his readers and communications on-line through Scholastic. In addition, Stine keeps tuned to youth popular culture through watching MTV and reading teen magazines. As Stine admits, this influence comes into play when he is writing dialogue. His minimalist narrative style fits perfectly with his ideas about teenspeak as he observes, "Kids aren't really eloquent. They never speak in paragraphs . . . . In fact, they mostly grunt" (Donahue).

While Stine's dialogue is more than grunting, it is short and to the point. The characters sound like teenagers because the dialogue reflects teen concerns written with the appropriate cadence. Although he keeps up and the books have some pop culture references, they are not loaded with them or with slang. Stine says, "I don't have them saying things like 'gnarly' and other stuff. . . . I'd like these books to be read five years from now and that kind of slang really dates them fast" (*Authors,* 216).

NORMAL KIDS, SAFE SCARES

Although he uses his son, his son's friends, and some basic research to construct the outward life of a character, the scare comes from what goes on inside. Stine jokes that he writes for twelve-year-olds because "my mental age is 12" (*Scholastic*). He says the key to writing horror is to "try to remember what scared you as a kid" (Santow, 115). In the *Goosebumps* books, the fears are those of most children: monsters, disappearing parents, pets dying, and all things slimy. Part of Stine's particular genius comes from his ability to find fright in all sorts of places. Stine says that he "once wrote a *Goosebumps* about these kids who find a sponge under the sink. It's just a sponge but it brings them horrible luck. I'm the kind of person who can find a sponge scary" (*TBR*). In *Fear Street*, the fears are those of normal teens—being popular, getting along with people, being safe.

"Safe." It is a term that Stine uses in just about every interview to describe his writing. Stine explained, "I try not to put in anything that is too close to their lives. . . . I wouldn't do child abuse, or AIDS, or suicide, or anything that could really touch someone's life like that. The books are supposed to be just entertainment, that's all they are" (*Authors,* 216). But it is the reaction to those things in their lives that cause children to gravitate toward horror fiction, according to editor Nancy Pines. She noted that "these are scary times. . . . Children are exposed regularly to the horrors of crime, war, drugs . . . what these books can do is to provide a safe place to be scared. It all ends with the last page" (Bates).

There are lots of reasons for this. If the books were loaded down with "problems" they would become realistic teen novels, which is not Stine's genre. Further, the problem would overwhelm the story: who is afraid of a few scary phone calls if the real source of stress in a teen's life is a relative dying of AIDS or a drug problem? That is not the type of fright Stine has dealt with, either in his writing, or—one suspects—in his own childhood growing up in Bexley. Stine says, "I'm pretty careful what I put in these books, and I don't go too far. . . . They all take place in suburban settings, just like Bexley."[5]

In fact, most of the characters in his books would be right at home in Stine's childhood. The names have changed, but the kids living in the nice houses with the nice green lawns of *Fear Street* and *Goosebumps* could just as well be growing up in Bexley in the fifties right next door to Stine. While the clothing styles are different, the rest of the environment remains the same. There is no talk of drugs, crime, AIDS, or any other contemporary social problem. Everyone is white and it looks as if any moment the Cleavers are going to drop in with some brownies. These are 1950s childhoods—or the image of them as displayed by that era's sit-com families.

When setting up his safe scares Stine taps into kids' natural inclination towards fright. Stine often compares his books to that juvenile obsession, the roller coaster. Stine offered:

I think kids like the books because they're like roller coaster rides. They're very fast. They're very exciting. You think you're going to go in one direction—they take you off in another direction. So they tease you. They fool you. . . . [These] books let you off safe and sound and you know—no matter how scary it is, or how thrilling or how exciting—you know that you're safe the whole time. (*Alderdice*, 209)

Part of Stine's ability to reach this audience is not only his long experience—over twenty-five years in the children's publishing industry—but also his knack of visualizing his audience. He remembers what scared him as a child and he tries to imagine what would scare a ten-year-old now. To get these scares to work—to be not too mild or too wild—Stine packs his books with, in his own words, "cheap thrills" (*Gray*, 54). One variety of those thrills are gross outs. Stine said he looks for "disgusting, gross things to put in the book they'll like: the cat is boiled in the spaghetti, a girl pours honey over a boy and sets ants on him. They [kids] like this gross stuff" (*Gray*, 54).

When Stine ventured away from writing for youth in *Superstitious*, he found difficulty in knowing what adults would find "cheap thrills." He recalled, "Writing *Superstitious* felt like writing a first novel. I think every writer, when they are writing picture their audience in their mind. When I write my scary books for kids, I picture these 10-year-old faces. When I started to write *Superstitious*, I had to change all the faces" (*Webchat*). Part of the problem with *Superstitious* as a horror novel is that while it does deliver the cheap thrills and gross outs, it does not deliver in other areas that readers of adult horror novels expect. Stine's venture in the adult arena falls short of the standards set by Stephen King.

About King, Stine says, "I'm a big admirer of Stephen King. I've been called the Stephen King for kids, and that is a great compliment" (*Sell*, D4). Stine's thrillers were once called "a sort of literary training bra for younger YA readers who like horror fiction but can't cope yet with King/Koontz/Straub/Andrews" (*Eaglen*, 49). Although Stine says being dubbed a literary training bra was "the worst thing I was ever called,"[6] he knows that part of his mission is to provide books that will keep kids reading through the school years.

UNDER THE INFLUENCE

Stine's influences are also the writers he read through his school years and the authors he continues to read as an adult. Stine recalled, perhaps tongue-in-cheek, that as a child "my favorite book was *Pinocchio*. In the original version, Pinocchio takes a big wooden mallet and smashes Jimmy Cricket [sic] flat against the wall! Then Pinocchio falls asleep with his feet on the stove and burns off his feet!! This was very influential" (*AOL*). Although Stine is certainly playing up the gory elements here, he really was a serious reader as a child. As a boy he read "Norse legends, Greek myths, Edgar Allan Poe, baseball stories" (*Scholastic*). As noted, Stine also mentions horror comics like *Tales from the Crypt* and science fiction writers like Isaac Asimov as influences. Stine says:

> I think Rod Serling was a very big influence on me. He was also from Ohio. . . . When I was a kid, I don't think I ever missed a *Twilight Zone*. When I was my readers' age I also loved Ray Bradbury. In fact, I think the scariest book I ever read was a Ray Bradbury book called *Something Wicked This Way Comes*. (*Webchat*)

Other authors continue to influence Stine, who said, "I've been reading a lot of Agatha Christie mysteries. She wrote 79 mysteries and they have wonderful tricky plots. I read a lot of novels, a lot of mysteries and I really enjoy humor books" (*AOL*). Stine also relates not only to Christie's talent, but also her popularity. He says "Somebody once asked Agatha Christie why her books were so popular, and she said, 'I just stumbled on something that people wanted to read.' I think that's what happened to me" (Gilson, 1997).

The Christie influence is perhaps the most pronounced in *Fear Street* titles like *Beach House* or *Ski Weekend* where Stine uses the "locked room" formula with great effect. The difference, of course, is that the room is usually at some exciting location, the victims are all teenagers, and the murderer is also normally a teenager. Rather than relying on a Miss Marple or Hercule Poirot, Stine's characters solve their own mysteries. Stine is showing his young readers, in a very entertaining fashion, that kids can solve problems.

Stine himself is a huge influence on young writers. He is asked in almost every interview for advice for young writers, and his answer might surprise his critics:

> My advice is to read, read, read. Read all kinds of books. That way you pick up different styles and learn different ways to say things. Don't worry about sending your stories to be published. No one really wants to publish works by kids. Just keep writing—and mainly reading and reading. (*AOL*)

Stine advises that the most important thing for budding writers to do is to start "reading books by many different authors" (*Ohio*, 140). It is easy to spot in Stine's work how his reading played a role in his success as a writer. From the twisty plots of Agatha Christie to the speculative fiction of Isaac Asimov to the gross outs of *Tales from the Crypt* to the zany attitude of *Mad* magazine, Stine's writing reflects his reading life.

While Stine's writing process may not be unique among writers for youth, what is outstanding is his honesty about it. He admits that many of his ideas are not original to him. They are suggested by a friend, an editor, or even by *TV Guide*. He admits his writing contains cheap thrills and openly talks about how he constructs books backward to trick his readers. He talks about how   titles—not characters or scenes but just titles—inspire him to write. And he writes every day—he's not waiting for the sun to be shining through the kitchen window just right. Rather than going to the Scholastic office to write funny articles for eight hours a day as he did for a decade, he's at home churning out best sellers. He's doing what he has always done—working at it like any other job, just punching the clock and punching out best-sellers. His goal is to sell books, and he does that very well.

He does that by being entertaining, without remorse or reservation. This attitude shines through in his disdain for advice often given to young writers. Stine comments:

> I hate it when authors come to schools and tell kids to write from their heart. I don't think I've ever written a single word from my heart. I write to entertain. I've written all kinds of things. I've written bubble gum cards and coloring books. And each time I tried to the best I could. If you really love to write, you can write anything. (*TRB*)

It is Stine's desire to entertain, at all costs and above all other concerns, which fuels his writing attitudes, guides his writing process, and explains his commercial success. And it is his basic belief—that kids deserve, need, and maybe even have a right to mindless entertainment—that drives the Stine scary machine that delights and terrifies kids. But this same belief is also what scares adults even more.

NOTES

1. Shawn Sell, "Stine Gives Kids *Goosebumps* with Frightening Speed," *USA Today* (31 October 1996): D4; hereafter cited in text as Sell.

2. "Meet Matt Stine," *The Bumps.* http://www.thebumps.simplenet.com/gbmatt.htm (21 May 1997).

3. Deirdre Donahue, "R.L. Stine Has a Frightful Way with Pre-teen Readers," *USA Today* (3 December 1993): D6; hereafter cited in text as Donahue.

4. Graham Jefferson, "Fox Gets *Goosebumps,*" *USA Today* (24 October 1995): D3.

5. Nancy Gilson, "The Real King of Fear," *Columbus Dispatch* (5 June 1997): 8E; hereafter cited in text as Gilson 1997.

6. Joyce Rosenberg, "Goosebumps: So Successful It's Scary," *Source.* http://sddt.com/files/librarywire/DN0_96_10_22_1c.html (3 March 1997).

CHAPTER TWELVE
WHAT'S SO SCARY ABOUT R.L. STINE?

R.L. Stine writes books that kids, especially boys, read without prodding or parental pressure. He has made reading a cool thing to do in schools all over the country. He has done what many thought was not possible in the high tech/heavy video world of today's youth: he has created a community of readers. A community where kids set up web pages, E-mail, and chat about his books via computer networks. A community where kids will go to libraries and bookstores to participate in *Goosebumps* clubs and wear T-shirts brandishing the name of not the hottest rock star, sports team, or TV hero, but the name of a book. He has given huge visibility to books for youth by his popularity, and by crossing over to other media. Finally, with his books and the genre of YA and children's horror he helped create and popularize, Stine has probably done more for reading in the United States than any other writer in the past decade.

The scariest thing about R.L. Stine's success is that it has exposed the huge gap that exists between young readers and adults. In particular, children's literature professors, librarians, reviewers, and educators seem the most troubled by Stine's success. It's a defensive posture: this "community of readers" is very different from the one Stine claims as his constituency, but not just by age or education. Different in that they don't want simply to enjoy a book that entertains them but want to analyze that literature. Different in that they think kids who read Stine are lazy for not reading more demanding young adult literature. They dismiss his work as illiterate garbage. They dismiss it because of preconceived notions of what equals quality, dismiss it because of the horror genre, dismiss it because of the hype and the money being made, and maybe just dismiss it because it appears in a series.

A SERIOUS QUESTION ABOUT SERIES FICTION

The success of Stine and other writers in the genre is tied to the fact that their works appear as part of a series. Series fiction, due to the fad for the romance and then the thriller craze, has dominated bookstore and library shelves for almost twenty years. This distresses those who believe that series cannot be creative because they are packaged, marketed, and published monthly like a product, not like a work of literature. But series fiction is a fact. Sylvia Makowski advances the following reasons librarians should embrace, rather than be repelled by, youth series fiction:

1. Kids like them. They're a fast, easy read. Most of them are wonderful escapist entertainment. Modern kids can fit them into their busy lives.
2. They fill a collection need for which there is an unending voracious appetite, such as mystery, adventure, horror, science fiction, fantasy, romance, etc.
3. They allow you to fill that collection need with the least output of time and money.
4. It is your duty as a professional to be knowledgeable about every library genre and how it can be used to stimulate the interest or fulfill the needs of any young patron.["]1

Makowski further argues that the quality of series fiction is better than it has been in the past, in part because of an influx of skilled writers. Just as important, however, is the role of packagers. Book packagers develop ideas, find writers, and design

the concept of a series. The books are written not just to a formula, but within highly specific guidelines. By being first with
Fear Street, Stine wrote the rules for all subsequent YA thrillers.

A different view about the need to study and appreciate series
fiction is offered by Dr. Cosette Kies, who authored the books
Presenting Young Adult Horror Fiction and *Supernatural Fiction for Teens*. After reviewing various horror series, she writes
that "there is slightly more acceptance . . . by adults because the
kids are reading them, even if they may read little else through
choice. Alas, a pessimistic thought to use for the ending of this
piece" (*Kies 1994*, 19). That attitude seems indicative of propo-
nents of the reading escalator theory. Series books (or any
popular fiction) are only good as a means to an end—to move
the reader from the "substandard" to something of higher quality.

Perhaps reading of any kind by any teenager in a world so
full of other options is quality. Perhaps series fiction provides
teenagers with the type of reading experience they want at a
particular time of their lives, and once that time in their lives has
passed, they will move on to something else, not because they
want to move to quality literature, but because series reading no
longer meets their emotional or recreational needs.

And what are the emotional needs of YA readers? Not surprisingly, the emotional needs coincide with the developmental
needs of adolescence: achieving independence, gaining acceptance, forming an identity, and managing excitement. These
goals are manifested in many ways, one of which is reading.
Teens will enjoy books, even in recreational fiction, that speak
to these needs by showing people of their age being independent
and strong. Teens will enjoy books that validate their often
conflicting feelings, books where the characters are not just like
them but represent the person they would like to be, books that
show problem-solving, books that show characters overcoming
odds, books that display the changing nature of a teen's relationships, and books that capture the fullness of YA life, not just the

outward trappings and the internal emotions, but the sheer essence of adolescent life: intensity and uncertainty.

In Stine's books, the teens are independent, experience conflicting emotions, and are role (and anti-role) models. The books, as a mystery/horror hybrid, are about problem-solving (who done it?), and build heat throughout for the underdog protagonist who overcomes the odds and wins in the end. Finally, the books mirror the YA experience: lots of confusion about what is happening, an intensity of emotion, and a thin layer of everyday fear of humiliation. You could run the same list with *Sweet Valley High* or almost any other series and find the same result: series books are responsive to kids' emotional needs. Good young adult literature does the same and critics applaud it; when it happens in series fiction, they ignore it because those books are "illiterate garbage."

Series books offer a safe repeated experience. Once a reader learns and likes a series, they know they can trust it. There is a psychological reassurance to series fiction: while YAs see their lives and bodies in a state of flux, a series book provides a stable, known, and dependable experience. These books are everywhere, not just at libraries but at bookstores and discount stores. Their availability leads to popularity. Kids read them; because kids read them, other kids read them. It is a Mobius strip success story: *Fear Street* is popular because *Fear Street* is popular. This is the peer psychology that drives all marketing for YAs. Finally, series books respond to kids' need to escape.

The furor over series reading certainly did not begin (nor will it end) with R.L. Stine. The proliferation of mystery and romance series in the early 1980s produced studies about both the attraction and the effects of such reading. Barbara Moran and Susan Steinfirst surveyed kids' mystery novels in 1985. Their question was "What is the appeal of series mystery fiction?" They found that:

These stories are highly formulated, good guy wins out over bad fairy tales for the older child. They move along quickly, have lots of dialogue and little narrative description and are highly predictable. Some researchers believe that young children like and generally prefer stereotyped characters, and are comforted by the sameness and simplicity of the characters and plots. . . . They present puzzles to be solved and wrongs to be righted. Many readers respond to the intellectual challenge of trying to solve the mystery before the protagonist. The readers also gain satisfaction from the final restoration of harmony that is characteristic of all mysteries. . . . The conclusion reassures the reader of any age that there is order in chaos, and that in a disorderly world, justice can triumph. [2]

Moran and Steinfirst also asked: "Why do these things appeal to youth?" They found their answer in developmental psychology, particularly in the works of Eric Erikson. From Erikson's conception of adolescence as a time of "both identity crisis and psychosocial moratoriums" (*Moran*, 116), Moran and Steinfirst looked at how series related to the crisis of adolescence, and concluded that series are appealing because:

On a conscious level they allow the reader to dwell in the easily accessible land of 'trash' for a while. . . . Adolescents are struggling to realize they are competent human beings, capable of carrying on life independent of their families. . . . It is therefore no surprise that young people may very well find comfort in these repetitive plots, and guidance from the strength of the series characters who, despite the silliness and cocksureness of it all, are . . . young men and women successfully posed on the brink of adulthood. (*Moran*, 117)

When looking at teen romances, Doris Fong took a similar track by marrying the appeal of series fiction to teenagers with the uniqueness of teenagers. She wrote:

While trying to defend the literary merit in the teen romance is ludicrous as extolling the virtue of a steady diet of junk food to hospital dietitians, it seems to me that much of the controversy and all of the criticism of series romances has overlooked an important and obvious fact: YAs are not adults. They process what they read through a filter of young adult, not adult, experiences and concerns.[3]

Fong looked at two studies to back up her thesis. One 1985 study[4] concluded that romance fiction was more reflective of normal teen experience than realistic novels. More teen girls are worrying about romance than are concerned with the drama trauma of realistic fiction. A second study in 1990[5] found that series romances empower girls to resist and challenge various social pressures.

Just two months later, Mary Huntwork presented a much longer and more detailed analysis of romance fiction by asking, then answering the question "Why do girls flock to *Sweet Valley High*?" Huntwork advances that "not all teenagers identify with the characters of the heavier problem novels. Some teenagers want to read about situations closer to their own."[6]

Margaret Mackey investigated the appeal of series books by looking at the *Baby-Sitters Club*. She concludes it is

> not helpful to dismiss such series reading with a passing sneer. The experience of making patterns, putting stories together, extrapolating, and confirming may be providing a crucial step towards more substantial reading. It is too easy to label such work as reading rubbish or as merely 'better than reading nothing.' . . . it does not seem possible to dismiss [series books] completely. Kristy, Mary Anne and the others seem assured of a place in the minds and hearts of at least one generation of little girls and may even be remembered years from now, long after readers have outgrown the immediate reading lessons which the *Baby-Sitters* may have to offer.[7]

These articles suggest that such reading is probably not harmful and may possess some benefits. This idea, that reading series fiction is positive, strikes a negative chord with some as regards the work of R.L. Stine.

THE WICKEDNESS OF R. L STINE

One such individual who is not pleased by Stine is YA literature commentator (and editor of this book) Patty Campbell. In her first foray against Stine and paperback thrillers, she wrote, "The good news is that YA horror paperbacks are not as bad as their reputation or covers would have readers believe. The packaging is more sensational than the contents, and the nastiness is not quite in the same league as slasher films or even Stephen King novels."[8] Campbell quoted a teenager's list of explanations as to why she enjoyed scary books. Many sound like they came from Stine:

1. "When I read for pleasure I just want to read something trashy. Adults have their trashy reading—why can't kids?"
2. "I know these aren't real—that's why I read them."
3. "My friends are reading worse stuff." (by which she meant graphic sex novels)
4. "I am offended that adults would try to limit or change my reading habits."
5. "I'm reading the classics in school, so I deserve some light reading on my own time."
6. "I don't know any other reading for my age."
7. "I think it is important that I'm reading something." (*Campbell*, 237)

While not a ringing endorsement of thrillers by any means, Campbell wrapped up her essay with a challenge "to critics and adults who work with young people to stop wringing their hands and get busy finding constructive ways to take advantage of the appeal of these books for teens" (*Campbell*, 239).

Two years later, however, Campbell wouldn't be wringing her hands, she would be washing them of her early tepid endorsement as she said about Stine:

> I think he's wicked. . . . I think he's extremely destructive. He preys on the absolute worst instincts of the human soul. He's also an extremely bad writer. If any of his books were turned in as a 5th grade essay, he would get a D minus.[9]

The article in *Teacher Magazine*, from which Campbell is quoted, is one of many about Stine to appear in professional and popular magazines. Each article will quickly retrace Stine's biography, summarize the books, and then present the battle of the competing experts to argue the merits of R.L. Stine. The author of these articles will inevitably come down square in the middle: yes, it is not great literature but at least kids are reading something.

In addition to interviews with experts, the articles contain quotations from parents of Stine's readers. For example: "I would much prefer that he do this than a lot of other things, like Nintendo" (*Hill*, 39). Another said, "They don't seem evil to me. The important thing is that he is reading" (*Hill*, 39). These remarks are representative of many parents' position on Stine. While most parents in these articles express concern, the overwhelming majority, in particular the parents of boys, feel grateful that their kids are reading. Most suggest that if not for Stine, their children would not be reading for pleasure at all.

Those in the children's book business are of two minds. Many, especially those cashing in on the success of Stine, have little bad to say about him. Others, like Campbell, take a much harder line. Stephanie Loer, children's book editor of the *Boston Globe*, concluded:

> These books are not good literature, but they are not harmful. Enticing, recreational reading, they can be a hook to get reluctant readers into libraries where they will find books of more substance. . . . There will always be a new audience of children coming along and scary stories will inevitably cast their spell on the younger set. (*Hill*, 41)

Stine came along at the right time with the right tools—his writing skills and Scholastic's marketing genius—to take horror to new heights of popularity.

AUTHOR OR CATALYST?

Stine is a catalyst. Arguments about his work stem from the beliefs held by adults about reading, children, and values. The debates about his books, among critics and between school boards and parents, is about the power of reading and its impact upon children; about fear in the life of children and whether horror fiction reflects that fear or causes it, and the meaning and value of popular culture. Stine is grouped with *The X-Files*, Stephen Spielberg's *The Lost World*, and other "corrupters" of youth for their output in the new superscary 1990s. According to the *New York Times*, "Never before have the movie, TV and publishing industries seemed so adept and sophisticated in indulging their dark fascinations . . . books, TV programs, and films that are getting grittier, scarier, edgier and more violent than ever before."[10] The only problem with this argument is that one could easily find similar "it's the end of the world as we know it" predictions tied to the horror films of the 1930s, the horror comics and films of the 1950s, and now the horror industry of the 1990s. Each older generation seems to think the popular culture of children is the worst ever. Parents who claimed Elvis was the devil must not be able to comprehend Marilyn Manson at all.

The main concern isn't the scariness of the books, but the reactions which children have to them. Further, it is young children—ages five and six—who are in over their heads as "it also appears that the audience for kiddy horror is getting younger and younger" (*Carvajal*, E1). Librarians, therapists, and parents are worried that Stine's *Fear Street* titles, intended for teens, are being read not by teens but by third graders. This all begs the question: Is the "problem" with the people who create horror or those who allow young children to eat it up? Does anyone really think that R.L. Stine wants a seven-year-old reading *Fear Street*? Or kids under six watching or reading *Goosebumps*? If his concern was only maximum market share, wouldn't these books be "worse?" Stine could perhaps get more readers for his *Fear Streets* by adding sex or for *Goosebumps* by killing off authority figures with reckless abandon, but he doesn't. Stine and Parachute have pushed books for kids out to a new borderline, but they are quite aware of the necessary limits of the market.

In libraries, the doctrine that a third party be required to "protect" children from reading horror or viewing other materials is called "in loco parentis," and it is not a philosophy that is

willingly embraced by most librarians. Yet it rears its head when
libraries get into discussions of collections, in particular for
youth. The age-old debate between "quality vs. popularity" is
really an argument about the role of popular culture. For whatever R.L. Stine is, he is a part of American popular culture,
which is driven by an economic system allowing for free choice
and which allows profit to be the bottom line for most decisions.
The *Goosebumps* cash machine reminds too many people that
while books can be literature, they are always commerce. The
literary and liberal tradition of libraries is getting all stained up
with the smell of marketing, merchandising, and *Goosebumps*-
mania. Stine's blatant commercialism, his desire to produce
books with little literary merit, and the resulting popularity of
those books is a sore point for many.

STINE UNDER SIEGE

The first shot at Stine and other writers of popular youth fiction was a preemptive strike appearing in *Harper's Magazine* in
1989. Though he was not addressing *Fear Street* or *Goosebumps*,
the author, Tom Englehardt (a former editor at Pantheon books
and a recipient of a Guggenheim fellowship) was already calling
literature for youth of the late 1980s "harmful." He noted:

> No matter how the children's book business seems to be thriving, what
> is most striking about these bestsellers is their starved nature. . . . A
> formalistic literature of anxiety and reassurance, the reassurance,
> sometimes laying only in the fact that another book just like the first is
> still to be purchased and another . . .[11]

These arguments should sound familiar to Stine. This should
underscore the main point: it is sometimes not so much that
adults don't like Stine in particular, but the fact that something is
a best seller for children indicates it can't have any quality—
forgetting, of course, that the ability to entertain children with
reading   material in an age of video is a remarkable quality for
any book to have. It is worth noting that Englehardt's wrath was

directed at those books then topping the best-seller list for children, books like *Mutant Ninja Turtles*. There seems to be a widely held assumption that the children's literature industry used to be "pure" and everything published was of high quality (how does *Cherry Ames, Student Nurse,* fit into this equation?), but that is just not the fact. Publishing for children is a business, not a public service, and bookstore and library shelves have long been filled with series paperbacks. This argument isn't about Stine; it is about trying to turn back the clock to a past that wasn't that different.

The first direct shot at Stine came in *Time* magazine in 1993 with Paul Gray's article, "Carnage: An Open Book," which opens with the observation that "adolescents now constitute a booming niche market for the peddling of published gore and violence" (*Gray*, 54). One author of YA horror fiction told me she was interviewed for this story and the first question asked by the interviewer was along the lines of "How does it feel to be responsible for writing books that cause teens to be violent?" It is perhaps not a coincidence that the cover story of the same issue of *Time* was "Kids and Their Guns." Somehow it didn't get mentioned in Gray's article that guns are almost never used in YA horror, especially not in Stine. Gray quotes a passage from Stine about a baby's head being pulled off, yet he fails to mention that it is a doll's head. Gray also quotes both Stine and Pike in the essay for the sake of equal time, but then compares them unfavorably to "classical children's literature" of a scary variety. The piece ends, predictably, with the call to move beyond Stine: "Maybe the youngsters will move upward in their tastes, through Stephen King and V.C. Andrews to Hemingway, Joyce and Shakespeare" (*Gray*, 54). Gray's closing thought and that of the librarians quoted are boilerplate—they'll move on to something else. Hopefully they'll use another list than Gray's, which puts King below Andrews and would wish teenagers to read James Joyce.

An article in *U.S. News & World Report* a few years later

was very similar. The author, Marc Silver, rounded up the usual suspects, quoting librarians and professors. The piece is much less critical, even citing a child psychologist as saying parents shouldn't worry about kids reading scary books because "most kids can separate fiction from real life."[12] Silver also perceptively writes, "What makes adults nervous is that they don't understand the *Goosebumps* phenomenon" (*Silver*, 96). Still, the editors ran a sidebar, "Getting Beyond *Goosebumps*," although listing YA and children's literature rather than James Joyce.

The next big attack came in the *New York Times Book Review* from Ken Tucker. Tucker's piece starts off with a series of quotations from some horror books, then goes on to point out the literary faults of the genre. After dismissing the "at least they are reading something" theory, Tucker takes off: "It seems just as likely, however, that all an adolescent's passion for Mr. Pike and Mr. Stine will lead to is an itch for Stephen King and Dean R. Koontz. . . . The authors tend to be too busy accommodating MTV attention spans to create real personalities; instead they race from one cheap jolt to the next."[13] "Accommodating MTV attention spans" is an interesting phrase, implying that rather than meeting the audience at its level, authors should aim higher. Rather than giving the audience "what they need"—books they will read—authors should instead provide books "they should read" (but probably won't) to challenge them. The flaw is simple: everyone doesn't want to be challenged; they just want to be entertained. If they can't find books that do that, then they can just go watch MTV. It is called "pleasure reading" because it is supposed to be pleasing, not demanding.

Tucker is also concerned that the young women in the book are not "strong, active protagonists" (*Tucker*, 27). Again, that is one of those statements that seems to go against the facts. Almost all of Stine's books feature young women who are strong and active, not like Jamie Lee Curtis in *Halloween*, but not helpless, hopeless heroines. Stuff happens to them, and they want to know why. They don't call the police or tell their parents; they want to solve it themselves. They are afraid, yet also courageous in taking risks. Most become heroic, as they come to the rescue of a sibling or friend to protect them from harm.

After comparing Stine and Pike to Poe, Stoker, and Shelley (unfavorably of course), Tucker takes a dig at Stine: "Most of these books seem to be textbook examples of how not to tell a story. Plowing through an R.L. Stine novel is exhausting because of its endless seesawing rhythm" (*Tucker*, 27). It is ironic that Tucker chooses Stine's roller coaster pacing as his main criticism, when it is obviously one of Stine's greatest strengths. It is not the rhythm of art, but rather the snap and crackle speed of pop culture products. This pacing allows readers to participate, anticipate, and also congratulate themselves for making it "up another hill." After dumping on *Goosebumps* for not being scary enough and for being "trite," Tucker proceeds to suggest good authors in the genre. It's obvious from his main recommendation, Joan Lowery Nixon, that Tucker doesn't understand the genre. Nixon's titles were repackaged with new post-Stine covers so they would look like thrillers, which is perhaps how Tucker got confused.

Finally, Tucker ends with not so much a criticism as an insult:

> Too much young adult horror fiction gleams like assembly line product. Its commercial cynicism and market-driven precision lack the gleeful inventiveness and loose, juicy vulgarity of good, exciting pop culture. If there's one overriding lesson taught by young adult horror, it's this: We have less to fear from hacksaws than from hacks. (*Tucker*, 27)

It reads well—although I'm not sure what YA thriller has a hacksaw used as a weapon—but it is a strange analysis. Is Tucker really saying that YA horror needs more vulgarity? That is a strange argument for someone who just used Joan Lowery Nixon's squeaky-clean mysteries as an example of a good read. Further, the word "hack" in the writing world cannot have anything but a negative connotation, like calling someone in sports a choker: it is the ultimate professional dig. "Hack" seems to imply someone lacking talent and that certainly doesn't describe R.L. Stine. But perhaps if "hack" is a descriptor for an author who month after month delivers books that are popular because they are entertaining, then maybe Stine is guilty as charged.

THE ASSASSINATION OF R.L. STINE

If Tucker's piece was an accusation, then what came next was like an assassination. Diana West's "The Horror of R.L. Stine" first appeared in the conservative magazine, *The Weekly Standard*. It was later reprinted in the *American Educator* and West used it to form the core for an op-ed piece in *American Teacher*. She writes that "the literary universe of juvenile horror writer R.L. Stine . . . may be the most dangerous place on earth."[14] From that premise, West proceeds to catalog what she considers the "horror" of Stine's fiction. In doing so, she hauls out just about every accusation ever made against Stine. Her argument is worth looking at, and dissecting, in detail.

She calls Stine's world a place "where youngsters live in jeopardy, helpless against an assortment of evils" (*West*, 43). Helpless is a strange word choice, for in almost every Stine book, the main characters triumph through their own actions. Throughout the book they show courage, and at the end there will usually be an act of bravery on their part. While they cannot stop the violence menacing them, the teen and child protagonists are trying to avoid danger, trying to figure things out, trying to solve the problem and escape being in jeopardy. In all suspense stories—action, horror, mystery—characters must be in jeopardy. No jeopardy, no suspense; no suspense, no book.

Which would be fine with West, who complains that the horror genre has forced out other books, writing that "under the broad 'young adult banner,' scattered copies of *Kidnapped, The Yearling*, or *White Fang* may suggest familiar territory, but the section is otherwise unrecognizable, dominated by shelf upon

tightly packed shelf of horror books. . . . It has also propelled a
once-seedy sideline of children's publishing into the market's
mainstream" (*West*, 47). If by "seedy sideline" she means series
fiction, then she's misinformed, as series fiction has long been
dominant in the YA market. Looking at the shelves of a YA area
in the pre-Stine days, she would have seen all those spaces oc-
cupied not by classics, but by romance fiction.

If she means horror fiction, then she is correct, although it's
unclear what makes it seedy. The subject itself? The covers?
Perhaps what is bothering West here is not so much what is on
the shelf as, given the limited shelf space in any library or
bookstore, what is not. Judging from the rest of her piece, that
would mean children's classics. The thrust of this argument
seems to be along the lines of "look how lousy things are now"
and if we would only return to the "way things were" everything
would be better. It's a nice thought, but unless West has access
to the time machine in Stine's *The Time Raider*, it ain't gonna
happen. These comments, among many others, demonstrate
West's utter lack of knowledge of the history or the current
status of young adult literature. If she really knew something
about young adult literature, she could be trumpeting titles like
Rats Saw God by Rob Thomas or any of the titles from the
Young Adult Library Services Association's "Best Books" or
"Best of the Best" lists rather than "Booth Tarkington's seminal
coming-of-age novel *Seventeen*" (West, 45). For her, it is a
black-and-white world between juvenile junk and timeless classics.

Her primary beef is Stine's style, which she calls "shock fiction" that

> launches a beginning reader, pinball style, into a vapid quest for actual
> physical gratification, a bodily experience of accelerated pulse rates
> and queasy stomachs. . . .And so, reading becomes a crude tool of
> physical stimulation, wholly devoid of mental, emotional, or spiritual
> engagement. Does that sound like a working definition of pornogra-
> phy? (*West,* 43)

Actually it sounds more like "the physical thrill of horror" (Klause, 39), present in any scary entertainment, which Stine certainly didn't invent. The criticism that "kids get a physical rush from reading them. It's not necessarily sexual, but it's visceral" (*Hill*, 41) is on target. A physical rush could also be used to describe a roller coaster ride, to which Stine has always compared his books. There is no mental engagement—it is just a thrill. Should reading be thrilling? Should it be so engaging that it leads to a physical reaction? West thinks not, arguing that "the aim of shock fiction is the same: to set off a body response which debases the act of reading—and more important, the reader himself" (*West*, 44). Is fiction that so engages the readers or so entertains them that it causes them to respond "debasing?" What West sees as Stine's pinball style doesn't jibe: Stine's style, like that of a roller coaster, is about predictability. Readers know each chapter ends with a cliffhanger; it is suspenseful but it is also expected.

What cheapens or debases reading is the idea that any reading which prompts a physical reaction is pornography. People who read romances, mysteries, suspense, westerns, and horror fiction are so engaged. Any well-written story with suspense will cause the heart to race or the pulse to quicken. This seems not a description of pornography, but of a book that transcends being just something on a printed page. It becomes real to the reader— what happens in the book matters so much that the reader becomes physically involved. Yes, Stine wants to shock, not to debase reading, but rather to make it enjoyable with constant action designed to keep "the reader wired to the book."[15]

Another tactic used by West and others is to compare Stine to Edgar Allan Poe, noting Poe's mastery and comparing it to Stine's "raw catalogue of horror and grotesques" (*West*, 44). It's an interesting analogy, but is it proper? Is the teen or pre-teen reader choosing between reading Poe and reading Stine, or between reading Stine and watching television, playing a computer game, or viewing a video? That's Stine's real competition and that of anyone writing for youth. It is stereotypical to categorize every youngster growing up in the 1990s as having an MTV attention span (as Tucker did in his piece). It is equally ridiculous, however, to ignore the fact that children today are different than they were forty years ago in the way that they process information and what they consider entertaining. Finally, West is comparing the books that Stine writes with the books she thinks should be written, that require "a mental engagement with language, with character, with the author's interpretation of events that transforms the action and elevates it above the cheap thrills of a rap sheet" (*West*, 44). Yet horror or suspense doesn't work unless the shocks are more than just shocks. A book of nothing but gross outs means nothing; instead, Stine mixes in humor and the banality of teen gossip between his payoff scenes. West wants horror as art; Stine wants horror as show. West wants books with deep meanings; Stine wants books with high sales.

West quotes a mother who says, "I'm thrilled. He's literally reading a book a day. He always says 'Just a few more pages when it's time to go to bed'" (*West*, 44). And another says that Stine's books "weren't my choice of subject matter. . . . But I'm happy he's reading. If he wasn't reading this, he wouldn't be reading anything at all" (*West*, 44). West uses these two quotes as a basis for launching into a discussion of the escalator theory: "There they are, clinging to the hope that their children's enthusiasm for Stine will spread to, say, Henry James and his foray into horror fiction, *The Turn of the Screw*" (*West*, 44). Yet, to me, neither of the quotes reflect that feeling at all. Both show mothers who are happy their children are reading. Nowhere do they even suggest that they are hoping the books will lead to something different—they are just happy reading is taking place at all.

There are also two huge cultural assumptions—first, that these mothers would care if their children read Henry James. Maybe in some homes families sit around at night and read Henry James to each other, but in most homes this doesn't happen. Blame television, the breakdown of the American educa-

tional system, or even the fluoride in the water, but this isn't
Stine's doing. In fact, he's reversing the trend toward nonread-
ing as a recreational activity of kids. This escalator theory is
about pushing everyone to read demanding books. It also tells
the person who has no interest—for whatever reason—in
climbing the escalator that they are somehow cheating themselves by being lazy and that they are less of a person for it. This
is cultural elitism and an attitude that says, in effect, "If you
don't read and can't appreciate great literature then you are lazy
and not very bright, and you have not much worth as a person."
Now, that is debasing.

The second assumption running under the whole Stine controversy is that reading Henry James is considered "good" while
reading R.L. Stine is "bad."   Perhaps pushing Henry James
down kids' throats turns them off not just to Henry James but to
reading in general. A better approach to lead kids to Henry
James, if that is your goal for whatever reason, is to start kids
reading. The best way to do that—there seems to be a consensus
on this—is to allow kids to choose books, and hook them on
reading first. Readers will read other books, but nonreaders
won't.

West isn't conceding Stine even that function. Her theory is
that Stine's books not only won't lead to "better" reading, but
will "be a retarding, pre-literate experience" (West, 44). The
effect of Stine is to stunt reading growth, as West asks, "Will
they graduate from shock schlock to the best that's been thought
and said? Are you kidding? It's doubtful that they will be able
to go cover-to-cover with Dick Francis" (*West*, 44). My personal
experience in working with youth for about as long as Stine's
been pumping out *Fear Streets*, is that West is just plain wrong.
Not misinformed or out of touch, but *wrong*. Based on my ob-
servations and conversations with current and past Stine readers,
with librarians, and with reading teachers, West's theory just
isn't true.

I recently worked at a private high school, where everyone

who graduates goes to college, most to "good" schools. In the process of writing this book, I spoke with students about Stine, and many of them talked about reading him in the past, then outgrowing his books, although some of the ninth graders still enjoyed his work. None of them expressed any problems with handling the books they are required to read in school (the usual classics) and they have a wide variety of recreational reading tastes. Some go on to read Stephen King, Anne Rice, and Dean Koontz, which Stine's critics like Campbell see as proof of Stine's bad influence. Many start reading speculative fiction. Others polish off YA authors like Robert Cormier, Michael Cadnum, and Caroline Cooney, while others read Charles Dickens and the Bronte sisters for kicks. Kids who started reading *Goosebumps* when I first started managing a public library branch five years later were still readers and "unretarded" by their Stine years.

A friend of mine whose son is in sixth grade has been reading Stine, both *Goosebumps* and *Fear Street*s, for years. He is the number one reader in his school in the accelerated reading program, which uses many non-Stine titles. One of his favorite books is the Newbery-winning *The Giver*, and he likes the *Redwall* books (yes, those big books) by Brian Jacques. *Not a single young adult I've talked with about reading Stine told me it in any way retarded their reading, documented by the fact that they are still readers and able to read things other than "shock fiction."* Correct, I don't see any of these kids reading *Turn of the Screw*, but then again, neither do I see many adults reading it, and they don't have R.L. Stine to blame.

Stine repeatedly and emphatically states that he is not writing books where the characters grow nor does he have any pretensions toward art. Yet West can't resist making the comparison: "because his brand of literary junk food has become a bookshelf staple to millions of young readers, some comparison with the books of the past is inevitable, not in terms of art or craft (which would be unfair) but rather in terms of theme and purpose"

(*West,* 45). Stine's purpose is to sell books by making them popular, by making them entertaining, by making them scary, by filling them with recognizable characters, gross outs, and cliff-hangers. West is also diametrically opposed to Stine's entire philosophy about children's right to purely recreational reading: "Kids need some beach junk of no value to read, don't they? Emphatically, no, children need no such thing" (*West,* 46). That's a pretty extreme position that rewrites the history of children's literature. While West criticizes Stine for shock fiction that causes constant physical stimulation, she wants readers to undergo constant mental stimulation. I'm not sure that is the better deal.

Part of West's failure to accept Stine on his own terms is because he reflects conditions that she doesn't accept. For example, while many see Stine's teen characters as mirrors for his readers, West deplores those characters, writing how in Stine's world "boyfriends frustrate girlfriends, brothers are unpleasant to their sisters, parents are props, voices scream, blood flows" (*West,* 46). It's odd that West should attack these elements, because except for the blood flowing, the rest is a pretty good description of the adolescent experience. Instead of being a beautiful innocent *Anne of Green Gables* experience, adolescence is filled with a degree of nastiness, and Stine's books reflect that. In most families, teenagers do frustrate each other, act mean to each other, and raise their voices. Not nice, but normal.

After attacking Stine and "shock fiction," West's piece ends painting on a broader canvas: "Ours is, after all, a shock culture, all sensation and no feeling. . . . Is it any surprise we see this trend reflected in children's books?" (*West,* 46). For West, Stine's books are both a symptom and a by-product of a culture gone haywire, a culture that is obviously deeply different from the one she wants or wants back. Much of the criticism of Stine looks backward in this way, written by people who, perhaps, romanticize their own adolescence and that of their children as a beautiful time of innocence, when the reality is very different.

These critics perhaps didn't grow up reading books like this and they want children of today to duplicate, and thus validate, their formative reading experiences. Yet books, like all mass media products, reflect the culture, and the popular culture of the 1990s is filled with shocks: shock jocks on talk radio, shock rap and death rock filling record stores, action film after action film designed to pump up the adrenaline of the audience, shock TV like *The Jerry Springer Show*, *WWF Raw*, and *South Park*, and ultimately reading material which reflects the shock culture.

West's argument boils down to a diatribe against youth popular reading, which, like all popular culture, is not meant to be "treasured books—deep and satisfying entertainments, from *The Wind in the Willows* to *Charlotte's Web*, from *The Call of the Wild* to *Ramona* to *The Once and Future King*" (*West*, 46). Instead, the very nature of popular culture is that most of it is not treasured or lasting but temporary and satisfying: put it out, make a profit, put out another. That's what drives youth marketing—dollars and sense. One thing missing from youth popular culture has been reading. Stine managed to put that element back in, at least temporarily. Maybe it would be a better world if every child read *Charlotte's Web* and not *Monster Blood IV*, but they don't. The real horror is a culture where kids, especially boys, don't read—and Stine has done his best to stop that turn of the screw from happening in his lifetime.

AND THE RESEARCH SAYS . . .

West's arguments might sound familiar. They are similar in many ways to those advanced in the fifties against the horror comics that Stine himself loved so much. The writing was substandard, claimed the comics critics; they were nothing but a series of jolts; they weren't lasting, and they created a physical response in their readers. In this case, the physical response was thought to be juvenile delinquency, according to the anti-comics tome *Seduction of the Innocent* by Fredric Wertham.[16] The case against comics turned out to be false, as later studies have shown.[17-18] A similar protest arose in the mid-eighties with the proliferation of romance series and multiple storyline books and the concern that the works were not of quality, that they were all the same and written to formula, and again, that YAs would choose to read these titles rather than "real books."

One of the most compelling arguments against series fiction, and perhaps the strongest one made by West against Stine, wasn't just that light reading had no value, but that Stine might have a negative impact on reading. That was the theory, but it doesn't jibe with the facts. An award-winning research project by Dr. Catherine Sheldrick Ross found that series reading, far from being harmful, might be for some readers an essential stage in their development as powerful readers. After tracing the history of series books, looking at the texts themselves and working from the transcripts of 142 open-ended interviews with adult readers who read for pleasure, Ross concludes:

> Rhetoric to the contrary, series books do NOT enfeeble the reader or render them unfit for reading anything else. It is not helpful to establish a hierarchy in reading in which a reader's passionate engagement with a pleasure book somehow does not count as "real reading."[19]

She further advances that the best way to create readers is to have lots of books available, then let readers choose. This is nothing new—the value of voluntary free reading has been well documented, through readers' diaries and case studies, as well as anecdotal evidence.[20-22] What is new, and important, is Ross's finding that the idea that series reading is detrimental to other reading doesn't hold water. Ross writes that "when we listen to readers [talk about series books], it seems as if they are talking about a totally different phenomenon from the mind-weakening experience described so confidently by the reading experts" (Ross, 215).

Such research was necessary and long overdue. Ross writes:

Current critics who denounce series books as enemies of good reading
are likely to be influenced by the interpretive activity of prior readers
and certainly have the support of at least a hundred years of received
opinion against series book reading. It appears that hostility to series
books is part of a larger configuration of attitudes involving the place
of fiction in public libraries, attitudes that developed alongside the
revolution in reading and cheap book publishing that took place in
nineteenth century North America. Discourse on popular fiction has
changed very little over the past one hundred years, as becomes evident
if we compare what was said about 'trashy' fiction and dime novels in
the 1880s with what is being said now about the horror series for young
readers. (Ross, 205)

As part of her research, Ross followed a discussion on the
rec.arts.books.children newsgroup concerning the relative merits
of Stine. Ross reports back some of the better comments, noting
that rather than discussing the texts or merits of Stine's books,
"the main argument turned on beliefs about what people thought
was happening when children read" (*Ross*, 206). What Ross did
was fill in the blanks, substituting research for assumptions.
Rather than assuming what children should and should not read,
Ross writes, "The librarians quoted from the library literature of
the past 100 years seem, in hindsight, to have been overconfi-
dent in their ability to know better than the reader what choices
are best. Readers reject this presumption" (*Ross*, 233).

Ross's research seems to counter the assertion of West,
Campbell, et al. that Stine readers will be dead-ended by his
books. A second argument is that if series readers would have to
read "real" books, they would not be able to do so. There is new
research which seems to answer this charge. In an article in *The
Reading Teacher*, three college instructors reported back on interviews with eleven and twelve-year-olds about series reading
as they attempted to determine if "the reading of series books
interferes with reader appreciation for literature of high quality?
Our study would suggest that it does not."[23]   The authors of this
research article, like Ross, concluded by advocating that educators let children read what they want to read as the single best
method for creating lifelong readers.

Finally, what about the supposed harmful effects of recreational or light reading? What little research there is in this area seems to indicate that

> the fear that teachers, administrators and parents have about light reading is unfounded. Their belief that students will never advance beyond this beginning to intermediate stages has been contradicted by the evidence gathered in this pilot study. Light reading . . . includes comic books, magazines, newspapers, and novels which include adventure, mystery, romance, sports, folk-hero, science fiction, and serialized form.[24]

The authors of the study conclude that

> the findings support the hypothesis that enjoyment of light reading during youth continues throughout adulthood. Secondly, the hypothesis that light reading leads to more serious reading . . . is also supported.. Frequent light readers do become good readers who go on to advanced, complex reading tasks, an ironic finding given educational and parental concerns. Since people become good readers only by extensive reading . . . the development of reading skills needs to be nurtured at every opportunity. (*Russikoff*, 123)

The nature of the research—it involved doctoral students—didn't bring in readers weaned on Stine's scary books. But what about his and other authors' multiple storyline books, which were also examples of roller coaster style shock fiction? The descriptions of Stine's writing style by his critics, except for the gross outs, seem to apply to his early books as well. If you keep the jokes coming one after the other, is that the same dynamic as constant shocks? West wants all reading to be of high quality; Stine's not as concerned about improving the quality of a person's reading as much as making sure there is a quantity of it. There is no quality to books which remain unread.

Light reading *is* reading for lots of people. Some people want nothing more out of any book than simply to be mindlessly entertained. Witness any week on the *New York Times* best-seller list. So why this constant disrespect for popular reading coupled with the demand that people read classics? Could it be, as Dr. Mary K. Chelton suggests, because librarians are "in the seriously delusional business of improving the hell out of everybody, a questionable goal at best." [25] Is this delusion fueled by arrogance or ignorance? Regarding Stine, both play a part. From what we know about reading research, the best method to improve children's reading isn't to improve the quality of their choices, but rather the quantity of choices, which would include series fiction.

READING IS READING IS READING

Despite the criticism of Stine, reading Stine is still reading. It is still the experience of opening a book, imagining the scenes, and turning—or in Stine's case, rapidly turning—the pages. In his work *The Power of Reading* Stephen Krashen quotes from years and years of reading research and surveys. [26] The one inescapable conclusion is that readers read. It doesn't matter what they read, as long as they read. Secretary of Education Richard Riley in one of his State of American Education speeches said, "All of our research tells us that this [reading] is so important. Read a book, read the comics, or read R.L. Stine's *Goosebumps* and get scared together—it doesn't matter, just read." [27]

Many have advanced this position for some time. Professional literature exists from librarians and teachers in the "can't beat 'em, then join 'em" mode. Rather than rallying against series books, these educators have looked for ways to work the books into the classroom. As Richard Abrahamson noted in a pre-*Fear Street* article, "For many readers . . . series book reading taught them the most important lesson of all—there is something exciting to be found between the covers of a book. Perhaps all of us owe these series books and authors a debt of gratitude." [28] It seems counterproductive to actively discourage any reading behavior among young people, especially male readers, a huge chunk of the Stine audience. Give them something good to read—something interesting, exciting, and real to them because they become involved in the story, and make it easy to read—and they will read.

There is one last critical assumption that shows the division between those who like Stine and those who don't, and it is laced with irony. Those who argue against Stine want children to read better books, to read books to engage the intellect. Yet it seems in wanting these children to be smarter, they fail to give kids credit for already being smart. They seem to think that kids can be tricked into liking Stine books and that kids don't know any better than *not* to read them. They seem to assume that Stine's readers are a teeming mass of followers who don't know quality books, don't know how to spend their time, and don't know how to make decisions. Stine has a different set of assumptions toward his audience. He encourages his readers to read other authors, and one would expect that he knows he will lose them. He knows that kids who read his books are smart, they like action, and they like problem-solving, conquering fear, and feeling independent. His characters are who his readers want to be or already are. And he seems to know, like his readers and unlike West, that for kids reading is mainly fun and tries to make sure his books, as one child explained, are "never, ever boring" (Klause, 39). Bree Bristow (thirteen at the time) sums up the "kid" position on Stine nicely, saying, "We don't take these books seriously. They're scary, but they're not real."[29]

And not all teachers oppose Stine either. Writing about the effort to ban students from reading *Goosebumps* in school, teacher Maxine Kamin writes that

> as educators, we all owe R.L. Stine a big expression of thanks for generating an intense interest in reading by our young people. Many students who were not readers now voraciously read any Stine book they can get their hands on. Though his books will never be required reading, supernatural content aside, they certainly have made an impact. . . We all know that to become proficient at any skill, one must practice. If our students consider reading to be a chore, like practicing a musical instrument they aren't interested in, it's doubtful they will become lifelong readers. Stine books provide the motivation that it is so impor-

tant to progress. They also offer readers an escape, which is what the bulk of recreational reading is all about. . . . But on the whole, Stine's books do provide students with an opportunity to face their fears, and good triumphs over evil in most episodes. . . . Many young readers are already realizing the deficiencies in Stine's types of formula books. As their tastes mature, they will turn to more challenging books. [30]

Kamin's point about children realizing the problems with Stine's writing is interesting. She, unlike Stine's critics, seems to have faith in children's ability to choose better books and to grow out of reading series fiction.

But what will they grow into reading? Kristine Kathryn Rusch writing in *The Magazine of Fantasy and Science Fiction* views Stine's writing as a bridge for readers to adult speculative fiction. Like most writers new to Stine, she bought a bunch of his books, in particular *Goosebumps*, read them and looked for clues to his popularity. She found:

I had several shocks. First, I enjoyed myself. The books read quickly and scared me in a number of places. Second, I found myself wanting to read more. And third, Stine did things I didn't expect. . . . The blood and violence were offstage, however. The ghosts, zombies, phantoms, and witches I encountered were tough and scary—and all defeated by the ingenuity of the protagonists. . . . I would give R.L. Stine novels to my children. True, the books are horror, but the fears I remember from my childhood. . . . Stine is in touch and in tune with that child part of himself, and he explores it with gusto. The endings are all upbeat. . . . The books make kids examine the bogeyman in the closet and then turn on the light for reassurance. . . . My concern comes from two places. First, the assumption of the sales clerk angered me. When she mentioned that children 'don't learn anything' from these books, I snapped at her. . . . 'I think children learn a lot from Stine. They learn to enjoy reading.' She tried to argue with me that children should learn more than that until I reminded her that much of the population in this country is functionally illiterate. What children are reading matters less than the fact that they are reading and enjoying what they read. . . . We have to remember that a rollicking good story is twice as important as learning something from the text. Fiction is about adventures, excitement, and exploring ourselves. R.L. Stine has captured those elements."[31]

THE SAFE SCARE

In the big picture, the criticism of R.L. Stine is a controversy about literature, its role and influence, about a culture that is increasingly violent and whose media products reflect that. Like most issues dealing with children, it boils down to a controversy about protecting children from influences some see as harmful. The controversy has moved over from talk and writing to action in a growing number of attempts to ban *Goosebumps* from school libraries. In a school district in suburban Minneapolis, the effort to ban *Goosebumps* made national news when a complaint was filed with the school board. The complaint charged that *Goosebumps* was about children being "tormented and haunted by inanimate things coming to life."[32]

Some people like scary books; some people don't. Some people like books that are expertly written with great literary style; some don't care as long as the story is good. Some people hate horror fiction, while others enjoy it. Stine explains:

> When I visit schools and libraries I ask kids what do you like about these books. The reply is always the same: we like to be scared. . . . But why? I've thought about this question a lot, and my feeling is that the real world is a very scary place for kids these days—much scarier than my books or most TV shows and movies. In the world of *Goosebumps*, kids are independent and strong. They use their wits, their cleverness, and a little luck to defeat the scary monsters. In the stories, kids have power; in real life, childhood often means being powerless to solve the problems of the grown-up world. *Goosebumps* offers kids a chance for safe scares. They experience terrifying adventures —and they survive them—in the safety of their room. (*Stine*, 25)

Stine presents his readers with stories they know based on fears they have. He gives them, in the hour or so it takes to read his books, a chance to push through those fears, plus be entertained. Stine is, quite simply, not just a youth writer, but a youth advocate. He respects his audience, knows they are smart, certainly smarter than his critics give them credit for, and finally he believes that kids should have access to entertaining books. In particular, Stine seems most pleased that boys have taken to his books. In every interview Stine notes with pride the male readership of his work, even saying he wants his epitaph to read: "he got boys to read" (Gilson, 1997). What's so scary about that?

TOO BUSY RUNNING

Are we making too much of R.L. Stine? I think not. His books serve a purpose: they entertain. But more than that, they give kids a positive reading experience to which they can respond since the horror is fun, yet also familiar. While it might be easy to suggest that anyone could have written these books, the fact that Stine has outsold and outlasted almost everyone else working in this genre demonstrates that his genius is special and worthy of serious study. Yet, Stine knows most would disagree:

> If you want to be taken seriously as a children's book writer, the rule in all children's books is that characters have to learn to and to grow. I'm really proud that mine don't. They don't learn anything. They're too busy running. But the kids in both series solve their own problems. They use their ingenuity, their strengths, talent, and they defeat the evil in every book.[33]

Stine's doing nothing different than most other writers for kids; he just teaches his lesson by using one of the most engaging genres for kids: horror.

Stine also scares his readers by not being afraid to look at the "shadyside" of life. His characters are not all good; they are not all bad; they just are. Things happen to these characters that are both rational, yet unexplainable. As mysteries, the events in these books are mostly logical and rational, yet as horror stories they are told in an environment of the unexplainable. What drives his characters is simply their energy, their essence—the very essence of adolescence. There isn't time to focus on the issues these books explore on the shadyside, because as Stine said, his characters are too busy running. And his readers continue to run from one *Fear Street* and *Goosebumps* to the next.

NOTES

1. Sylvia Makowski, "Serious about Series: Selection Criteria for a Neglected Genre," *Voice of Youth Advocates* (February 1994): 355.

2. Barbara Moran and Susan Steinfirst, "Why Johnny (and Jane) Read Whodunits in Series," *School Library Journal* (March 1985): 116; hereafter cited in text as Moran.

3. Doris Fong, "From *Sweet Valley* They Say We Are Leaving," *School Library Journal* (January 1990): 38.

4. Susan Kundin, "Romance Versus Reality: A Look at YA Romantic Fiction." *Top of the News* (Summer 1985): 114 - 18.

5. Mary Ann Moffitt, *Understanding the Appeal of the Romance Novel for the Adolescent Girl: A Reader Response Approach,* ERIC_NO- ED 284190 (Syracuse NY: Educational Resources Information Center, 1990).

6. Mary Huntwork, "Why Girls Flock to *Sweet Valley High*," *School Library Journal* (March 1990): 140.

7. Margaret Mackey, "Filling the Gaps: *The Baby-Sitters Club*, the Series Book and the Learning Reader," *Language Arts* (September 1990): 489.

8. Patty Campbell, "The Sand in the Oyster." *The Horn Book* (March/April 1994): 234; hereafter cited in text as Campbell.

9. David Hill, "Who's Afraid of R. L. Stine?" *Teacher Magazine* (March 1996): 41; hereafter cited in text as Hill.

10. Doreen Carvajal, "In Kids' Pop Culture, Fear Rules," *New York Times* (1 June 1997): E1; hereafter cited in text as Carvajal.

11. Tom Engelhardt, "Reading May Be Harmful to Your Kids In the Nadirland of Today's Children's Books," *Harper's.* (June 1991): 56.

12. Marc Silver, "Horrors, It's R. L. Stine," *U.S. News & World Report* (23 October 1995): 95.

13. Ken Tucker, "Nameless Fear Stalks the Middle-Class Teenager," *New York Times Book Review* (14 November 1993): 27; hereafter cited in text as Tucker.

14. Diana West, "The Horror of R.L. Stine," *The Weekly Standard* (25 September 1995): 42; hereafter cited in text as West.

15. Patrick Jones, "Climbing Pike's Peak: Young Adult Thrillers," *Kliatt Paperback Book Guide* (September 1992): 4.

16. Frederic Wertham, *Seduction of the Innocent* (New York: Rinehart, 1954).

17. Larry Dorrell, "Why Comic Books?" *School Library Journal* (November 1987): 30-31.

18. Larry Dorrell, Larry Curtis, and Rampal Kuldip, "Book-worms Without Books? Student Reading Comic Books in the School House," *Journal of Popular Culture* (Fall 1995) : 223-34.

19. Catherine Sheldrick Ross, "If They Read Nancy Drew, So What? Series Book Readers Talk Back," *Library & Information Science Research* (Summer 1995): 234.

20. Robert G. Carlsen and Anne Sherrill, *Voices of Readers: How We Come to Love Books* (Urbana IL: National Council of Teachers of English, 1988).

21. Robert G. Carlsen, *Books and The Teenage Reader: A Guide to Teachers, Librarians, and Parents.* 2nd rev. ed. (New York: Bantam, 1967).

22. Mary Leonhardt, *Parents Who Love Reading, Kids Who Don't* (New York: Crown, 1993).

23. Adele Greenlee, Dianne L. Monson, and Barbara M. Taylor, "The Lure of Series Books?" *Reading Teacher* (November 1996): 224.

24. Karen Russikoff and James L. Pilgren, "Shaking the Tree of 'Forbidden' Fruit: A Study of Light Reading," *Reading Improvement* (Summer 1994): 122; hereafter cited in text as Russikoff.

25. Mary K. Chelton, "Unrestricted Body Parts and Predictable Bliss: The Audience Appeal of Formula Romances," *Library Journal* (July 1991): 49.

26. Stephen Krashen, *The Power of Reading: Insights from the Research.* (Littleton CO: Libraries Unlimited, 1993).

27. Richard Riley, "Third Annual State of American Education Address," *United States Dept. of Education* (28 February 1996) http://www.ed.gov/Speeches/02-1996/secretar.html (21 May 1997).

28. Richard E. Abrahamson, "They're Reading the Series Books So Let's Use Them," *Journal of Reading* (March 1979): 530

29. Jennifer Chauhan, "Hungry for Horror," *Teacher Magazine* (October 1992): 35.

30. Maxine Kamin, "Should Teachers Discourage R. L. Stine Books? You Don't Steer Students Away from Motivation," *American Teacher* (April 1996): 4.

31. Kristine Rusch, "Editorial: R.L. Stine's Books for Children," *The Magazine of Fantasy and Science Fiction* (August 1995): 9.

32. Tamara Henry, "*Goosebumps*' Series Scares Up More School Controversy," USA Today (13 May 1997): D7.

33. Wilder Penfield, "Chills! *Goosebumps*!" *Toronto Sun* http://canoe1.canoe.ca/JamBooksFeatures/stine_rl.html (20 May 1997).

BIBLIOGRAPHY

This bibliography is divided into four sections. The first section, "Primary Sources," is a listing of all of Stine's work as of January 1998. Stine's prodigious output posed a challenge: listing his books alphabetically would not serve the purpose of showing Stine's development as an author. Thus, I have opted for a chronological listing. Within each year, the books are in alphabetical order with series notes. Those books written by Stine under names other than R.L. Stine, including Jovial Bob, are included in this section as well and identified. Not included are those books bearing Stine's name on the cover, but written by another author. The second section, "Secondary Sources," presents books, articles, and documents about R.L. Stine and the thriller genre. The third section, "Background Sources," presents books, articles, and documents concerning the large issues discussed: popular reading, series fiction, and horror as entertainment. The fourth section, "Reviews," lists reviews of Stine's books.

New articles and web pages about Stine are constantly appearing on the Internet. A web page for this book has been prepared at the url: http://members.aol.com/naughyde/rlstine.htm.

I. PRIMARY SOURCES

BOOKS

1978
*The Absurdly Silly Encyclopedia &
Fly Swatter*. New York: Scholasitc.
As Jovial Bob Stine with Bob K.
Taylor, ill.

*How to Be Funny: An Extra-Silly
Guidebook*. New York: Dutton. As
Jovial Bob Stine with Carol
Nicklaus, ill.

1979
The Complete Book of Nerds. New
York: Scholasitc. As Jovial Bob
Stine.

*Going Out, Going Steady, Going
Bananas: The Bananas Dating
Guide*. New York: Scholasitc. As
Jovial Bob Stine.

1980
*The Dynamite Do-It-Yourself Pen
Pal Kit (Dynamite Books)*. New
York: Scholastic. As Jovial Bob
Stine with Jared D. Lee, ill.

*Dynamite's Funny Book of Sad
Facts (Dynamite Books)*. New York:
Scholastic. As Jovial Bob Stine.

The Pigs' Book of World Records.
New York: Random House. As
Jovial Bob Stine with Peter J.
Lippman, ill.

The Sick of Being Sick Book. New
York: Dutton, 1980; Scholastic. As
Jovial Bob Stine and Jane Stine,
with Carol Nicklaus, ill.

1981
*The Bananas Book of Foto Funnies
(Bananas Books)*. New York:
Scholasitc. As Jovial Bob Stine.

*Bananas Looks at Television
(Bananas Books)*. New York:
Scholastic. As Jovial Bob Stine.

*The Beast Handbook (Bananas
Books)*. New York: Scholasitc. As
Jovial Bob Stine with Bob K.
Taylor, ill.

*The Cool Kids' Guide To Summer
Camp (Vagabond Books)*. New
York: Scholasitc. As Jovial Bob
Stine and Jane Stine with Jerry
Zimmerman, ill.

Gnasty Gnomes. New York:
Random House. As Jovial Bob Stine
with Peter J. Lippman, ill.

1982
*Bored with Being Bored! How to
Beat the Boredom Blahs*. New York:
Four Winds Press, Scholastic. As
Jovial Bob Stine and Jane Stine.

*Don't Stand in the Soup: The
Funniest Guide to Manners*. New
York: Bantam. As Jovial Bob Stine
with Carol Nicklaus, ill.

The Time Raider. New York: Scholasitc.

1983
Blips: The First Book of Video Game Funnies. New York: Scholasitc. As Jovial Bob Stine.

Everything You Need to Survive Brothers & Sisters. (The Stines' Super Survival Kit ; #4) New York: Random House. As Jovial Bob Stine and Jane Stine with Sal Murdocca, ill.

Everything You Need to Survive First Dates (Stines' Super Survival Kit ; #1). New York: Random House. As Jovial Bob Stine and Jane Stine with Sal Murdocca, ill.

Everything You Need to Survive, Homework (Stines' Super Survival Kit ; #3). New York: Random House. As Jovial Bob Stine and Jane Stine with Sal Murdocca, ill.

Everything You Need to Survive Money Problems (The Stines' Super Survival Kit ; #2). New York: Random House. As Jovial Bob Stine and Jane Stine with Sal Murdocca, ill.

The Forest of Enchantment (An Advanced Dungeons & Dragons™). New York: Marvel.

Golden Sword of Dragonwalk (Twistaplot). New York: Scholasitc.

1984
Bananas Yearbook. New York: Scholastic. As Jovial Bob Stine.

The Great Superman Movie Book. New York: Scholastic.

Horrors of the Haunted Museum (Twistaplot). New York: Scholastic.

Indiana Jones and the Curse of Horror Island (Find Your Fate). New York: Ballantine Books.

Indiana Jones and the Giants of the Silver Tower (Find Your Fate). New York: Ballantine Books.

Instant Millionaire (Twistaplot). New York: Scholastic.

The Siege of the Dragonriders (Wizards, Warriors & You). New York: Avon. As Eric Affabee.

Through The Forest of Twisted Dreams (Wizards, Warriors & You). New York: Avon.

1985
The Badlands of Hark. New York: Scholastic.

Challenge of the Wolf Knight (Wizards, Warriors & You). New York: Avon Books.

Conquest of the Time Master (Wizards, Warriors & You). New York: Avon Books.

Demons of the Deep (Masters of the Universe). New York: Golden Books.

Indiana Jones and the Cult of the Mummy's Crypt (Find Your Fate). New York: Ballantine Books.

Indiana Jones and the Ape of Howling Island (Find Your Fate). New York: Ballantine Books.

The Invaders of Hark. New York: Scholastic.

James Bond in Win, Lose, or Die (Find Your Fate). New York: Ballantine Books.

Jovial Bob's Computer Joke Book. New York: Scholastic. As Jovial Bob Stine.

1986
101 Silly Monster Jokes. New York: Scholastic. As Jovial Bob Stine with Bob K. Taylor, ill.

Attack on the King (Wizards, Warriors & You). New York: Avon Books. As Eric Affabee.

Blind Date. New York: Scholastic.

Cavern of the Phantoms (Wizards, Warriors & You). New York: Avon Books.

Doggone Dog Joke Book. New York: Scholasitc. As Jovial Bob Stine.

G.I. Joe: Operation Deadly Decoy (Find Your Fate). New York: Ballantine Books.

G.I. Joe: Operation Mindbender (Find Your Fate). New York: Ballantine Books.

G.I. Joe: Operation Star Raider (Find Your Fate). New York: Ballantine Books. As Eric Affabee.

G.I. Joe and the Everglades Swamp Terror (Find Your Fate). New York: Ballantine Books. As Eric Affabee.

Golden Girl and the Vanishing Unicorn (Find your Fate). New York: Ballantine Books.

Miami Mice. New York: Scholasitc. As Jovial Bob Stine with Eric Gurney, ill.

Mystery of the Impostor (Wizards, Warriors & You). New York: Avon Books.

1987
Dragon Queen's Revenge (Wizards, Warriors & You). New York: Avon Books. As Eric Affabee.

G.I. Joe: Serpentor and the Mummy Warrior (Find Your Fate). New York: Ballantine Books.

Jet Fighter Trap (The Protectors). New York: Scholastic. As Zachary Blue.

The Petrova Twist (The Protectors). New York: Scholastic. As Zachary Blue.

Spaceballs. London: Hippo. As Jovial Bob Stine.

Twisted . New York: Scholastic.

1988
101 Wacky Kid Jokes. New York: Scholasitc. As Jovial Bob Stine with Don Orehek, ill.

Big Top Pee Wee: A Color and Fun Book. New York: Scholasitc. As Jovial Bob Stine with Paul Reubens.

Big Top Pee Wee: The Movie Storybook. New York: Scholasitc. As Jovial Bob Stine with Paul Reubens.

Broken Date (Crosswinds). New York: Pocket Books.

G.I. Joe: Jungle Raid (Find Your Fate). New York: Ballantine.

Look Out! Here Come the Raisinbusters! New York: Trumpet Club. As Jovial Bob Stine.

Siege of Serpentor (G. I. Joe). New York: Ballantine.

1989
The Baby Sitter. New York: Scholastic.

Ghostbusters II: a Novelization. New York: Scholasitc. As Jovial Bob Stine.

Missing (Fear Street). New York: Archway.

My Secret Identity: a Novelization. New York: Scholasitc. As Jovial Bob Stine.

The New Girl (Fear Street). New York: Archway.

The Overnight (Fear Street). New York: Archway.

Pork and Beans: Play Date. New York: Scholasitc. As Jovial Bob Stine with Jose Aruego, ill.

The Surprise Party (Fear Street). New York: Archway.

1990
101 Creepy Creature Jokes. New York: Scholasitc. As Jovial Bob Stine with Don Orehek, ill.

101 School Cafeteria Jokes. New York: Scholasitc. As Jovial Bob Stine with Don Orehek, ill.

101 Vacation Jokes. New York: Scholasitc. As Jovial Bob Stine with Rick Mujica, ill.

Beach Party. New York: Scholastic.

The Boyfriend. New York: Scholasitc.

Curtains. New York: Archway.

The Good News, Bad News Joke Book. New York: The Trumpet Club. As Jovial Bob Stine with Bob K. Taylor, ill.

Halloween Party (Fear Street). New York: Archway.

Haunted (Fear Street). New York: Archway.

How I Broke Up with Ernie. New York: Archway.

Phone Calls. New York: Archway.

The Stepsister (Fear Street). New York: Archway.

The Wrong Number (Fear Street). New York: Archway.

1991
The Amazing Adventures of Me, Myself and I. New York: Bantam.

The Baby Sitter II. New York: Scholastic.

The Fire Game (Fear Street). New York: Archway.

The Girlfriend. New York: Scholastic.

Jerks-in-Training (Space Cadets). New York: Scholasitc.

Lights Out (Fear Street). New York: Archway.

Losers in Space (Space Cadets). New York: Scholasitc.

Party Summer (Fear Street Super Chiller). New York: Archway.

The Secret Bedroom (Fear Street). New York: Archway.

Silent Night (Fear Street Super Chiller). New York: Archway.

Ski Weekend (Fear Street). New York: Archway.

The Sleepwalker (Fear Street). New York: Archway.

The Snowman. New York: Scholasitc.

1992
Beach House. New York: Scholastic.

The Best Friend (Fear Street). New York: Archway.

Bozos on Patrol (Space Cadets). New York: Scholastic.

Broken Hearts (Fear Street Super Chiller). New York: Archway.

First Date (Fear Street). New York: Archway.

The First Evil (Fear Street Cheerleaders). New York: Archway.

Goodnight Kiss (Fear Street Super Chiller). New York: Archway.

Hit and Run. New York: Scholasitc.

The Knife (Fear Street). New York: Archway.

Monster Blood (Goosebumps). New York: Scholastic.

The Prom Queen (Fear Street). New York: Archway.

Say Cheese & Die! (Goosebumps). New York: Scholastic.

The Second Evil (Fear Street Cheerleaders). New York: Archway.

Silent Night #2 (Fear Street Super Chiller). New York: Archway.

Stay Out of the Basement (Goosebumps). New York: Scholastic.

The Third Evil (Fear Street Cheerleaders). New York: Archway.

Welcome to Dead House (Goosebumps). New York: Scholastic.

1993
Baby Sitter III. New York: Scholastic.

Be Careful What You Wish For (Goosebumps). New York: Scholastic.

The Betrayal (Fear Street Saga). New York: Archway.

The Burning (Fear Street Saga). New York: Archway.

The Cheater (Fear Street). New York: Archway.

The Curse of the Mummy's Tomb (Goosebumps). New York: Scholastic.

The Dead Girlfriend. New York: Scholastic.

The First Horror (Fear Street: 99 Fear Street). New York: Archway.

The Ghost Next Door (Goosebumps). New York: Scholastic.

The Girl Who Cried Monster (Goosebumps). New York: Scholastic.

Halloween Night. New York: Scholastic.

The Haunted Mask (Goosebumps). New York: Scholastic.

Hitchhiker. New York: Scholastic.

Let's Get Invisible (Goosebumps). New York: Scholastic.

Night of the Living Dummy (Goosebumps). New York: Scholastic.

Piano Lessons Can Be Murder (Goosebumps). New York: Scholastic.

The Secret (Fear Street Saga). New York: Archway.

Sunburn. (Fear Street). New York: Archway.

Welcome to Camp Nightmare (Goosebumps). New York: Scholastic.

The Werewolf of Fever Swamp (Goosebumps). New York: Scholastic.

1994
Attack of the Mutant (Goosebumps). New York: Scholastic.

Bad Dreams (Fear Street). New York: Archway.

The Beast. New York: Archway.

Call Waiting. New York: Scholastic.

The Cheerleaders: The New Evil (Fear Street Super Chiller). New York: Archway.

The Dare (Fear Street). New York: Archway.

Deep Trouble (Goosebumps). New York: Scholastic.

The Dead Lifeguard (Fear Street Super Chiller). New York: Archway.

Double Date (Fear Street). New York: Archway.

Ghost Beach (Goosebumps). New York: Scholastic.

Go Eat Worms! (Goosebumps). New York: Scholastic.

Halloween Night II. New York: Scholastic.

Horrors of the Haunted Museum (Goosebumps). New York: Scholastic.

I Saw You That Night! New York: Scholastic.

The Mind Reader (Fear Street). New York: Archway.

Monster Blood II (Goosebumps). New York: Scholastic.

My Hairiest Adventure (Goosebumps). New York: Scholastic.

The New Boy (Fear Street). New York: Archway.

One Day at Horrorland (Goosebumps). New York: Scholastic.

One Evil Summer (Fear Street). New York: Archway.

Phantom of the Auditorium (Goosebumps). New York: Scholastic.

Return of the Mummy (Goosebumps). New York: Scholastic.

The Scarecrow Walks at Midnight (Goosebumps). New York: Scholastic.

The Second Horror (Fear Street: 99 Fear Street). New York: Archway.

Tales to Give You Goosebumps. New York: Scholastic.

The Third Horror (Fear Street: 99 Fear Street). New York: Archway.

The Thrill Club (Fear Street). New York: Archway.

Why I'm Afraid of Bees (Goosebumps). New York: Scholastic.

You Can't Scare Me! (Goosebumps). New York: Scholastic.

1995
The Abominable Snowman of Pasadena (Goosebumps). New York: Scholastic.

The Barking Ghost (Goosebumps). New York: Scholastic.

The Baby Sitter IV. New York: Scholastic.

Bad Moonlight (Fear Street Super Chiller). New York: Archway.

The Beast II. New York: Archway.

College Weekend (Fear Street). New York: Archway.

The Cuckoo Clock of Doom (Goosebumps). New York: Scholastic.

The Dark Secret (Fear Street: The Cataluna Chronicles). New York: Archway.

Dead End (Fear Street). New York: Archway.

The Deadly Fire (Fear Street: The Cataluna Chronicles). New York: Archway.

Evil Moon (Fear Street: The Cataluna Chronicles). New York: Archway.

Final Grade (Fear Street). New York: Archway.

The Haunted Mask II (Goosebumps). New York: Scholastic.

The Headless Ghost (Goosebumps). New York: Scholastic.

The Horror at Camp Jellyjam (Goosebumps). New York: Scholastic.

It Came from Beneath the Sink (Goosebumps). New York: Scholastic.

Monster Blood III (Goosebumps). New York: Scholastic.

More Tales to Give You Goosebumps. New York: Scholastic.

The New Year's Party (Fear Street Super Chiller). New York: Archway.

A Night in Terror Tower (Goosebumps). New York: Scholastic.

The Night of the Living Dummy (Goosebumps). New York: Scholastic.

Revenge of the Lawn Gnomes (Goosebumps). New York: Scholastic.

A Shocker on Shock Street (Goosebumps). New York: Scholastic.

The Stepsister II (Fear Street). New York: Archway.

Superstitious. New York: Warner.

Switched (Fear Street). New York: Archway.

Truth or Dare (Fear Street). New York: Archway.

Wrong Number II (Fear Street). New York: Archway.

1996
Attack of the Jack-O'-Lanterns (Goosebumps). New York: Scholastic.

Bad Hare Day (Goosebumps). New York: Scholastic.

The Beast from the East (Goosebumps). New York: Scholastic.

The Boy Next Door (Fear Street). New York: Archway.

Calling All Creeps! (Goosebumps). New York: Scholastic.

The Confession (Fear Street). New York: Archway.

Egg Monster from Mars (Goosebumps). New York: Scholastic.

The Face (Fear Street). New York: Archway.

The Fear Street Saga Collector's Edition. New York: Archway.

The First Scream (Fear Street: Fear Park). New York: Archway.

Ghost Camp (Goosebumps). New York: Scholastic.

Goodnight Kiss II (Fear Street Super Chiller). New York: Archway.

House of Whispers (Fear Street Sagas) . New York: Archway.

How I Got My Shrunken Head (Goosebumps). New York: Scholastic.

How to Kill a Monster (Goosebumps) . New York: Scholastic.

The Last Scream (*Fear Street: Fear Park*). New York: Archway.

Legend of the Lost Legend (*Goosebumps*). New York: Scholastic.

Loudest Scream (*Fear Street: Fear Park*). New York: Archway.

A New Fear (*Fear Street Sagas*). New York: Archway.

Night Games (*Fear Street*). New York: Archway.

The Night of the Living Dummy III (*Goosebumps*). New York: Scholastic.

The Perfect Date (*Fear Street*). New York: Archway.

Say Cheese & Die, Again! (*Goosebumps*). New York: Scholastic.

Secret Admirer (*Fear Street*). New York: Archway.

Silent Night III (*Fear Street Super Chiller*). New York: Archway.

Vampire Breath (*Goosebumps*). New York: Scholastic.

What Holly Heard (*Fear Street*). New York: Archway.

1997
All-Night Party (*Fear Street*). New York: Archway.

The Best Friend II (*Fear Street*). New York: Archway.

Beware the Snowman (*Goosebumps*). New York: Scholastic.

The Blob That Ate Everyone (*Goosebumps*). New York: Scholastic.

Cat (*Fear Street*). New York: Archway.

Chicken Chicken (*Goosebumps*). New York: Scholastic.

The Curse of Camp Cold Lake (*Goosebumps*). New York: Scholastic.

Deep Trouble II (*Goosebumps*). New York: Scholastic.

Don't Go to Sleep! (*Goosebumps*). New York: Scholastic.

Fear Hall: The Beginning (*Fear Street*). New York: Archway.

Fear Hall: The Conclusion (*Fear Street*). New York: Archway.

Goodnight Kiss Collector's Edition (*Fear Street*). Includes short story "The Vampire Club." New York: Archway.

Goosebumps Triple Header: Three Shocking Tales of Terror (*Goosebumps*). New York: Scholastic.

The Haunted School (Goosebumps).
New York: Scholastic.

*High Tide (Fear Street Super
Chiller).* New York: Archway.

*How I Learned to Fly
(Goosebumps).* New York:
Scholastic.

*I Live in Your Basement
(Goosebumps).* New York:
Scholastic.

Into the Dark (Fear Street). New
York: Archway.

Killer's Kiss (Fear Street). New
York: Archway.

Monster Blood IV (Goosebumps).
New York: Scholastic.

*More & More & More Tales to Give
You Goosebumps.* New York:
Scholastic.

*My Best Friend is Invisible
(Goosebumps).* New York:
Scholastic.

Rich Girl (Fear Street). New York:
Archway.

Runaway (Fear Street). New York:
Archway.

Trapped (Fear Street). New York:
Archway.

Werewolf Skin (Goosebumps). New
York: Scholastic.

*Who Killed the Homecoming
Queen? (Fear Street).* New York:
Archway.

AUTOBIOGRAPHICAL WORKS

"Ghost Writer." *Life* (December 1994): 12-13.

It Came From Ohio: My Life as a Writer, as told to Joe Arthur. New York: Scholastic, 1997.

"R.L. Stine." *Speaking for Ourselves, Too : More Autobiographical Sketches by Notable Authors of Books for Young Adults.* Edited by Donald R. Gallo. Urbana: National Council of Teachers of English, 1993.

"Why Kids Love to Get *Goosebumps.*" *TV Guide* (28 October 1995): 24-25.

UNCOLLECTED SHORT STORIES

"The Homemade Monster." *TV Guide* (15 March 1997): 26.

"The Spell." *Thirteen: 13 Tales of Terror.* Edited by Tonya Pines. New York: Scholastic, 1991.

II. SECONDARY SOURCES

BOOKS

Commire, Anne, ed. *Something About The Author.* Vol. 31. Detroit: Gale Research, 1983.

Drew, Bernard A. *The 100 Most Popular Young Adult Authors: Biographical Sketches and Bibliographies.* Littleton, CO: Libraries Unlimited, 1996.

Hedblad, Alan, ed. *Children's Literature Review,* Vol. 37. Detroit: Gale Research, 1996.

Hile, Kevin S. and E.A. DesChenes, eds. *Authors and Artists for Young Adults.* Vol. 13. Detroit: Gale Research, 1994.

Holtze, Sally Holmes, ed. *Seventh Book of Junior Authors & Illustrators.* New York: H.W. Wilson, 1996.

Hubbard, Andrea. "An Analysis of the Incidence of Havighurst's Developmental Tasks in the Adolescent Horror Novels of R. L. Stine and Christopher Pike." Master's Theses, University of North Carolina at Chapel Hill, 1994.

Jones, Patrick. "Thrillers." In *Children's Books and Their Creators,* edited by Anita Silvey. New York: Houghton Mifflin, 1996.

— "R.L. Stine." In *Twentieth Century Young Adult Writers.* Detroit: Gale Research, 1995.

Keaton, Claudia. *Teacher's Guide to Young Adult Mystery/Horror Bestsellers.* New York: Archway, 1991.

Locher, Francis, ed. *Contemporary Authors.* Vol. 105. Detroit: Gale Research, 1982.

Powell, Steven L. "Fright Light: A Content Analysis of R. L. Stine's 'Goosebumps,' and Selected Other Juvenile Horror Fiction Series." Masters Theses, University of North Carolina at Chapel Hill, 1995.

Roginski, James W. *Behind The Covers: Interviews with Authors and Illustrators of Books for Children and Young Adults*. Littleton, CO : Libraries Unlimited, 1985

Straub, Deborah, ed. *Contemporary Authors*. New Revision Series. Detroit: Gale Research, 1988.

Telgen, Diane, ed. *Something About the Author*. Vol. 76. Detroit: Gale Research, 1994.

Wheeler, Jill C., *R.L. Stine*. Minneapolis: Abdo & Daughters, 1996.

MAGAZINE AND JOURNAL ARTICLES

"1996 Shows Decline in Book Challenges." *Library Journal* (1 April 1997): 18-19.

Alderdice, Kit. "R. L. Stine: 90 Million Spooky Adventures." *Publishers Weekly* (17 July 1995): 208-9.

"Attack of the Thriller Books." *Time for Kids* (1 November 1996): 4-5.

Benezra, Karen. "Scholastic's Cool Ghouls." *Brandweek* (3 June 1996): 46-48.

— "Kraft Foods Contracts *Goosebumps*." *Brandweek* (22 January 1996): 37-40.

Bethune, Brian. "Master of Thrills and Chills." *Maclean's* (11 December 1995): 46.

"Big Deal: *Goosebumps*." *Mediaweek* (8 July 1996): 8.

Bodart, Joni Richards. "In Defense of Horror Fiction." *Book Report* (March April 1994): 25-6.

Budge, David. "Schlock of the New Craving for Horror." *The Times Educational Supplement* 4116 (19 May 1995): 8.

Campbell, Patricia, "The Sand in the Oyster." *The Horn Book* (March/April 1994): 234-38.

— "The Sand in the Oyster." *The Horn Book* (November/December 1994): 756-59.

Chauhan, Jennifer. " Hungry for Horror." *Teacher Magazine* (October 1992): 18-19+.

Claro, Danielle. "The *Goosebumps* Guy." *Nickelodeon Magazine* (April-May 1995): 10.

Cornwell, Tim. "Children Crazy for 'Easy Read' Horror." *The Times Educational Supplement* 4181 (16 August 1996): 12.

Dugan, Jeanne. "The Thing That Ate the Kids' Market." *Business Week* (11 November 1996): 174-76.

Dunleavey, M. P. "Children's Writers Plumb the Depths of Fear." *Publishers Weekly* (27 March 1995): 28-29.

— "Books that Go Bump in the Night." *Publishers Weekly* (5 July 1993): 30-31.

Eaglen, Audrey B. "New Blood for Young Readers." *School Library Journal* (December 1989): 49.

Engelhardt, Tom. "Reading May Be Harmful to Your Kids In the Nadirland of Today's Children's Books." *Harper's* (June 1991): 55-62.

Ermelino, Louisa. "Talking with . . . R.L. Stine." *People Weekly* (9 October 1995): 32.

Flamm, Matthew. "Between the Lines." *Entertainment Weekly* (14 March 1997): 72.

— "Between the Lines." *Entertainment Weekly* (9 January 1998): 63.

Freeman, Laurie. "Searching for the Next *Goosebumps*." *Advertising Age* (12 February 1996): S4-S6.

"*Goosebumps* Author Primed for TV." *Mediaweek* (24 March 1997): 5.

"*Goosebumps* Promotion." *Mediaweek* (8 July 1996): 28.

"*Goosebumps* with Every Gulp." *Publishers Weekly* (2 September 1996): 41.

Gray, Paul. "Carnage: An Open Book." *Time* (2 August 1993): 54.

Girxit, Joe. "Fear, Fiction and the Adolescent." *New University Quarterly* (Summer 1992): 243-51.

Hill, David. "Who's Afraid of R.L. Stine?" *Teacher Magazine* (March 1996): 38-41.

"The Horror Book Explosion." *Zillions* (1 July 1997): 22.

"The Horror, The Horror: The Pros and Cons of Series Fiction Take on a New Dimension with the Advent of Young-Adult Horror." *Quill & Quire* 60, no. 5 (1994): 34-35.

Hughes, Susan. "Scare Tactics." *Chatelaine* (June 1996): 24.

Jensen, Jeff. "*Goosebumps* Goes to Extremes." *Advertising Age* (28 October 1996): 8.

— "*Goosebumps* Promotion Lures Taco Bell, General Mills." *Advertising Age* (9 June 1997): 53.

Johnson, Sharlene King. "Tales from the Crypt." *Ladies Home Journal* (October 1992): 117.

Jones, M. "R.L. Stine: Big Scares for Small Readers." *Newsweek* (30 October 1995): 80.

Jones, Patrick. "Climbing Pike's Peak: Young Adult Thrillers." *Kliatt Young Adult Paperback Guide* (September 1992): 3-4.

— "Have No Fear: Scary Stories for the Middle Grades." *Emergency Librarian* (September/October 1993): 30-32.

Kamin, Maxine. "Should Teachers Discourage R. L. Stine Books? You Don't Steer Students Away from Motivation." *American Teacher* (April 1996): 4.

Kanner, Bernice. "Too Much Ado about *Goosebumps*." *Journal of Commerce and Commercial* (31 July 1996): 7A.

Kaplan, James. "Scare Tactics." *TV Guide* (26 October 1996): 30.

"Kids' Book Licenses Become Best Sellers." *Discount Store News* (18 November 1996): 39-40.

Kies, Cosette. "EEEK! They Just Keep Coming! YA Horror Series." *Voice of Youth Advocates* (April 1994): 17-19.

— "Horror Fiction in School Library Media Centers." *School Library Media Activities Monthly* (May 1993): 29-30.

La Franco, Robert. "Page Turners." *Forbes* (8 May 1995): 131.

Lodge, Sally. "Life After *Goosebumps*: Kids' Horror Genre Assumes Monstrous Proportions." *Publishers Weekly* (2 December 1996): 24-27.

Mallory, Michael. "Scare Fare." *Variety* (9 December 1996): 46-7.

Matas, Alina. "Popular *Goosebumps* Kids' Books Spawn Clothes Line." *Knight-Ridder/Tribune Business* (12 July 1996): unpaged.

McCoy, Tim. "Is There Life After *Goosebumps*?" *The Literature Base* (August 1996): 24.

McGillis, Roderick. "R. L. Stine and the World of Child Gothic." *Bookbird* 33, no. 3-4 (1995): 15+.

"Meet R.L. Stine." *Waldenbooks Kid's News* (Spring 1995): 1.

Miller, Cyndee. "Scary, but Nice." *Marketing News* (7 October 1996): 2.

Milliot, Jim. "Retail Sales, Media Ventures Spur Growth at Scholastic." *Publishers Weekly* (23 September 1996): 11.

— "Scholastic Plans Consolidation After Overexpansion." *Publishers Weekly* (5 May 1997): 10.

Moy, Suelain. "To Shock Is the System: Teen Thriller Novels." *Entertainment Weekly* (31 January 1992): 68.

"One for the Books for Kraft: *Goosebumps* Tie-in." *Supermarket News* (12 February 1996): 12.

"R. L. Stine." *Biography Today* (April 1994): 106-11.

"R. L. Stine: The 25 Most Intriguing People '95." *People Weekly* (25 December/ 1 January 1996): 102-3.

Reid, Calvin. "Golden to Publish New Series by R.L. Stine." *Publishers Weekly* (18 August 1997): 10-12+.

Roback, Diane. "Hollywood and Horror." *Publishers Weekly* (7 March 1994): S14.

— "*Lion King* Roars, *Goosebumps* Soar." *Publishers Weekly* (20 March 1995): S17-S23.

— "The Year of the Paperback." *Publishers Weekly* (4 March 1996): S24+.

Rud, Rita. "How about Asking a Child for a Change? An Interview with a Ten-Year-Old *Goosebumps* Fan." *Bookbird* (Fall 1995): 22.

Rusch, Kristine. "Editorial: R.L. Stine's Books for Children." *The Magazine of Fantasy and Science Fiction.* (August 1995): 5-9.

Santow, Dan and Tony Kahn. "The Scarier the Better." *People Weekly* (14 November 1994): 115-16.

Sarland, Charles. "Attack of the Teenage Horrors." *Signal* 74, no. 1: 49-62.

— "Revenge of the Teenage Horror." *Signal* 74, no. 2: 113-132.

"The Scary Truth About R. L. Stine." *Scholastic Scope* (20 October 1995): 10.

Silver, Marc. "Horrors, It's R. L. Stine." *U.S. News & World Report* (23 October 1995): 95-96.

Stanley, T. L. "Scaring Kids for a Living." *Mediaweek* (4 November 1996): 9-12.

Stalter, Katharine. "*Goosebumps*' Stirs Rights Talk." *Variety* (2 October 1995): 91.

Stasio, Marilyn. "Children's Books: Under the Spell of Scary Stuff." *New York Times Book Review* (9 June 1991): 53.

Tabor, Mary B. W. "Grown-Ups Deserve Some Terror, Too." *The New York Times Biographical Service* (September 1995): 1316-18.

Tobenkin, David. "Fox Gets *Goosebumps*." *Broadcasting & Cable* (17 April 1995): 16.

Tucker, Ken. "Nameless Fear Stalks the Middle-Class Teenager." *New York Times Book Review* (14 November 1993): 27+.

Turbide, Diane. "The Kidlit Boom." *Maclean's* (11 December 1995): 44-48.

Unger, Jeff. "Get *Goosebumps*." *Parenting* (October 1996): 72.

Voight, Joan. "*Goosebumps* Characters Enliven Pizza Hut Ad Touting Promotion." *Adweek - Western Ed.* (5 May 1997): 5.

West, Diana. "The Horror of R.L. Stine." *The Weekly Standard* (25 September 1995): 42-46.

— "The Horror of R. L. Stine." *American Educator* (Fall 1995): 39-41.

— "Should Teachers Discourage R. L. Stine Books?" *American Teacher* (April 1996): 4.

Zancanella, Don. "The Horror, the Horror." *English Journal* (February 1994): 9-11.

NEWSPAPER ARTICLES

"Author Donates $30,000 to Bexley Schools." *Columbus Dispatch* (31 May 1996): C5.

Bash, Alan. "*Goosebumps* Spreading Fast." *USA Today* (1 December 1995): D1.

Bates, Steve. "The Thrill of the Fright." *Washington Post* (7 August 1994): B1.

Becker, Eve. "The King of Creepy." *Chicago Tribune* (12 July 1994): sec. 7: p. 1.

Bertelson, Christine. "Goosebumps Gives Educator the Creeps." *St. Louis Post-Dispatch* (19 October 1996): B1.

Blais, Jacqueline. "Sales of Early Goosebumps Chill." *USA Today* (27 February 1997): D6.

— "Spooky Stine Tackles TV Next." *USA Today* (6 April 1995): D4.

Blumefeld, Laura. "Frightfully Glad to Meet You." *Washington Post* (8 December 1995): F1.

Bonne, Lori. "R.L. Had Some Time to Kill. . . . So He Chilled with US!" *Chicago Tribune* (27 May 1997): G1.

Brownlee, Lisa L. "*Goosebumps* Deal Is in the (Doritos) Bag." *Wall Street Journal* (10 July 1996): B1.

Carvajal, Doreen. "In Kids' Pop Culture, Fear Rules." *New York Times* (1 June 1997): E1.

Deep, Said. "Scary Tale Books Hot with Kids." *Detroit News & Free Press* (9 April 1995): D5.

"Boo Is for Books." *Wall Street Journal* (27 October 1994): A1.

Donahue, Deidre. "Going On-line with R.L. Stine." *USA Today* (27 October 1994): D8.

— "R.L. Stine has a Frightful Way with Pre-teen Readers." *USA Today* (3 December 1993): D6.

Favre, Jeff. "He Has Scared Kids For Years." *Chicago Tribune* (11 October 1995): C1.

Gabriel, Trip. "Real Goose Bumps for Scholastic As Its Share Price Plunges 40%." *New York Times* (22 February 1997): A35.

Gammerman, Amy. "Gnarliatious Novels." *Wall Street Journal* (29 November 1991): A20.

Gelene, Denise. "Scary Up Scads of Young Readers." *Los Angeles Times* (7 August 1996): A1.

"Getting a Grip on Goosebumps." *Chicago Tribune* (7 April 1997): A12.

Gilson, Nancy. "Of Shivers & *Goosebumps*." *Columbus Dispatch* (30 March 1995): H1.

— "The Real King of Fear." *Columbus Dispatch* (5 June 1997): E8.

— "Safely Scary." *Columbus Dispatch* (10 March 1994): G8.

"*Goosebumps* Books Too Scary For Kids?" *Reuters News Service* (3 January 1997).

Halls, Kelly Milner. "It's Getting Bumpier! R.L. Stine Kills Off Old *Goosebumps* for Scarier Tales in His *Series 2000*." *The Atlanta Constitution* (12 January 1998): D3.

Harris, Roy. "Children's Bookshelf." *Los Angeles Times* (13 March 1996): BR11.

Henry, Tamara. "Goosebumps Series Scares up More School Controversy." *USA Today* (29 January 1997): D7.

Howard, Susan. "Fairy Tales from Hell: Between Dr. Seuss and Stephen King are Authors like R.L. Stine Who Write, Like, Really Scary Books." *Newsday* (21 July 1994): B4.

Jefferson, Graham. "Fox Gets *Goosebumps*." *USA Today* (24 October 1995): D3.

Kaplan, Fred. "*Goosebumps* for Grown-Ups." *Boston Globe* (31 October 1995): 61.

King, Susan. "Giving Kids Big *Goosebumps*." *Los Angeles Times* (29 June 1997): TV5.

Malitz, Nancy. "CD Romp: Goosebumps Scares Up Fun in New Game." *Detroit News* (2 October 1997): E6.

Minzesheimer, Bob. "The Leaders of the Banned." *USA Today* (18 September 1997): D6.

Morgan, Heather. "Making It Cool to Read." *Los Angeles Times* (7 April 1995): Valley Edition 11.

O'Briant, Don. "Giving Adults *Goosebumps*." *Atlanta Constitution* (18 September 1995): B1.

O'Harrow, Robert Jr. "Budding Bookworms." *Washington Post* (8 December 1995): C1.

Peace, Sara. "Books for Children: Chills and Thrills from R.L. Stine." *Gannett News Service* (5 August 1996).

Salliant, Catherine. "Things that Go *Goosebumps* in the Night." *Los Angeles Times* (30 October 1995): A3.

School Becomes Nightmare for Parents." *Washington Post* (22 January 1997): A3.

Sell, Shawn. "Stine Gives Kids *Goosebumps* with Frightening Speed." *USA Today* (31 October 1996): D4.

Stepp, Diane R. "Panel to Decide Book Ban." *The Atlanta Constitution* (14 May 1997): A1.

Tabor, Mary B. "Grown-Ups Deserve Some Terror, Too." *New York Times* (7 September 1995): C1.

— "Hints of Horror, Shout of Protest." *New York Times* (2 April 1997): A16.

"Talking with R.L. Stine." *Kidsday/Newsday* (14 April 1996): n.p.

Tobin, James. "Kids' Love of Gore Horrifies Parents but Not Librarians." *Detroit News* (10 April 1997): C1.

Vogt, Amanda. "*Goosebumps;* The Books Are a Thrill, But." *Chicago Tribune* (16 April 1996): E1.

Warrick, Pamela. "Nightmare on Wall Street." *Los Angeles Times* (13 June 1997): E1

Will, Ed, "Frightfully Good Books." *Denver Post* (22 December 1993): F1.

Yip, Pamela. "A Big Scare for Investors." *Houston Chronicle* (22 February 1997): C1.

Yon-Smith, Song-Mee. "*Goosebumps* Books Are the Best." *Washington Post* (19 January 1997): C7.

Zaslow, Jeffrey. "R.L. Stine" *USA Weekend* (27 April 1997): 22.

ARTICLES FROM THE INTERNET

Casini, Dave. "Things That Goosebump in the Night." *PC World*, http:/
www.pcworld.com/annex/games/articles/nov_96/goosebump.html (7
March 1997).

Erbe, Bonnie and Josette Shiner. "Should Schools Ban *Goosebumps*?
Pro/Con" *The Journal*, http://www.jrnl.com/news/97/February/
jrn81130297.html (7 March 1997).

Hart, Michael. "*Goosebumps* Fans Meet Their Scary Hero." *Fort Worth Star-
Telegram*, http://www.star-telegram/CLASSACTS10/
1:CLASSACTS10031396.html (7 March 1997).

Larabee, John. "Fears: Mask *Goosebumps* or Terror." *Detroit News*,
http://detnews.com/menu/stories/41516.htm (14 February 1997).

Lippman, L. "R.L. Stine Still Giving Children *Goosebumps*." *Salt Lake Tribune*, http://www.sltrib.com:80/96/FEBRUARY/02/thf
/21011513.htm (7 March 1997).

Maurstad, Tom. "A Night in Terror Town." *Dallas Morning News*,
http://www.newstimes.com/archive/February2396/tv.htm (7 March 1997).

Penfield, Wilder. "Chills! *Goosebumps*!" *Toronto Sun*, http://canoe1.
canoe.ca/JamBooksFeatures/stine_rl.html (20 May 1997).

Rosenberg, Joyce. "*Goosebumps* Books Take Over." *Houston Chronicle*,
http://www.chron.com/content/chroncile/business/96/10/27/*Goosebumps*.ht
ml (14 February 1997).

— "*Goosebumps*: So Successful It's Scary." *Source*, http://sddt.com/
files/librarywire/DN0_96_10_22_1c.html (3 March 1997).

Soucy, Glenn. "Escape from Horrorland." *Coming Soon*,
http://www.csoon.com/issue23/goosebmp.htm (17 May 1997).

Stavish, Monica. "Children's Writer Worth Wait for Fans." *Fort Worth Star-
Telegram*, http://neterrant.net:80/news/doc/1047/1:NE11/
1:NE11031096.html (14 February 1997).

— "Signing by *Goosebumps* R.L. Stine Will Thrill Young Fans." *Fort Worth
Star-Telegram*, ttp://neterrant.net:80/news/doc/1047/1:NE24/
1:NE2403041096.html (14 February 1997).

"Talking Back: Censorship of *Goosebumps*." *Houston Chronicle*,
http://www.chron.com:80/content/chronicle/yo/97/01/30/yo-
talkingback.html (21 May 1997).

Thorn, Patti. "*Goosebumps* So Successful It's Scary." *Detroit News*,
http://detnews.com/menu/stories/46217.htm (14 February 1997).

Tobin, James. "Children's Books: Kids' Love of Gore Horrifies Parents But
Not Librarian." *The Detroit News*, http://detnews.com/1997/metro/9704/
10/04/0400164.htm (19 December 1997).

Van Dine, Lynn. "Library Ignores Calls to Ban Books by Defending the *Goosebumps* Novels as Entertaining for Kids." *The Detroit News*,
http://detnews.com/1997/metlife/9710/08/10080015.htm (7 May 1997).

Warrick, Pamelia. "*Goosebumps* Creator Sees Nightmare Come True." *Augusta Chronicle,* http://augustachronicle.com/stories/062997 /fe_stine.html (19 December 1997).

OTHER INTERNET DOCUMENTS

"All-Time Best-Selling Paperback Children's Books." *Publishers Weekly Online Edition,* http://www.bookwire.com/pw/articles/childrens/all-time-paperbacks.html (7 May 1997).

"Authors Online, Interview Transcript: R.L. Stine." *The Scholastic Network,* http://network.scholastic.com/network/authors/gallery/stine/transcript.htm (14 February 1997).

"Authors Online, Meet the Author: R.L. Stine." *The Scholastic Network,* http://network.scholastic.com/network/authors/gallery/stine/index.htm (14 February 1997).

"Conversation with R.L. Stine: Archive." http://www.ralphbunche.rbs.edu/ WW/pr9697/rlstine (7 May 1997).

"Exclusive TBR Interview with R.L. Stine." *The Book Report,* http://steamship.bookwire.com/TBR/transcripts.article$4178 (19 December 1997).

Kersten, Katherine. "Goosebumps Is Shock Fiction." *Center for the American Experiment,* http://www.amexp.org/strib12997.htm (7 May 1997).

"A Live Chat with R.L. Stine." *The Scholastic Network* via America Online (conducted 31 October 1994).

MacDonald, J.D. "R.L. Stine Meets Diana West." http://www.sff.net/ eople/doylemacdonald/r_rant01.htm (7 May 1997).

"Meet Matt Stine." *The Bumps,* http://thebumps.simplenet.com/gbmatt.htm (7 May 1997).

"Minnesota Parents Want to Ice the *Goosebumps* Book Series." *CNN Interactive,* http://cnn.com/US/9701/24/goosebumps.index.html (7 May 1997).

"Online Focus: Pulp Friction." *Online News Hour,* http://www1.pbs.org:80 /newshour/bb/education/Februaryruary97/ (14 February 1997).

Riley, Richard. "Third Annual State of American Education Address." *United States Department of Education* (28 February 1996) http://www.ed.gov/Speeches/02-1996/secretar.html (21 May 1997).

"Robert Lawrence Stine." *Internet Roundtable,* http://www.irsociety.com/ stine.html (5 May 1997).

"Webchat Broadcasting System Interview with R.L. Stine." *Internet Roundtable,* http://www.irsociety.com/recent/transtin/html (5 May 1997).

"YA Mystery/Horror Titles." *Simon Says,* http://www.simonsays.com/ 4785657017/01716861/kidzone/teach/mystery/stine.html (7 May 1997).

OTHER DOCUMENTS/UNPUBLISHED MANUSCRIPTS

Christenbury, Leila. *Things That Go Bump in the Night: Recent Developments in Horror Fiction for Young Adults* ERIC_NO- ED360638 (Syracuse NY: Educational Resources Information Center).

Kies, Cosette. *Cover Art, Consumerism, and YA [Young Adult] Reading Choices.* ERIC_NO- ED391487 (Syracuse: NY: Educational Resources Information Center).

Makowski, Silvia. *Serious About Series.* Lanham MD: Scarecrow Press, forthcoming 1998.

Nodelman, Perry. "The Ordinary Monstrosity: the World of *Goosebumps.*" (unpublished)   Winnipeg, Manitoba, Canada: University of Winnipeg, 1997.

III.   BACKGROUND SOURCES

POPULAR READING AND SERIES FICTION

Abrahamson, Richard E. "They're Reading the Series Books So Let's Use Them." *Journal of Reading* (March 1979): 523-30.

Bardola, Nicola. "The Sense of Violence in Children's Literature." *Bookbird* (Fall 1993): 6.

Browder, Rusty. "The Password is Paperbacks." *The Horn Book* (February 1981): 30-37.

Campbell, Patty. "The Sand in the Oyster." *The Horn Book* (December 1996): 776-80.

Carlsen, G. Robert. *Books and The Teenage Reader: A Guide to Teachers, Librarians, and Parents.* 2nd rev. ed. New York: Bantam, 1967.

— and Anne Sherrill. *Voice of Readers: How We Come to Love Books.* Urbana IL: National Council of Teachers of English, 1988.

Cart, Michael. *From Romance to Realism: 50 years of Growth and Change in Young Adult Literature.* New York: HarperCollins, 1996.

Caywood, Caroline. "Series Fiction." *School Library Journal* (August 1992): 94.

Chelton, Mary K. "Unrestricted Body Parts and Predictable Bliss: The Audience Appeal of Formula Romance." *Library Journal* (July 1991): 44-49.

Copeland, Jeffrey S. "Multiple Storyline Books for Young Adults." *English Journal* (December 1987): 52-54.

Deane, Paul. "Violence in Children's Fiction Series." *Journal of Popular Literature* (Fall 1990): 67-74.

Dorrell, Larry. "Why Comic Books?" *School Library Journal* (November 1987): 30-32.

— Larry Curtis and Rampbal Kuldip. "Book-worms Without Books? Student Reading Comic Books in the School House." *Journal of Popular Culture* (Fall 1995) 223-34.

Fader, Daniel. *Hooked on Books*. New York: Berkley, 1966.

Fong, Doris. "From *Sweet Valley* They Say We Are Leaving." *School Library Journal* (January 1990): 38-39.

Genco, Barbara, et al. "Juggling Popularity and Quality." *School Library Journal* (March 1991): 115-19.

Greenlee, Adele A., Dianne L. Monson, and Barbara M. Taylor. "The Lure of Series Books: Does it Affect Appreciation for Recommended Literature?" *Reading Teacher*. (November 1996): 216-25.

Huntwork, Mary. "Why Girls Flock to *Sweet Valley High*." *School Library Journal* (March 1990): 137-40.

Jones, Patrick. "A Series of Choices; A Choice of Series." *The Booktalker* 2 (Fall 1995): 59-62.

— *Connecting Young Adults and Libraries*. 2nd ed. New York NY: Neal-Schuman, 1998.

Krashen, Stephen. *The Power of Reading*. Littleton CO : Libraries Unlimited, 1993.

— and Joanne Ujiie. "Comic Book Reading, Reading Enjoyment, and Pleasure Reading Among Middle Class and Chapter 1 Middle School Students." *Reading Improvement* (Spring 1996): 51-54.

Kundin, Susan G. "Romance Versus Reality: A Look at YA Romances." *Top of the News* (Summer 1985): 114-18.

Leonhardt, Mary. *Parents Who Love Reading, Kids Who Don't*. New York: Crown, 1993.

— *Keeping Kids Reading*. New York: Crown, 1996.

Mackey, Margaret. "Filling the Gaps: *The Babysitters Club*, the Series Book and the Learning Reader." *Language Arts* (September 1990): 484-89.

Makowski, Silvia. "Serious About Series: Selection Criteria For a Neglected Genre." *Voice of Youth Advocates* (February 1994): 349-51.

McCrackin, Mark. "Like Cereals and Soaps: the Marketing of Paperbacks." *Top of the News* (Spring 1982): 247-50.

Meagher, Joe. *Readioactive: How to Get Kids Reading for Pleasure*. New York: Paperjacks, 1985.

Moffett, Mary Anne. *Understanding the Appeal of the Romance Novel for the Adolescent Girl*. ERIC DOC NO 2841940 . Syracuse, NY: Educational Resources Information Center, 1985.

Moran, Barbara. "Why Johnny (and Jane) Read Whodunits in Series." *School Library Journal* (March 1985): 113-17.

Nell, Victor. "The Psychology of Reading for Pleasure." *Reading Research Quarterly* (Winter 1988): 21+.

— *Lost in a Book: The Psychology of Reading for Pleasure.* New Haven: Yale University Press, 1988.

Nilsen, Alleen Pace. "Big Business, Young-Adult Literature and The Boston Pops." *English Journal* (February 1993): 70-5.

Reid, Louann and Ruth Cline. "Our Repressed Reading Addictions: Teachers and Young Adult Series Books." *English Journal* (March 1997): 86-72.

Roback, Diane. "Selling Young Adult Books." *Publishers Weekly* (19 October 1984): 24-27.

Ross, Catherine Sheldrick. "If They Read Nancy Drew, So What? Series Book Readers Talk Back." *Library & Information Science Research* (Summer 1995): 201-36.

— "Reading Series Books: What Readers Say." *School Library Media Quarterly* (Spring 1986): 165-71.

— "Reading the Covers off Nancy Drew." *Emergency Librarian* (1 May 1997): 19.

Russikoff, Karen A. "Shaking the Tree of 'Forbidden' Fruit: A Study of Light Reading." *Reading Improvement* (Summer 1994): 122-24.

Saltman, Judith. "Groaning Under the Weight of Series Books." *Emergency Librarian* (May 1996): 23.

Sutton, Roger. "Librarians and the Paperback Romance." *School Library Journal* (November 1985): 25-29.

Wertham, Frederick M. *Seduction of the Innocent.* New York: Rinehart, 1954.

HORROR AS ENTERTAINMENT

Bettelheim, Bruno. *The Uses of Enchantment.* New York: Dial Books, 1983.

Dika, Vera. *Games of Terror: Halloween, Friday the 13th, and The Films of the Stalker Cycle.* Rutherford NJ : Fairleigh Dickinson University Press, 1990.

Grixti, Joseph. *Terrors of Uncertainty : The Cultural Contexts of Horror Fiction.* London and New York: Routledge, 1989.

Hainer, Cathy. "*Animorphs* Evolve into a Kids' Hit." *USA Today* (25 September 1997): D8.

Huang, Thomas. "Oh That's Gross! Pop Culture Has Developed a Taste for the Tasteless." *Dallas Morning News* (7 January 1998): C1.

Ingrassia, Michelle. "What if the Three Little Pigs Tried Conflict Mediation?" *Newsweek* (31 January 1994): 63.

Johnson, Deirdre D. "Adolescents' Motivations for Viewing Graphic Horror." *Human Communications Research* (June 1995): 522-52.

Kendrick, Walter. *The Thrill of Fear: 250 Years of Scary Entertainment.* New York: Grove Weidenfeld, 1991.

Kies, Cosette. *Presenting Young Adult Horror Fiction.* Boston: Twayne, 1988

— *Supernatural Fiction for Teens: More than 1300 Paperbacks to Read for Wonderment, Fear and Fun.* 2nd ed. Littleton CO: Libraries Unlimited, 1992.

King, Stephen. *Stephen King's Dance Macabre.* New York: Everet House, 1991.

Klause, Annette Curtis. "The Lure of Horror." *School Library Journal* (November 1997): 38-39.

Molitor, Fred and Barry S. Sapolsky. "Sex, Violence and Victimization in Slasher Films." *Journal of Broadcasting and Electronic Media* (Spring 1993): 233-42.

Oliver, Mary Beth. "Adolescents Enjoyment of Graphic Horror." *Communication Research* (February 1993): 30-50.

Paul, William. *Laughing, Screaming: Modern Hollywood Horror and Comedy.* New York : Columbia University Press, 1994.

Pinsker, Beth. "When Movies Get Medieval: Gothic Traditions Underlie Hollywood's Latest Screaming Fad." *Dallas Morning News* (20 December 1997): C5.

Skal, David J. *The Monster Show: A Cultural History of Horror.* New York: Norton, 1993.

Smalley, Barbara. "Are Horror Movies Too Horrible for Kids?" *Redbook* (October 1990): 36-37.

Twitchell, James B. *Dreadful Pleasures: An Anatomy of Modern Horror.* New York : Oxford University Press, 1985.

IV. Reviews

ALA Booklist = BL
Book Report = BR
Children's Book Watch = CBW
Emergency Librarian = EL
English Journal = EJ
Library Journal =LJ
Locus Science Fiction Review =
    Locus
New York Times Book Review =
    NYTBR
Publishers Weekly = PW
Reading Teacher = RT
School Library Journal = SLJ
Voice Of Youth Advocates =
    VOYA

99 Fear Street: The First Horror
    Locus (Sept. 1994) : 64.
    VOYA (Dec. 1994) : 290.
99 Fear Street: The Second Horror
    Locus (Oct. 1994) : 55.
    VOYA (Aug. 1995) : 144.
Attack of The Mutant
    RT (Oct. 1995) : 144.
The Baby Sitter
    PW (14 July 1989) : 79.
    VOYA (Feb. 1990) : 347.
The Baby Sitter II
    JR (Nov. 1993) : 223.
    VOYA (April 1992) : 36.
The Baby Sitter III
    VOYA (April 1994) : 40.
Badlands of Hark
    SLJ (Jan. 1986) : 82.
Beach House
    Kliatt (Nov. 1992) : 12.
    VOYA (April 1993) : 47.
Beach Party
    SLJ (Nov. 1981) : 151.
    BR (Jan. 1991) : 66.

SLJ (Jan. 1991) : 97.
    VOYA (Feb. 1991) : 368.
The Beast
    Locus (July 1994) : 61.
The Best Friend
    Kliatt (March 1993) : 10.
    VOYA (April 1993) : 47.
Blind Date
    BL (15 Sept. 1986) : 121.
    EJ (April 1989) : 88.
    Kliatt (Fall 1986) : 18.
    PW (22 Aug. 1986) : 102.
    SLJ (Nov. 1986) : 108.
    VOYA (April 1987) : 33.
Bored with Being Bored
    SLJ (Jan. 1983): 79.
The Boyfriend
    BR (May 1991) : 66.
    Locus (April 1991) : 44.
    VOYA (June 1991) : 114.
Broken Date
    CBW (Nov. 1981) : 7.
Broken Hearts
    Kliatt (March 1993) : 10.
    VOYA (June 1993) : 105.
Call Waiting
    RT (Oct. 1995) : 141.
    VOYA (Aug. 1994) : 150.
Challenge of The Wolf Knight
    SLJ (Jan. 1986) : 82.
    VOYA (Feb. 1986) : 400.
The Cheater
    VOYA (Aug. 1993) : 158.
Cheerleaders: The First Evil
    CBW (Oct. 1993) : 2.
    Locus (Jan. 1995) : 51.
    VOYA (Feb. 1993) : 360.
Cheerleaders: The Second Evil
    Kliatt (Jan. 1993) : 13.
    CBW (Oct. 1993) : 2.
    VOYA (Feb. 1993) : 360.

Cheerleaders: The Third Evil
  CBW (Oct. 1993) : 2.
  Kliatt (Jan. 1993) : 13.
  VOYA (June 1993) : 105.
*The Cool Kids' Guide to Summer
  Camp*
  Kirkus (1 April 1981) : 436.
  NYTBR(26 April 1981) : 69.
  SLJ (Nov. 1981) : 98.
Curtains
  BR (Jan. 1991) : 66.
  Kliatt (Jan. 1991) : 14.
  PW (28 Sept. 1990) : 104.
The Dare
  VOYA (April 1994) : 41.
The Dare (Audio Version)
  BL (1 July 1995) : 1804.
  Kliatt (July 1995) : 44.
The Dead Girlfriend
  Locus (Oct. 1993) : 55.
The Dead Lifeguard
  VOYA (Aug. 1995) : 144.
Don't Stand in The Soup
  SLJ (April 1982) : 122.
Double Date (Audio Version)
  Kliatt (Nov. 1985) : 46.
*Dynamite Funny Book of Sad
  Facts of Life*
  SLJ (Sept. 1981) : 126.
*Everything You Need to Know to
  Survive: BroThers and Sisters*
  BR (March 1984) : 47.
  SLJ (March 1984) : 166.
*Everything You Need to Know to
  Survive: First Dates*
  BR (March 1984) : 47.
  SLJ (March 1984) : 166.
*Everything You Need to Know to
  Survive: Homework*
  BR (March 1984) : 47.
  SLJ (March 1984) : 166.

*Everything You Need to Know to
  Survive: Money Problems*
  BR (March 1984) : 47.
  SLJ (March 1984) : 166.
Fear Street Saga: The Betrayal
  Kliatt (Nov. 1993) : 11.
  Locus (Jan. 1994) : 46.
  VOYA (April 1994) : 41.
Fear Street Saga: The Burning
  Locus (Jan. 1994) : 46.
Fear Street Saga: The Secret
  Locus (Jan. 1994) : 46.
  VOYA (April 1994) : 41.
The Fire Game
  VOYA (June 1992) : 102.
First Date
  VOYA (Oct. 1992) : 232.
The Girlfriend
  VOYA (April 1992) : 36.
Gnasty Gnomes
  SLJ (Sept. 1981) : 130.
Golden Sword of Dragonwalk
  VOYA (June 1984) : 94.
Goodnight Kiss
  VOYA (Dec. 1992) : 296.
Halloween Night
  Kliatt (Jan. 1994) : 13.
  PW (20 Sept. 1993) : 31.
Halloween Night II
  PW (19 Sept. 1994) : 261.
  VOYA (Aug. 1995) : 144.
Halloween Party
  BR (Jan. 1991) : 66.
  VOYA (Feb. 1991) : 368.
Haunted
  BR (Nov. 1990) : 66.
  SLJ (Oct. 1990) : 145.
Hit and Run
  Kliatt (Sept. 1992) : 16.
  VOYA (April 1993) : 30.

The Hitchhiker
    Kliatt (May 1993) : 11.
    VOYA (April 1993) : 20.
How I Broke Up With Ernie
    BL (July 1990) : 2098.
    SLJ (Nov. 1990) : 142.
How to Be Funny
    Kirkus (15 July 1978) : 753.
    PW (10 July 1978) : 136.
    SLJ (Nov. 1979) : 82.
I Saw You That Night
    RT (Oct. 1995) : 142.
    VOYA (Aug. 1995) : 144.
Indiana Jones and The Curse of
    Horror Island
    VOYA (Dec. 1984) : 260.
Indiana Jones and The Giants of
    The Silver Tower
    SLJ (Jan. 1985) : 91.
It Came From Ohio
    SLJ (July 1997): 112.
James Bond in Win, Place or Die
    VOYA (Feb. 1986) : 388.
The Knife
    VOYA (June 1992) : 115.
Lights Out
    VOYA (June 1992) : 102.
The Mind Reader
    Locus (Jan. 1995) : 52.
    VOYA (Aug. 1995) : 144.
The New Boy (Audio Version)
    Kliatt (Jan. 1996) : 47.
The New Girl
    EJ (Sept. 1990) : 95.
    EL (March 1990) : 62.
    Kliatt (Sept. 1989) : 106.
    PW (9 June 1989) : 68.
    SLJ (Aug. 1989) : 154.
One Evil Summer
    VOYA (Dec. 1994) : 290.
The Overnight
    BL (15 Dec. 1989) : 827.

Party Summer
    Wilson Library Bulletin (Oct.
    1991) : 101.
The Petrova Twist
    SLJ (Dec. 1987) : 83.
Phone Calls
    BR (Nov. 1990) : 66.
    Kliatt (Sept. 1990) : 16.
    PW (8 June 1990) : 56.
    SLJ (Oct. 1990) : 145.
    VOYA (Oct. 1990) : 220.
Pigs' Book of World Records
    BL (1 May 1980) : 1299.
    NYTBR(27 April 1980): 62.
    PW (25 April 1980) : 80.
    SLJ (Oct. 1980) : 139.
Pork and Beans: Play Date
    Kirkus (15 May 1989) : 771.
The Prom Queen
    VOYA (Aug. 1992) : 180.
The Secret Bedroom
    BL (15 Sept. 1991) : 171.
    VOYA (June 1992) : 102.
The Sick of Being Sick Book
    Kirkus (1 July 1980) : 840.
    RT (Oct. 1981) : 67.
    SLJ (Aug. 1980): 71.
Silent Night
    VOYA (April 1992) : 36.
Ski Weekend
    VOYA (May 1991) : 66.
The Sleepwalker
    Locus (Sept. 1990) : 61.
    SLJ (Sept. 1990) : 258.
    VOYA (Feb. 1991) : 368.
The Snowman
    VOYA (Dec. 1991) : 319.
Stay Out of The Basement
    Locus (Aug. 1982) : 55.
The Stepsister
    BR (March 1991) : 60.

Sunburn
  VOYA (Feb. 1994) : 386.
Superstitious
  BL (Aug. 1995) : 1911.
  Kirkus (15 July 1995) : 981.
  LJ (Aug. 1995) : 120.
  People (9 Oct. 1995) : 32.
  PW (19 June 1995) : 47.
  SLJ (Nov. 1995) : 140.
  USA Today (14 Sept. 1995) :
  D6.
  Washington Post (18 Sept.
  1995) : B2.
Superstitious (Audio Version)
  Book Watch (Nov. 1985) : 2.
  Kliatt (Jan. 1986) : 51.

Switched
  CBW (July 1995) : 5.
Twisted
  EJ (March 1988) : 86.
  PW (10 July 1987) : 71.
  VOYA (Dec. 1987) : 238.
Welcome to Dead House
  Locus (Aug. 1992) : 55.
Werewolf of Fever Swamp
  VOYA (Aug. 1995) : 146.
The Wrong Number
  SLJ (June 1990) : 126.
The Wrong Number II
  VOYA (June 1995) : 99.

INDEX

ABOUT THE AUTHOR

Patrick Jones is a librarian in Houston, Texas. He is the author of *Connecting Young Adults and Libraries: A How To Do It Manual* (Neal-Schuman, 1992). A second revised and expanded edition was published in 1998. Jones has written over forty articles for such library professional publications as *The Horn Book, School Library Journal, Voice of Youth Advocates,* and *The Journal of Popular Culture in Libraries* as well as essays for reference books such as *Children's Books and Their Creators* (Houghton Mifflin, 1995). He is a frequent speaker at library conferences about young adult literature and library services. He created the *Young Adult Librarian's Help/Homepage* (http:// www.kcpl.lib.mo.us/ya). He edited a column for *Voice of Youth Advocates* about web sites of interest to young adults, and maintains the *Connecting Young Adults and Libraries* homepage (http://members.aol.com/ naughyde/connecting). He is a graduate from the School of Library Science at the University of Michigan. He is currently working on a young adult novel called *Things Change.*